Oliver Optic, Richard Hooker Wilmer

Brother against Brother

The War on the Border

Oliver Optic, Richard Hooker Wilmer

Brother against Brother
The War on the Border

ISBN/EAN: 9783337336851

Printed in Europe, USA, Canada, Australia, Japan

Cover: Foto ©ninafisch / pixelio.de

More available books at **www.hansebooks.com**

*The Blue and the Gray
Army Series*

Brother against Brother

OR

THE WAR ON THE BORDER

BY

OLIVER OPTIC

AUTHOR OF "THE ARMY AND NAVY SERIES" "YOUNG AMERICA ABROAD, FIRST AND SECOND SERIES" "BOAT-CLUB STORIES" "THE GREAT WESTERN SERIES" "THE ONWARD AND UPWARD SERIES" "THE WOODVILLE STORIES" "THE STARRY FLAG SERIES" "THE YACHT-CLUB SERIES" "THE LAKE SHORE SERIES" "THE RIVERDALE STORIES" "THE ALL-OVER-THE-WORLD LIBRARY" "THE BLUE AND THE GRAY NAVY SERIES" "THE BOAT-BUILDER SERIES" ETC.

BOSTON
LEE AND SHEPARD PUBLISHERS

COPYRIGHT, 1894, BY LEE AND SHEPARD

All Rights Reserved

BROTHER AGAINST BROTHER

ELECTROTYPING BY C. J. PETERS & SON, BOSTON, U.S.A.

PRESSWORK BY S. J. PARKHILL & CO.

TO

My Son-in-Law

GEORGE W. WHITE, Esquire

ONE OF TWO WHO HAVE ALWAYS BEEN THE SAME TO
ME AS REAL SONS

This Book

IS AFFECTIONATELY AND GRATEFULLY
DEDICATED

PREFACE

"Brother Against Brother" is the first of "The Blue and the Gray Army Series," which will include six volumes, though the number is contingent upon the longevity of one, still hale and hearty, who has passed by a couple of years the Scriptural limit of "threescore years and ten" allotted to human life. In completing the first six books of "The Blue and the Gray Series," the author realized that the scenes and events of all these stories related to life in the navy, which gallantly performed its full share in maintaining the integrity of the Union. The six books of "The Army and Navy Series," begun in the heat of the struggle thirty years ago, were equally divided between the two arms of the service; and it has been suggested that the equilibrium should be continued in the later volumes.

In the preface of "A Victorious Union," the consummation of the terrible strife which the navy had reached in that volume, the author announced his intention to make a beginning of the books which are to form the army division of the series. Soon after he had returned from his sixteenth voyage across the Atlantic, he found himself in excellent condition to resume the pleasurable occupation in which he has been engaged for forty years in this particular field. It seems to him very much like embarking in a new enterprise, though his work consists of an attempt to enliven and diversify the scenes and incidents of an old story which has passed into history, and is forever embalmed as the record of a heroic people, faithfully and bravely represented on hundreds of gory battle-fields, and on the decks of the national navy.

The story opens in one of the Border States, where two Northern families had settled only a few years before the exciting questions which immediately preceded organized hostilities were under discussion. Considerable portions of the State in which they were located were in a condition of violent agitation, and outrages involving wounds and death were perpetrated. The head of one of these two families was a man of stern integrity,. earnestly loyal to the Union and the government which was forced into a deadly strife for its very existence. That of the other, influenced quite as much by property considerations as by fixed principles, becomes a Secessionist, fully as earnest as, and far more demonstrative than, his brother on the other side.

In each of these families are two sons, just coming to the military age, who are not quite so prominent in the present volume as they will be in those which follow it. "Riverlawn," the plantation which came into the possession of the loyal one by the will of his eldest brother, became the scene of very exciting events, in which his two sons took an active part. The writer has industriously examined the authorities covering this section of the country, including State reports, and believes he has not exaggerated the truths of history. As in preceding volumes relating to the war, he does not intend to give a connected narrative of the events that transpired in the locality he has chosen, though some of them are introduced and illustrated in the story.

The State itself, as evidenced by the votes of its Legislature and by the enlistments in the Union army, was loyal, if not from the beginning, from the time when it obtained its bearings. As in other Southern States, the secession element was more noisy and demonstrative than the loyal portion of the community, and thus obtained at first an apparent advantage. The present volume is largely taken up with the conflict for supremacy between these hostile elements. The loyal father and his two sons are active in these scenes; and the taking possession of a quantity of military supplies by them precipitates actual warfare, and the question as to whether or not a company of cavalry could be recruited at Riverlawn had to be settled by what amounted to a real battle.

To the multitude of his young friends now in their teens, and to the greater multitude now grown gray, who have encouraged his efforts during the last forty years, the author renewedly acknowledges his manifold obligations for their kindness, and wishes them all health, happiness, and all the prosperity they can bear.

WILLIAM T. ADAMS.

DORCHESTER, JULY 4, 1894.

CONTENTS

	PAGE
CHAPTER I.	
TROUBLESOME TIMES IN KENTUCKY	17
CHAPTER II.	
SOMETHING ABOUT THE LYON FAMILY	29
CHAPTER III.	
A NORTHERN FAMILY IN KENTUCKY	41
CHAPTER IV.	
THE ARRIVAL AND WELCOME AT RIVERLAWN	54
CHAPTER V.	
THE DISTRESS OF MRS. TITUS LYON	66
CHAPTER VI.	
THE NIGHT ADVENTURE ON THE CREEK	78
CHAPTER VII.	
A STORMY INTERVIEW ON THE BRIDGE	90
CHAPTER VIII.	
AN OVERWHELMING ARGUMENT	102

CHAPTER IX.
A Most Unreasonable Brother 114

CHAPTER X.
The Sink-Cavern near Bar Creek . . . 126

CHAPTER XI.
Aroused to the Solemn Duty of the Hour . . 138

CHAPTER XII.
The Night Expedition in the Magnolia . . 150

CHAPTER XIII.
At the Head Waters of Bar Creek . . . 162

CHAPTER XIV.
The Transportation of the Arms 174

CHAPTER XV.
The Establishment of Fort Bedford . . . 186

CHAPTER XVI.
The Union Meeting at Big Bend 198

CHAPTER XVII.
The Ejection of the Noisy Ruffians . . . 210

CHAPTER XVIII.
The Demand of Captain Titus Lyon . . . 222

CHAPTER XIX.
The Conference in Fort Bedford 234

CONTENTS

CHAPTER XX.
The Approach of the Ruffian Forces . . . 246

CHAPTER XXI.
The Beginning of Hostilities 258

CHAPTER XXII.
The First Shot from Fort Bedford . . . 270

CHAPTER XXIII.
The Party Attacked in the Cross-Cut . . 282

CHAPTER XXIV.
The Encounter with the Ruffians . . . 294

CHAPTER XXV.
The Gratitude of Two Fair Maidens . . . 306

CHAPTER XXVI.
The Skirmish on the New Road 318

CHAPTER XXVII.
An Unexplained Gathering on the Road . . 330

CHAPTER XXVIII.
The Result of the Flank Movement . . . 342

CHAPTER XXIX.
The Humiliating Retreat of the Ruffians . 354

CHAPTER XXX.
Levi Bedford and his Prisoner 366

CONTENTS

	PAGE
CHAPTER XXXI.	
DR. FALKIRK VISITS RIVERLAWN	378
CHAPTER XXXII.	
THE ARRIVAL OF THE RECRUITING OFFICER	391
CHAPTER XXXIII.	
ONE AGAINST THREE ON THE ROAD	403
CHAPTER XXXIV.	
THE FIRE THAT WAS STARTED AT RIVERLAWN	415
CHAPTER XXXV.	
A BATTLE IN PROSPECT ON THE CREEK	427
CHAPTER XXXVI.	
THE SECOND BATTLE OF RIVERLAWN	438

ILLUSTRATIONS

"The overseer elevated his rifle"   Frontispiece

	PAGE
"Then you mean I am drunk"	121
"He grappled with the fellow"	212
"I had to be careful not to hit the lady" . . .	299
"It won't go off again until you load it" . . .	372
"Stop, Boy! shouted the man"	413
"The boys climbed a big tree to obtain a better view"	431

BROTHER AGAINST BROTHER.

CHAPTER I

TROUBLESOME TIMES IN KENTUCKY

"NEUTRALITY! There is no such thing as neutrality in the present situation, my son!" protested Noah Lyon to the stout boy of sixteen who stood in front of him on the bridge over Bar Creek, in the State of Kentucky. "He that is not for the Union is against it. No man can serve two masters, Dexter."

"That is just what I was saying to Sandy," replied the boy, whom everybody but his father and mother called "Deck."

"Your Cousin Alexander takes after his father, who is my own brother; but I must say I am ashamed of him, for he is a rank Secessionist," continued Noah Lyon, fixing his gaze on the planks of the bridge, and looking as grieved as though one of his own blood had turned against him. "He was born and brought up in New Hampshire, where about all the people believe in the Union as they do in their own mothers, and a traitor would be ridden on a rail out of almost any town within its borders."

"Well, it isn't so down here in the State of Kentucky, father," answered Deck.

"Kentucky was the second new State to be admitted to the Union of the original thirteen, and there are plenty of people now within her borders who protest that it will be the last to leave it," replied the father, as he took a crumpled newspaper from his pocket. "Here's a little piece from a Clarke County paper which is just the opinion of a majority of the people of Kentucky. Read it out loud, Dexter," added Mr. Lyon, as he handed the paper to his son, and pointed out the article.

The young man took the paper, and read in a loud voice, as though he wished even the fishes in the creek to hear it, and to desire them to refuse to be food for Secessionists: "Any attempt on the part of the government of this State, or any one else, to put Kentucky out of the Union by force, or using force to compel Union men in any manner to submit to an ordinance of secession, or any pretended resolution or decree arising from such secession, is an act of treason against the State of Kentucky. It is therefore lawful to resist any such ordinance."

"That's the doctrine!" exclaimed Mr. Lyons, clapping his hands with a ringing sound to emphasize his opinion. "Those are my sentiments exactly, and they are political gospel to me; and I should be ashamed of any son of mine who did not stand by the Union, whether he lived in New Hampshire or Kentucky."

"You can count me in for the Union every time, father," said Deck, who had read all the newspapers, those from the North and of the State in which he resided, as well as the history of Kentucky and the current exciting documents that were floating about the country, including the long and illogical letter of the State's senator who immediately became a Confederate brigadier.

"I haven't heard your Cousin Artie, who is just your age, and old enough to do something on his own account, say much about the troubles of the times," added Mr. Lyon, bestowing an inquiring look upon his son. "I have seen Sandy Lyon talking to him a good deal lately, and I hope he is not leading him astray."

"No danger of that; for Artie is as stiff as a cart-stake for the Union, and Sandy can't pour any Secession molasses down his back," replied Deck.

"I am glad to hear it. I heard some one say that Sandy had joined, or was going to join, the Home Guards."

"He asked me to join them, and wanted me to go down to Bowling Green with him in the boat. He had already put his name down as a member of a company; but of course I wouldn't go."

"The Home Guards thrive very well in Bar Creek; and I noticed that all who joined them are Secessionists, or have a leaning that way," added the father. "The avowed purpose of these organizations is to preserve the neutrality of the State; but that is only another name for treason; and when affairs have progressed a little farther, the Home Guards will wheel into the ranks of the Confederate army. President Lincoln made a very guarded and non-committal reply to the Governor's letter on neutrality; but it is as plain as the nose on a toper's face that he don't believe in it."

"I think it is best to be on one side or the other."

"Isn't Sandy trying to rope Artie into the Home Guards, Dexter?" asked Mr. Lyon with an anxious look on his face.

"Of course he is, as he has tried to get me to join."

"Artie is a quiet sort of a boy, and don't say much; but it is plain that he keeps up a tremendous thinking all the time, though I have not been able to make out what it is all about."

"He is considering just what all the rest of us are thinking about; but I am satisfied that he has come out just where all the rest of us at Riverlawn have arrived, father. He and I have talked a great deal about the war; and Artie is all right now, though he may have had some doubts about where he belonged a few months ago."

"But Sandy was over here no longer ago than yesterday, and he was talking for over an hour with Artie on this bridge where we are now," said Mr. Lyon.

"They were talking about the Union meeting to be held to-morrow night at the schoolhouse by the Big Bend," added Deck.

"What interest has Sandy in that meeting? He does not train in that company."

"He advised Artie not to go to the meeting, for it was gotten up by traitors to their State."

"That's a Secessionist phrase which he borrowed from some Confederate orator, or at Bowling Green, where he spends too much of his time; and his father had better be teaching him how to lay bricks and mix mortar."

"But Uncle Titus is over there half his time," suggested Deck.

"He had better be attending to his business; for the people over at the village say they will have to get another mason to settle there, for your uncle Titus don't work half his time, and the people can't get their jobs done. There is a new house over there waiting for him to build the chimney."

"Why don't you talk to him, father?" asked Deck very seriously.

"Talk to him, Dexter!" exclaimed Mr. Lyon. "You might as well set your dog to barking at the rapids in the river. For some reason Titus seems to be rather set against me since we settled in Barcreek. We used to be on the best of terms in New Hampshire, for I always lent him money when he was hard pressed. I don't know what has come over him since we came to Kentucky."

"I do," added Deck, looking earnestly into his father's face.

"Well, what is it, I should like to know? I have always done everything I could since I came here for him."

"Sandy told me something about it one day, and seemed to have a good deal of feeling about it. He says you wronged Uncle Titus out of five thousand dollars," said Deck, wondering if his father had ever heard the charge before.

"I know what Sandy meant. Of course Titus must have been in the habit of talking about this matter in his family, or Sandy would not have known anything about it," replied Mr. Lyon, evidently very much annoyed at the revelation of his son.

"I did not know what Sandy meant, and I thought I had better not ask him; for of course I knew there was not a particle of truth in the charge," added Deck, surprised to find that his father knew something about the accusation.

"I don't talk with my children about troublesome family matters, Dexter, and your Uncle Titus ought not to do so. "I shall only say that there is not the slightest grain of reason or justice in the charge against me; and Titus knows it as well as I do. If anybody has wronged him, it was your deceased Uncle Duncan. Let the matter drop there, at least for the present. Why does Sandy wish to prevent Artie from attending the Union meeting to-morrow night?"

"He said it was likely to be broken up by the Home Guards."

"Then he probably knows something about a plot to interfere with the gathering. I rode up to the village this morning, and I was quite surprised to find that several whom I knew to be loyal men did not intend to be present. When I urged them to be there, they hinted that there would be trouble at the schoolhouse."

At this moment a bell was rung at the side-door of the mansion, about ten rods from the bridge where the father and son had been discussing the situation. It crossed the creek a quarter of a mile from the river, which has a course of three hundred miles through the State, and is navigable from the Ohio two-thirds of its length during the season of high water. The mansion was the residence of Noah Lyon; and after the green field, ornamented with stately trees, which extended from the house to the river, it had taken the name of "Riverlawn" in the time of the former proprietor. The plantation extended along the creek more than half a mile, including over five hundred acres of the richest land in the State.

Above the bridge was a little village of negro houses, so neat and substantial that they deserved a better name than "huts," generally given to the dwellings of the slaves of a plantation. Each had its little garden, fenced off and well cared for. It was evident that the occupants of these cottages were subjected to few if any of the hardships of their condition. Many of them were just returning from the hemp fields and the horse pastures of the estate; and they seemed to be happy and contented, with no care for the troubles that were then agitating the State.

The bell had been rung at the side-door of the mansion by a black woman, very neatly dressed. Back of the dwelling was the kitchen in a separate building, according to the custom at the South. Mr. Lyon, though he was the present proprietor of this extensive estate, was dressed in very plain clothes, and had none of the air of a Kentucky gentleman. Deck was clothed in the same manner; but both of them looked very neat and very respectable in spite of their plain clothes.

They came from the bridge at the sound of the bell. On the left of the entrance was the dining-room, a large apartment, with the table set for dinner in the middle of it. Two young octoroon girls were standing by the chairs to wait upon the family, which consisted of six persons.

"You have been shopping this forenoon, haven't you, Ruth?" asked Mr. Lyon, addressing his wife, who was seated at one end of the table while he was at the other.

"I did not do much shopping; but I called upon Amelia, and found her very much troubled," replied Mrs. Lyon, alluding to the wife of Titus Lyon.

"I should think she might be troubled," replied Mr. Lyon. "She does not take any part in politics; but one of her brothers is a captain in a New Hampshire regiment, and another is a major, and all her family are loyal to the backbone. She has not said much of anything, but I know she does not approve the attitude of her husband and her two sons. The last time I saw her, she was afraid they would enlist in the Confederate army. Titus won't hear a word of objection from her."

"She told me an astonishing piece of news this forenoon," continued Mrs. Lyon.

"I shall not be much astonished at anything Titus does," added the husband. "But what has he done now? Has he enlisted in the Confederate army?"

"Not yet; but Amelia says he has been offered the command of a company of Home Guards if he will pay for the arms and uniform of it. He agreed to do so, and has already paid over the money, five thousand dollars."

"Is it possible!" exclaimed Mr. Lyon; and the two boys dropped their knives and forks in their astonishment. "I did not think he would go as far as that. He could not be a ranker Secessionist if he had lived all his life in South Carolina, instead of nine or ten years in Kentucky."

"This happened a month ago, and Amelia says the arms are hidden somewhere on the river."

"Does she know where?"

"She did not tell me where if she knew.

More than this, she says he is drinking too much whiskey, and that the Secessionists have made a fool of him. She is afraid he will throw away all his property."

"I have noticed several times that he has been drinking too much, though he was not exactly intoxicated."

"Oh! Amelia said he meant to make you pay for the arms and uniforms," said Mrs. Lyon, with some excitement in her manner. "He insists that you owe him five thousand dollars."

"If I did, he gives me a good excuse for not paying it; but I do not owe him a nickel. Home Guards and Confederates here are all the same; and no money of mine shall go for arming either of them."

"Titus's wife says you are denounced as an abolitionist, Noah, and they will drive you out of the county soon," added Mrs. Lyon.

"When they are ready to begin, I shall be there," replied Mr. Lyon with a smile.

The dinner was finished, and the family separated, Deck and his father returning to the bridge, followed by Artie.

CHAPTER II

SOMETHING ABOUT THE LYON FAMILY

THE grand mansion and the extensive domain of Riverlawn had been occupied by the Lyon family hardly more than a year when the political excitement in Kentucky began to manifest itself, though not so violently as in some of the more southern States. Abraham Lincoln had been elected President of the United States, and south of Mason and Dixon's line he was regarded as a sectional president whose term of office would be a menace and an absolute peril to the institution of slavery. Senator Crittenden of Kentucky proposed certain amendments to the Constitution to restore the Missouri Compromise, by which slavery should be confined to specified limits, and Congress prevented from interfering with the labor-system of the South.

Before Christmas in 1860, South Carolina had unanimously passed its Ordinance of Secession, the intelligence of which was received with enthusiasm by the Gulf States, all of which soon followed her example. The more conservative States held back, and all but the four on the border seceded in one form or another after some delay.

In Kentucky the wealthy planters and slaveholders, with many prominent exceptions, were inclined to share the lot of the seceding States; but the majority of the people still clung to the Union. Both sides of the exciting question were largely represented, and the contest between them was violent and bitter. For a time the specious compromise of neutrality was regarded as the panacea for the troubles of the State by the less violent of the people on both sides. Home Guards were enlisted and organized to protect the territory from invasion by either the Federal or the Confederate forces.

The occupation of Columbus and Hickman on the Mississippi River by Southern troops, immediately followed by the taking of Paducah by General Grant with two regiments of Union soldiers from Cairo, practically dissolved the illusion of neutrality. The government at Washington never recognized this makeshift of those who loved the Union, but desired to protect slavery.

It was honestly and sincerely cherished by good men of both parties, who desired to preserve the Union and save the State from the horrors of civil war.

The government did not regard the seceded States as so many independent sovereignties, as the Secessionists claimed that they were, but as part and parcel of a union of States forming one consolidated nation, with no provision in its Constitution for a separation of any kind, or for the withdrawal of one or more of the individual members of the Union. The States which had pretended to dissolve their connection with the other members of the compact were considered as refractory members of the Union, in a state of insurrection against the sovereign authority of the nation, who were to be reduced to obedience and subjection by force of arms; for they had appealed to the logic of bayonets and cannon-balls in carrying out their disruption.

With the duty of putting down the insurrection and subduing the refractory elements in the South on its hands, the government could not respect or even tolerate a neutrality which placed the State of Kentucky, four hundred miles in extent from east to west, between the loyal and the disloyal sections of its domain. If for no other purpose, armies of Federal troops must cross the country south of the Ohio in order to reach the seat of the Rebellion.

The Home Guards were powerless to prevent the passage of the loyal armies through the State; and any attempt to do so would have been to fight the battle of the Confederate armies, and would have at once robbed neutrality of its transparent mask. A portion of these military bodies were doubtless honest in their intentions. Those who were not for the Union in this connection were practically against it. Later in the course of events, the Home Guards were incorporated in the armies of the Rebellion; and no doubt these organizations were used to a considerable extent to recruit the forces of the enemy.

For a period of several months the State was not in actual possession of either party in the conflict. One was struggling within its territory to keep it in the Union, and the other to force it into the Southern Confederacy. Irresponsible persons formed what they called a "Provisional Council," elected a governor, and sent delegates to the

Confederate Congress, who were admitted to seats in that body.

During this chaotic state of affairs, Kentuckians were joining both armies, though the great body of them enlisted in the forces of the Union. At the close of 1861 it was estimated that Kentucky had twenty-six thousand men, cavalry and infantry, enrolled to fight the battles of the loyal nation, including those who had joined the regiments of other States.

Deeds of violence were not uncommon in many parts of the State, growing out of the excited state of feeling. Confederate emissaries were busy in the territory, and armed bodies of them foraged for provisions and fodder in the southern portions. Unpopular men were hunted down and shot or hanged, and the reign of disorder prevailed. Such was the condition of Kentucky soon after the Lyon family took possession of Riverlawn; and some account of its several members becomes necessary.

The first of the name in America had been one of the earliest English settlers in Massachusetts; but one of his descendants, more than a hundred years later, had moved to the colony of New Hampshire. Early in the present century, one of his grandchildren was a farmer in Derry, in that State. This particular Lyon had four sons, two of whom have already been mentioned in this story.

Duncan Lyon was the eldest of them, and seems to have been the most enterprising of the four; for he emigrated to Kentucky, and purchased the extensive tract of land which now formed the estate of Riverlawn. He became a planter in due time from his small beginnings, raising hemp, tobacco, and horses, without neglecting the productions necessary for the support of his household. He was very prosperous in his undertakings; and being a man of good sense and excellent judgment, he became a person of some distinction in his county. He was known as "Colonel Duncan Lyon," though he never held any military position; but his title clung to him, and even his brothers in New Hampshire always spoke of him as the " colonel."

He never married; but he made a modest fortune of one hundred thousand dollars, including the value of his estate, though not including the value of about fifty negroes, men, women, and

SOMETHING ABOUT THE LYON FAMILY 35

children, which for some reason he never disclosed, he did not put into the inventory that accompanied his will.

The colonel's estate was on Bar Creek, at its junction with Green River. One mile from Riverlawn was the village of Barcreek, a place with three churches, several stores, a blacksmith's and a wheelwright's shop, with a carpenter and a mason. It supplied the needs of the country in a circuit of eight or ten miles. In fact, it was a sort of market town.

There was not a great deal of building done in this region; but the mason residing there had made a comfortable living, jobbing and erecting an occasional chimney, till he died in 1852. The colonel notified his brother, Titus Lyon, who was a mason in Derry, that there was an opening for one of his trade in Barcreek, but he could not advise him to move there.

Titus was not a prosperous man; for he was rather lazy, and greatly lacking in enterprise. The colonel did not believe he would do any better in a new home than in the old one, and he bluntly wrote to him to this effect. The planter had a suspicion that his brother drank too much whiskey, for he could not account for his poverty in any other way; but he had no evidence on the point. Titus decided to move to Kentucky; and he did so, though he had to borrow the money of his brother Noah to enable him to reach his new home.

Business in his trade happened to be usually good after his arrival, and for several years he did tolerably well. Then he desired to buy a house and some land which were for sale in Barcreek. The colonel loaned him five thousand dollars for this purpose, and to pay off his note to Noah, mortgaging the estate he had purchased as security.

From this time Titus did not do as well as before. He seemed to regard himself as a landed proprietor, and the equal of the planters of Kentucky. He neglected his work, feeling rather above it, negroes doing most of the jobs in his line. He employed a couple of them, but they did not earn their wages. The colonel had to help him out several times.

As a planter in good standing among his neighbors in the county, Colonel Lyon, who was not a profound thinker, fell in with the views and opinions of those in his grade of society. He was not a strong pro-slavery man, but he owned half a hundred negroes, who had been necessary to enable him to carry on his planting operations; but he treated them as well as though he had paid them wages.

He was not inclined to make any issue with his neighbors on the labor question, though some of them thought he was not entirely reliable on this subject. He attended to his business, and did not vex his spirit over extraneous matters. When the protection of the South against the aggressions of the North in connection with slavery was agitated, he followed his Kentucky leaders.

On the question of any interference on the part of Congress or the people of the free States he had very decided opinions. If he had ever intended to manumit his negroes, as had been hinted in the county, no one could object to his position after the subject began to be agitated in the State. After eight years' residence in Barcreek, his brother Titus was a more thorough-going pro-slavery man than the planter; in fact, he had had a strong tendency in that direction when he lived in Derry.

Titus's wife was not a happy woman in her domestic relations. She was better educated than her husband, and emphatically more sensible; and she could not help seeing that Titus was frittering away his opportunities, drinking too much whiskey, and associating with reckless and unprincipled characters. Their two sons, Alexander and Orlando, were following in the footsteps of their father. Even the three daughters had imbibed strange notions from their associates, and belonged on the Secession side of the house.

Colonel Lyon was not permitted to witness the wild disorder which pervaded the State after the election of the Republican President; for he died suddenly in a fit of apoplexy, after he had eaten his Christmas dinner, in 1858. He was only fifty years old, and perhaps if he had taken more exercise and been more prudent in his eating and drinking, he might have taken part in the stormy events of the later period.

Colonel Cosgrove, a prominent lawyer residing at the county seat, and an intimate friend of the deceased, was present at the funeral. Titus took charge of the affairs of the mansion, and the lawyer intimated to him that he should be present at opinions of those in his grade of society. He was not a strong pro-slavery man, but he owned half a hundred negroes, who had been necessary to enable him to carry on his planting operations; but he treated them as well as though he had paid them wages.

He was not inclined to make any issue with his neighbors on the labor question, though some of them thought he was not entirely reliable on this subject. He attended to his business, and did not vex his spirit over extraneous matters. When the protection of the South against the aggressions of the North in connection with slavery was agitated, he followed his Kentucky leaders.

On the question of any interference on the part of Congress or the people of the free States he had very decided opinions. If he had ever intended to manumit his negroes, as had been hinted in the county, no one could object to his position after the subject began to be agitated in the State. After eight years' residence in Barcreek, his brother Titus was a more thorough-going pro-slavery man than the planter; in fact, he had had a strong tendency in that direction when he lived in Derry.

Titus's wife was not a happy woman in her domestic relations. She was better educated than her husband, and emphatically more sensible; and she could not help seeing that Titus was frittering away his opportunities, drinking too much whiskey, and associating with reckless and unprincipled characters. Their two sons, Alexander and Orlando, were following in the footsteps of their father. Even the three daughters had imbibed strange notions from their associates, and belonged on the Secession side of the house.

Colonel Lyon was not permitted to witness the wild disorder which pervaded the State after the election of the Republican President; for he died suddenly in a fit of apoplexy, after he had eaten his Christmas dinner, in 1858. He was only fifty years old, and perhaps if he had taken more exercise and been more prudent in his eating and drinking, he might have taken part in the stormy events of the later period.

Colonel Cosgrove, a prominent lawyer residing at the county seat, and an intimate friend of the deceased, was present at the funeral. Titus took charge of the affairs of the mansion, and the lawyer intimated to him that he should be present at

Riverlawn the next morning to carry out the wishes and intentions of his departed friend.

Titus did not understand this notice, and supposed that the duty of settling the estate of his brother rested entirely upon him. Colonel Cosgrove came as he had promised, with a will in his hands, of which he had been the custodian. He proceeded to read it without any ceremony, Titus being the only other person present.

The deceased valued his property at one hundred thousand dollars, Riverlawn being placed at twenty-five thousand, the rest being in cash, stocks, and other securities. The estate, including the negroes, everything in the house or connected with the place, and ten thousand dollars, half cash and half stocks, were given to Noah Lyon. The document explained that he gave the money and stocks to Noah, because he had supported and brought up the two children of his deceased brother Cyrus.

To his brother Titus he gave twenty-five thousand dollars, including the mortgage note he held against him, half the balance in cash, and half in stocks and bonds. To his brother Noah, in trust for the two children of his brother Cyrus, deceased, twenty-five thousand dollars, to be paid over to them when they were of age. Colonel Cosgrove said the deceased had apportioned the stocks as they were to be given to the legatees, and the money was in the county bank. He would come to Barcreek in about a week to pay over the cash, and deliver the stocks to Titus.

The lawyer was appointed executor of the estate, and he would hold the property given to Noah Lyon until he came to receive it, or made other arrangements in regard to it. Then he showed a letter, with a great seal upon it, which he had been directed to deliver to Noah in person. Titus wanted to know what the letter was about; but if the lawyer knew its contents, he avoided making any revelation.

It was evident to Colonel Cosgrove that Titus was dissatisfied with the will, for a heavy frown had rested on his brow since the reading of the first item of the instrument; but he said nothing, and very abruptly left the legal gentleman.

CHAPTER III

A NORTHERN FAMILY IN KENTUCKY

Titus's eldest daughter, Mildred, had written to her Uncle Noah in New Hampshire the particulars of the death of his brother after the fact had been telegraphed to him by Colonel Cosgrove. The letter was hardly more than an announcement of the decease of her Kentucky uncle, and the date of the funeral. It was not possible for Noah to reach Barcreek in season to be present at the last rites; but he wrote to Titus without delay.

A few days after the telegram a letter from Colonel Cosgrove, the executor, came to Noah Lyon, containing a copy of the will of his brother. The lawyer, who had been the intimate friend and confidant of Colonel Lyon, wrote with entire freedom to the distant brother. He stated that his deceased friend had little confidence in Titus, and in Barcreek he was not considered as an entirely reliable man.

The most important item in the letter was that Colonel Lyon had passed a whole day with him only a week before his death, talking most of the time about his estate. He had lived at Riverlawn twenty-five years, had developed the place from a wilderness, and was very much attached to it. In his will he had left it to Noah, and he desired that he should move to Kentucky and take possession of the estate.

It required a week of consideration in the comfortable home of the Derry farmer, in which the children, their own and the adopted ones, took part, before a conclusion could be reached; but it was a compliance with the request of Colonel Lyon. Within a year before his death the planter had spent a month with the New Hampshire farmer, during which he had told him all about his estate and his surroundings at Barcreek. They had not met before since the elder brother first went to Kentucky; and the Kentuckian formed a very high opinion of his New England brother, which was quite in contrast with his estimate of Titus, who had been his neighbor for six years.

The colonel's will was dated within two months of this visit, and doubtless he was thinking of his last testament when he went to New Hampshire. As soon as it was settled that the family should make their home in Kentucky, Noah wrote a long letter to his only surviving brother, announcing his intention to leave Barcreek as soon as he could settle up his business in Derry. He expressed himself with all brotherly kindness, and was glad that they were again to live near each other.

Titus did not even reply to this letter, though his wife wrote to Mrs. Noah, expressing the pleasure she felt that they were again to be neighbors. It was about two months after the death of Colonel Lyon that Noah and his family arrived at Bowling Green, the county town, which was the nearest railroad station to Barcreek, fifteen miles distant. Noah Lyon had kept up his correspondence with the executor of his brother, and Colonel Cosgrove was at the station when the family arrived. Titus was not there, and he did not manifest much interest in the coming of his only remaining brother.

The distinguished lawyer extended a hearty welcome to the family, and invited them all to dinner at his mansion. He wondered that Titus or some member of his family was not there to greet the new-comers; but he said little about him, though enough to show that he had not a very exalted opinion of him.

"You will find the mansion of your late brother in perfect order, Mr. Lyon," said Colonel Cosgrove, as they rose from the dinner-table. "I was over there yesterday, and satisfied myself that every thing was in condition for your reception. The furniture remains just as it was in the time of Colonel Lyon."

"You have been very kind, Colonel Cosgrove, and I am very grateful to you for all the attention you have given to my brother's affairs and to me," replied Noah, taking the hand of the hospitable executor. "Does my brother Titus live near Riverlawn?"

"About a mile from it, in the village of Barcreek," answered the lawyer. "Your brother, the colonel, had several boats; and when he went to the village in the open season he usually made the trip by the river, rowed by half a dozen of his boys."

"I was not aware that he had any boys," added Noah.

"His hands, his negroes; and he always called

them boys. He was the best friend they ever had," the colonel explained. " That reminds me that I have a letter which your late brother required me to deliver personally into your hands;" and the lawyer went to his office for it.

He returned in a few minutes, and gave the letter, which was heavily sealed with wax, to the new owner of Riverlawn. He had mentioned this epistle in one of his letters to the new proprietor, and Noah wondered as he looked upon its elaborate seals what could be the subject of the communication. The colonel was speaking of the boys, which reminded him of the letter; and he suspected that it had some connection with the negroes. He put it in his pocket very carefully, and then looked at his watch.

"How far is it from this town to Barcreek?" he asked, still holding the watch in his hand.

"Fifteen miles; and as the roads are not in the best condition at this season of the year, it will take about two hours and a half to make the trip," replied the lawyer. "But it is only two o'clock, and you have plenty of time."

"But I must look up a conveyance," suggested the new proprietor of Riverlawn.

"A conveyance is all ready for you, Mr. Lyon," added the colonel. "I directed Mr. Bedford to come over for you and your family, and he has been here since nine o'clock this morning. He came with the road-wagon, which will comfortably accommodate your whole family; and one of the boys came over with another wagon to tote your baggage over."

"You have been very thoughtful and considerate, Colonel Cosgrove, and I am under very great obligations to you," said Noah.

"Don't mention it, Mr. Lyon. I should be happy to have you spend the night with me, for we have still a great deal to talk about," answered the executor.

"My family, as well as myself, are naturally quite impatient to see our new home," suggested the New Hampshire farmer. "Fifteen miles is not a very long distance even in New England, and I hope we shall meet often."

"I shall visit Riverlawn often until you are well settled in your new home. I have a plantation myself on the road to Barcreek, and about half way there, which I visit two or three times a week; and I shall be glad to give you all the information you need in regard to your surroundings, or in relation to the management of your estate. You will see me occasionally at Riverlawn, and I shall hope to meet you and your family here, or at my estate, which is called Belgrade."

"Thank you, Colonel; I am sure we shall be good friends in spite of my antecedents as a Northern farmer, for I am not a bigot or a fanatic."

"I have no doubt we shall be good friends and good neighbors," said the Kentuckian, as he took the hand of his new client, and struck the bell on the table. "Now I will send for Mr. Bedford, who has been the overseer or manager of your brother for the last ten years. As the colonel was, he is a bachelor of fifty, and has been one of the family at Riverlawn. He is a thoroughly reliable man, and one of the late colonel's best friends."

A servant was sent for the overseer, and presently he appeared. He was a rather stout man, and his round face seemed to be overflowing with pleasantry and good-nature. He was duly presented to all the six members of the family, and heartily shook the hand of each of them. He did not at all answer to the description of plantation overseers which Noah Lyon had obtained from the books he had read, depicting the horrors of slavery. In spite of his occupation he took a fancy to him at first sight; and all the family were pleased with him.

The manager, as Noah preferred to call him, was Levi Bedford. He had never been very successful in the management of his own affairs; but he was a man after Colonel Lyon's own heart, and in his will he had given him five thousand dollars, which was one of the grievances Titus had against the testament. One of the virtues of Levi, as his late employer always called him, was his extreme fondness for horses, with his skill in raising and managing them; for this had been an important branch of the planter's business.

"I have started Pink over to the place with all your baggage, Major Lyon, and I am ready to leave with the family when you say the word," said Mr. Bedford, after they had conversed a few minutes.

"I am not a major, Mr. Bedford," replied Noah; and all the family laughed when they heard the military title applied to him.

"Your brother was not exactly a colonel; but

that is a fashion we have down here of expressing our respect for a man by giving him rank in the military," laughed the manager. "But I want you to call me 'Levi,' as your brother did, and as Colonel Cosgrove does when there is no company present."

"Very well, Levi; I intend to conform to the customs of the country. We are all ready to leave at once," added Noah.

"My team will be at the door in four minutes and three-quarters, Major Lyon," answered the manager as he left the room.

"Call it five, Levi," added the colonel.

"Less than that, Colonel," replied Levi as he closed the door.

"I would give that man double the wages I pay my present overseer if I could have him at Belgrade; and I should make money by the change," said the host, as he went to the window of the drawing-room, to which the party had retired from the dining-room. "The only fault he has is that he is too gentle and indulgent to the negroes. The neighbors say he is spoiling the niggers all over two counties. But I reckon the colonel was more to blame for that, if anybody was to blame, for he had a soft heart. I never saw two men less alike than your two Kentucky brothers," continued Colonel Cosgrove, as Noah joined him at the window. "There is your team, and Levi hasn't been gone quite five minutes."

"Four horses!" exclaimed Noah.

"Levi likes a good team and enough of it," added the lawyer.

"And I never saw four handsomer horses in all my life," added the new owner of Riverlawn, as he gazed with admiration on the magnificent animals; and all the family hastened to the windows to see the turnout.

"You will find at least thirty more of them when you get to Riverlawn."

The road-wagon was a covered vehicle with four seats, large enough for a dozen passengers. It was neatly painted and upholstered, and the harnesses on the horses were elegant enough for a city turnout. The whole family promptly realized that they were entering upon a style to which they had never been accustomed. But Noah Lyon had suddenly become a rich man.

The colonel gallantly assisted the ladies to their seats. The horses danced and pranced; but they were so well trained that they did not offer to start till Levi drew up his four reins and gave them the word to go. Hasty adieux were spoken, and the horses went off, gently at first, but soon put in a lively pace.

Noah and his wife took the back seat, Dorcas and Hope took the next one, for all of them had been handed to these places by the colonel; Dexter installed himself at the side of Levi, and Artemas had a seat all to himself behind them. All was new and strange to them, and they observed the buildings in the town till they passed out of the village. Then the scenery was quite different from that of their former home.

Only two of the four children were those of Noah and his wife. Dexter was his son, and was sixteen years old at this time, while his sister Hope was thirteen. Both of them had received a high-school education in part, and they were both very bright scholars. People in Derry called Deck an "old head," which meant that his judgment and knowledge had ripened beyond his years. Without being a "goody," he was a good boy, with high aims and noble impulses.

Ten years before, Cyrus Lyon, one of the four

brothers of whom Colonel Duncan was the eldest, was a resident of Hillsburg in the State of Vermont, where he had settled on a valley farm, which he had hired with the intention of buying it when he was able to do so. He was married in Derry, and had two children, with whom he moved to his new home. He lived in an old house, between which and the public road flowed a small river, nearly dry most of the year, but exceedingly turbulent in the spring when the snow melted on the mountains.

A freshet came, and the house was surrounded by water. The bridge over the stream was raised, and Cyrus went out to secure it. His wife followed to assist him, and while both of them were on it, a rush of waters came which tore the structure into fragments, and both of them were swept away by the mad torrent. They were drowned in spite of the efforts of the neighbors to rescue them. But they saved the two children who remained in the house.

Noah had taken these two children and brought them up as his own, for the father did not leave property enough to pay his debts. Artemas was fifteen and Dorcas was seventeen. The colonel paid for their support for ten years, and left each a handsome legacy, in trust with Noah.

In two hours from the county town, Levi Bedford reined in his four horses at the front door of the Riverlawn mansion.

CHAPTER IV

THE ARRIVAL AND WELCOME AT RIVERLAWN

IT was about five o'clock in the afternoon when the road-wagon drew up in front of the mansion at Riverlawn. Less than a week before the Northern family had left the deep snows and the icy cold of New Hampshire, and the air of the Southern clime was comparatively mild and soft. The magnolias were as green as in summer; certain flowers had pushed their way out of the ground, and blossomed in the garden.

The young people in the wagon had been delighted with the ride, the air was so mild, and everything was so new and strange. They had struck the river road leading from the estate to the village, and the rest of the way was along Bar Creek to the bridge which crossed it to the mansion. They had passed Pink, the old negro who came with the baggage, at Belgrade, where he had stopped to water his two horses. Levi Bedford had talked all the way, pointing out every object of interest to the new-comers, telling stories, repeating all the old jokes of the locality, which were quite new to his audience.

As the manager wheeled his horses from the creek road upon the bridge, he cracked his whip, which seemed to be the signal for the four spirited horses to dance and prance, in order to make a proper display as they reached the end of their journey. Gathered in the walks in front of the house were all the servants of the mansion, and all the field-hands belonging to the place, to welcome the family.

There were just fifty-one of them, Levi said, and they all broke out in a yell, which was intended for a cheer, as the magnificent animals danced up to the front door. It was a cordial welcome, and the "people" put their whole souls into it. Noah Lyon took off his Derby hat and waved it to the crowd; Deck and Artie followed his example, all of them bowing; while Mrs. Lyon and the girls flaunted their handkerchiefs vigorously to the assembled population of the plantation.

Most of them were somewhat shy at first, though they intended to give a proper welcome to the family of the new proprietor, and they were rather restrained in their demonstration; but as soon as the party waved their hats and handkerchiefs, with pleasant smiles on their faces, all of them shouted, "Glad to see you!" their enthusiasm being limited only by the vigor of their voices and the strength of their lungs.

The Lyons were intensely amused at the earnestness of the demonstration, and they laughed heartily. They retained their seats in the wagon after it stopped, more interested in the gathering around them than in anything else for the time. The crowd closed up around the vehicle in order to obtain a nearer view of their new masters and mistresses. They had known and loved as a patriarch the colonel, for he had always been kind and indulgent to them. Unfortunately they also knew Titus Lyon, by reputation if not personally, and for a month they had been wondering whether the new proprietor was like the colonel or his Kentucky brother.

The "people" were of all ages, from the bald-headed old negro with a flaxen fringe around his rear head on a level with his ears, down to the infant in arms, whose toothless grin contrasted with the ivory display of its mother. They were of all the hues of the colored race, from the ebony face whereon charcoal could make no mark to the light saffron tint of the octoroon.

There was a plentiful sprinkling of "mammies" and "uncles" among them, for all the older ones are called by these names. But the great body of them were young or middle-aged men and women, able-bodied and fit for regular work. Noah Lyon and his wife were particularly struck with the appearance of two girls sixteen to eighteen years old, who were nearly as white as their own children. They were neatly and modestly dressed, and both of them had very pretty faces. They were employed in the house as waiters at the table, and in other general work.

"Glad to see you, mars'r!" shouted a score of the tribe in unison. "Glad to see you, missus!" "Gib you welcome to Barcreek, mars'r and missus!" "Glad to see de young mars'rs and missusses!"

Levi, with a very broad and cheerful smile upon his round face, descended from the wagon with the reins in his hand, which he handed to a mulatto whom he called Frank, who had been the colonel's coachman. He proceeded to assist

Mrs. Lyon to alight, and her husband followed her without any of the assistance tendered to him, for he was only forty years old, and almost as nimble as he had ever been. The manager handed the girls to the ground as politely as though he had served his time as a dancing-master, and the young ladies smiled upon him as sweetly as though he had been a younger beau.

"This is Diana, Mrs. Lyon, the cook and housekeeper," said Levi, taking a yellow woman of fifty by the arm, and presenting her to the new lady of the house.

"Diana, missus, and not Dinah," added the housekeeper, as the lady took her hand.

"I will always call you Diana, and never Dinah," replied Mrs. Lyon. "I have no doubt we shall be good friends, though I am not used to your ways in Kentucky."

"This girl is Sylvie," said Diana, drawing the elder of the two octoroons into the presence of the lady; and her color was light enough to make her blushes transparent. "This is Julie," she added, bringing the other of the pretty pair to the front. "Both of them wait on the table, and 'tend on missus. Both of them come from New Orleans when they were little girls, and both of them speak French like a pair of mocking-birds."

"I am very happy to see you, girls, and I think we shall get along very well together, for I have never been used to having any one to wait on me," said the lady, as she took each of them by the hand; and they were so pretty that she was disposed to kiss them.

The rest of the family were presented in like manner to the house servants, and Levi introduced them to the rest of the people in a mass. The Lyons all felt that they had suddenly become lions, at least so far as Riverlawn was concerned. Noah had been a prosperous farmer in New Hampshire, engaged in some outside operation in which he had been successful; but even in haying-time he had never had more than three hired men. This avalanche of half a hundred servants suddenly attached to him was a new and novel experience; and the situation was just as strange to his wife and the young people.

Aunty Diana conducted the family into the

house with many bows and flourishes, followed by the pretty octoroons, and ushered them into the drawing-room, which had seldom been used when the colonel was alive; for he was as simple in his manners as Noah, though he felt obliged to keep up the style of the mansion.

"Help you take your things off, missus?" said Diana to Mrs. Lyon, while Sylvie and Julie tendered their services to Dorcas and Hope.

"We should like to go to our rooms, Diana," replied the lady. "I suppose they are all ready for us."

"All ready, missus."

"Of course you can take your choice of the rooms, Mrs. Lyon," interposed Levi, who had come into the house as soon as he had sent the people to their cottages. "There are eight rooms on the second floor, besides two company chambers; and I suppose Diana has already picked out one for the owner and his wife."

"You can take just what room you like, missus, but I picked out the colonel's chamber for mars'r and missus, 'cause it is the biggest, has a dressing-room and four great closets. I think that one suit missus best," added Diana.

"We will all go up-stairs and look at the rooms," replied Mrs. Lyon.

She concluded to take the colonel's room, to which Noah assented; and it was a palatial apartment to both of them. The girls were next provided with rooms, and the two octoroons were unremitting in their attentions to them. Though they knew that these girls were slaves, they treated them like sisters, and before the day was over they were fast friends; for both of them were utterly devoid of any Southern prejudices against those who were so nearly of their own color. They were disposed to treat all the servants kindly, but they had not the same feeling towards those of ebony hue.

The same sentiment prevailed through the family; and as a rule it pervaded most of the enlightened families of the South. The girls as well as the mother — and Dorcas and Artie looked upon and called Mrs. Lyon by this endearing name — had been accustomed to wait upon themselves, and they found it rather difficult to economize the willing hands of Sylvie and Julie. But when Pink arrived with the trunks and other baggage, the field-hands "toted" them to the proper chambers, and the aid of the servants was very welcome, for both of them were tired after the long journey they had made.

As the great clock in the spacious hall below struck six, the family were summoned to supper. Levi acted as master of ceremonies, for Diana was busy in the kitchen, with her two assistants; but he seemed to have some doubts about seating himself at his employer's table, though he had always had a place there in the colonel's time.

"Sit here, if you please, Levi, and always consider yourself as one of the family," said Noah, after he had asked Deck to take the second seat on the right, giving the manager the first, which is the seat of honor; and the question of Levi's position at Riverlawn was settled once for all.

"Thank you, Major Lyon," replied he, as he took the place assigned to him. "I always sat at the table with Colonel Lyon, even when he had guests; but it isn't always the rule with planters to have the overseer at his table, and I am much obliged to you for your consideration."

"When I had two or three hired men on my farm, they always came to the table with me, and would have thought they were abused if they had been placed at a separate board." laughed the embryo planter. "But they were the 'mud-sills' of the North, you know."

"I was raised in Tennessee, Major, and was tolerably well educated. I was in business for myself in Shelbyville, the capital of our county, which was named for one of my ancestors. But I did not succeed, for the place was not big enough. I bought some nice horses of Colonel Lyon, and for some reason he took a fancy to me."

"I don't think that was very strange," added Noah.

"When I failed, he wanted me to come and manage this place for him; and I have been here ever since. He paid me well, and I have always done the best I could for him. He was a good man; and it looks to me just as though his successor was as good a man as he was."

"Thank you, Levi; I believe we shall be friends."

"Betwixt you and me, Major," continued the manager in a low tone, "when the colonel's health began to be rather shaky, though I had no idea he was so near his end, I had a mortal dread that a certain other man would come into possession of this place. Excuse me for saying that, but I couldn't help it. Since I met you this noon, Major, I have been lifted up to the seventh heaven."

Noah did not deem it wise to make any reply to this remark then; but he intended to inquire more particularly in regard to his Kentucky brother when he had an opportunity; and it appeared that the manager had some very pronounced opinions in regard to Titus. He changed the subject, and continued to eat his supper.

The meal was elaborate enough for a family feast. After the fried ham and bacon, the fried chicken, with baked potatoes and the nicest white cornbread the family had ever eaten, came hot biscuits, waffles, and griddle-cakes, and cake of several kinds, which were fully approved by Mrs. Lyon. Diana came in before the party rose from the table, and the praises bestowed upon her handiwork in the kitchen would have made her blush if she had been as light-colored as the two girls that waited upon the table.

When Noah Lyon went to his room after supper, and was alone there, he took from his pocket the letter from his deceased brother which Colonel

Cosgrove had given him. It was with no little emotion that he broke the cumbrous seals. It looked very much like a mystery to him, for the estate had been duly divided in the will.

It was a very kindly and brotherly letter for the first page. Then the colonel stated that Noah had by the time he received the letter discovered that the value of the fifty-one negroes on the estate had not been included in his valuation of the property. They were worth at least twenty-five thousand dollars. They had been given to him with the plantation, but he enjoined it upon him on no account to sell one of them.

In the letter he found another as carefully sealed as the one that enclosed it, directed to his successor, with the direction: "Not to be opened till five years from the date of my death. Duncan Lyon."

The letter evidently related to the slaves on the plantation; but the mystery in regard to them was still unsolved.

CHAPTER V

THE DISTRESS OF MRS. TITUS LYON

IN the rear of the drawing-room was the library. It contained about five hundred bound volumes, and more than this number of pamphlets and documents, which had accumulated in a quarter of a century. It contained a large desk and a safe, and the apartment was an office rather than a library, though the owner of Riverlawn had largely improved his education by reading in his abundant leisure. The shelves were piled high with newspapers and magazines, which appeared to have been the staple of his intellectual food.

Levi had given the key of the safe to the new proprietor; and after Noah had read and reread the open letter, and pondered its contents, he carried the one which was not to be opened for five years to the library, and deposited it in the safe with the explanatory epistle which left the whole subject a mystery. What was eventually to become of the negroes was not indicated, but he was enjoined not to sell one of them on any account.

" Though opposed to the extension of slavery, Noah Lyon did not believe that Congress had any constitutional right to meddle with the system as it existed in the States. He had never been brought into contact with slavery, and did not howl when his brother became a slaveholder. Like the majority of the people of the North, he was instinctively, as it were, opposed to human bondage; but he had never been considered a fanatic or an abolitionist by his friends and neighbors. He simply refrained from meddling with the subject.

The fifty-one negroes on the estate had been willed to him, and he was as much a slaveholder as his brother had been. The injunction not to sell one of them was needless in its application to him, for he would as readily have thought of selling one of his own children as any human being.

It would require a bulky volume to detail the experience of Noah Lyon and his family during the years that followed his arrival at Barcreek. He was an intelligent man, richly endowed with saving common-sense, and soon made himself familiar with all the affairs of the plantation. He made the acquaintance of the servants, which was no small matter in itself, for he ascertained the history, disposition, and character of all of them.

He found that his brother had not over-estimated the worth of Levi Bedford, who soon became a great favorite with all the family. The new proprietor found no occasion to change the conduct of affairs in the management of the place, even if he had felt that he was competent to improve the methods and system of his late brother. Everything went on as before. Levi made the crops of hemp, tobacco, corn, and vegetables, and raised horses, marketing everything to be sold. He consulted his employer, but he had little to say.

The family became acquainted with their neighbors within a circuit of ten miles, and in spite of their origin they were kindly and hospitably received by the best families.

At the end of a year the Lyons had practically become Kentuckians. In the following year came the great political campaign which resulted in the election of Abraham Lincoln to the presidency.

Ominous growls had been heard from the South, and even in the border State of Kentucky. Noah regarded the situation with no little anxiety; but he continued to attend to his own affairs, and it was not till the bombardment of Fort Sumter that he began to take an active part in the agitation which was shaking the entire nation.

Titus Lyon was one of the most stormy and aggressive of the Southern sympathizers. Even neutrality was a compromise with him. When Noah's family took possession of Riverlawn, he did not call at the mansion for several days, though his wife and Mabel, his eldest daughter, had spent the day after their arrival with them. Though Titus said nothing at first, or for months to come, it was very evident to Noah that he was intensely dissatisfied with the distribution the colonel had made of his property.

The state of affairs in Barcreek has been shown in the conversation between the planter and his son on the bridge. This seemed to be a favorite resort for conferences, and they returned to it after dinner. On one side of it was a seat which had been put up there years before; for it was shaded by a magnificent tree which grew by the side of the creek road, and the bridge was the coolest place on the estate in a hot day.

"Of course you heard what your mother said about her visit to Titus's house to-day, Dexter," said the father, as he seated himself on the bench.

"I could not well help hearing it," replied Deck.

"If there is anything in this world I abominate, it is a family quarrel," continued Noah, fixing his gaze upon the dark waters of the creek. "Your uncle seems to be disposed to be at variance with me, though I am sure I have done nothing of which he can reasonably complain. He is down upon every Union man in the county. I should say that Barcreek was about equally divided between the two parties. But he does not talk politics to me, as he does to every other man in the place."

"I don't know what he means when he says you owe him five thousand dollars, for I thought the boot was on the other leg," said Deck, looking into the troubled face of his father.

"He owes me several hundred dollars I lent him before he sold his railroad stock. He is able to pay me now, for he has turned his securities into money, and he seems to be flinging it away as fast as he can. He must be worth twenty-five thousand dollars, including his house and land; but I don't know how much of it he has thrown away."

"If he has spent five thousand dollars for arms, ammunition, and uniforms, he must have made a big hole in it," suggested Deck. "He keeps three horses when he has no use for more than one."

"He never had a tenth part as much money before in his life, and he does not know how to use it. He will be the captain of a Home Guard as soon as he can enlist the men, and the people on his side of the question at the village have begun to call him 'Captain Lyon,' or 'Captain Titus.'"

"Sandy told me that he, his father, and Orly had been drilling for three months with an old soldier who was in the Mexican War," added Deck. "There comes Artie in one of the boats."

"Where is he going?" asked Noah.

"I'm sure I don't know; Artie don't always tell where he is going," answered Deck.

His cousin, whom he regarded and treated as his brother, was pulling a very handsome keel boat leisurely up the creek. The colonel appeared to have had some aquatic tastes, for at a kind of pier half-way between the bridge and the river were a sailboat and two row-boats, all of which were kept in excellent condition. In places the river was wide enough to allow the use of a boat with a sail, and the colonel had had some skill in managing one; but neither Noah nor his boys could handle such a craft, and it was never used.

The creek extended back some ten miles through a flat, swampy region, and Deck and Artie had explored it almost to its source in some low hills not a dozen miles from the Mammoth Cave. Like most boys, they were fond of boats, and nothing but the forbidding command of the planter prevented them from experimenting with the Magnolia, as the sailboat was called by the colonel.

If the boys had explored Bar Creek to its source, they would have discovered that it came out of the numerous "sinks" to be found in this portion of the country, and streams flowed in subterranean channels which honeycombed the earth at a greater or less depth below the surface.

"What are you up to, Deck?" shouted Artie, as he approached the bridge.

"Nothing particular," replied the one on the bridge. "Where are you going?"

"Up the creek," answered Artie very indefinitely. "Can't you go with me? It is easier for two to row this boat than for one."

"I don't want to go now," returned Deck, who was too much interested in the conversation with his father to leave him.

"You may go with him if you want to, Dexter," interposed Mr. Lyon.

"I don't care about going now, father. Do you suppose Uncle Titus has really bought the arms and things as mother says?" asked Deck.

"Your aunt is very much worried about the actions of your uncle. I suppose he told her what he had done, for she would not make up such a story out of whole cloth. Besides, it seems to be in keeping with a dozen other things he has done; and he is certainly doing all he can to raise a company in Barcreek," replied Mr. Lyon.

"Isn't it strange that he never says anything to you about politics, especially such as we are having now?" asked the son.

"I don't see him very often; he is at Bowling Green half the time. Besides, he and I never agreed on politics. By the great George Washington, there he is now!" exclaimed Noah Lyon, springing up from his seat on the bench.

Titus Lyon was seated with his wife in a stylish buggy. He stopped his horse on the bridge when he came opposite to his brother, and passing the reins to Mrs Lyon he descended to the planks. His wife drove on, and stopped at the front door of the mansion. Frank the coachman ran with all his might from the stable to take charge of the team, and the lady went into the house.

"How do you do, Titus?" said Noah, extending his hand to his brother.

"I think it is about time for me to have some talk with you, Noah," replied Titus, ignoring the offered hand, and bestowing a frowning look upon Deck. "Send that boy away."

"Dexter knows all about my affairs, and I don't have many secrets from him," replied Noah very mildly, and somewhat nettled to have his son treated in that rude manner.

"I came over here on purpose to talk with you; and what I have to say is between you and me — for the present. If you don't wish to talk with me on these terms, that's the end on't," added Titus, rising from the seat he had taken.

"I will go with Artie, father," interposed Deck, who did not wish to prevent an interview between the brothers, though he thought his uncle behaved like a Hottentot.

"Very well, Dexter; but you needn't go if you don't want to," said his father, who evidently did not believe that the proposed interview with Titus would be conducted on a peace basis.

"I think I will go," added Deck, who hailed Artie from the bridge, and then hastened to a plank where he could get into the boat.

For a reason which he would not have explained if he had been interrogated by his father, or by any other person except Deck, Artie was very desirous to have his cousin go with him; in fact, he was thinking of postponing his excursion, whatever its object, till his cousin could accompany him, when the hail came to him from the bridge. He pulled up to the plank, the outer end of which was supported by stakes driven into the bottom of the stream, with a cross-piece above the water. It had been built for the convenience of those taking one of the boats near the mansion. Deck took an oar, and they pulled together up the creek.

Mrs. Titus Lyon was cordially welcomed at the door of the house by Mrs. Noah, who had seen her coming from the window. The lady from the village was in a high state of perturbation, and her eyes looked as though she had been weeping.

"I have had an awful time since you called upon me this morning," said she, wiping her eyes with her handkerchief. "I don't know what we are coming to at our house. For the first time in my life my husband struck me after we got up from dinner, and then hurried me down here with hardly time to change my clothes!"

"Struck you, Amelia!" exclaimed Mrs. Noah with an expression of horror.

"Perhaps it was all my own fault," groaned the poor woman.

"No fault could justify your husband in striking you. But what was it for?" inquired Mrs. Noah, overflowing with sympathy for her sister-in-law.

"You remember that story about the arms and equipments I told you this morning? Well, it seems that my son Orly was listening at the half-open door when I supposed that no one but myself was in the house, for the girls had all gone off to the store. He heard the whole of it, and told his father when he came in to dinner," gasped the abused lady in short sentences.

"He struck you for telling me, did he?" demanded Mrs. Noah indignantly. "I should like to give him a piece of my mind!"

"Don't you say a word to him about it, for that would only make it all the worse for me. Titus says there is no truth at all in the story. He has bought no arms. I misunderstood him; he was telling about a committee in Logan County that had bought the arms and ammunition for a company. It is all a mistake; and if you have told any of your family, do take it all back, and say there is not a word of truth in the story."

Mrs. Titus could see from the window that the two brothers were having a stormy interview on the bridge; but she stayed till long after dark, and had recovered her self-possession before she left. Noah had no supper till she had gone, and the boys had not yet returned.

CHAPTER VI

THE NIGHT ADVENTURE ON THE CREEK

If Deck Lyon had particularly noted the actions of his cousin in the boat he would have noticed that he was less decided in his movements than usual. He stopped rowing several times in the ten minutes or more that elapsed after he had invited Deck to go with him; and one who had been near enough to study his expression would have understood that he had a purpose before him which he was not prepared to execute under present circumstances.

He had listened with the closest attention to Mrs. Lyon's report of her visit at the house of Titus, and he was in a revery after dinner as he observed Noah and his son walking to the bridge. He waited till he had seen them seated on the bench, and then he walked slowly to the boat pier. He was disappointed when his cousin refused to go with him; but he was not inclined to persuade him to leave his father, for he concluded that something of importance was under discussion between them.

He was relieved, and all his vigor and animation came back to him as he pulled to the house landing. Artie was more inclined than Deck to keep within his own shell; but it was not for the want of native energy, and both of the boys were disposed to do whatever they had in hand with all their might. He brought the boat up abreast of the pier, and Deck stepped into the bow without any further invitation. He took one of the light pine oars from his cousin.

"If you don't object, Deck, I would like to pull the forward oar," said Artie, as his companion was seating himself.

"It is all the same to me which oar I take," replied Deck, as he changed his place.

"I want to talk with you, and I can do it better when you are in front of me," added Artie, as he shoved the boat out into the stream.

"Where are you going? You seem to have something in your head besides bones," said Deck curiously.

"Besides the bones I've got a big notion in my head."

"Is it a Yankee or a Kentucky notion, Artie?"

"I picked it up here, and it is Kentuckish. But I don't want to say anything now; for I'm afraid some one might hear me, more particularly Uncle Titus," replied the bow oarsman as he took the stroke from his cousin. "I wonder what brought him over here, for he don't come to Riverlawn much oftener than he goes to church."

"He acts like a regular Hottentot just out of the woods; and if there are any bears in Kentucky they would behave like gentlemen compared with Uncle Titus," added Deck, who proceeded to describe the manner of the visitor on the bridge when the two brothers met.

"Uncle Titus has got something besides bones in his head this afternoon, and when he started to come over here he meant business," suggested Artie. "Something is in the wind."

"I wanted to stay and hear what was said, but Uncle Titus drove me off as he would have kicked a snake into the creek. He was as grouty and as savage as a she-lion that had lost all her cubs."

"Did he say anything about that story your mother told at dinner?" asked Arty.

"Not a word; he drove me off as though I had

been a cur dog before he said a word about anything else," replied Deck, who could not easily forget the brutal manner of his uncle. "But you have not told me yet where you are going, Artie. You haven't any fishlines or bait, and I suppose you are not going a-fishing."

"Not up the creek, for the river suits me better for that business; but I'm going a-fishing for something that won't swim in the water," replied the undemonstrative boy.

"What do you mean by that?" demanded Deck; and his interest in the subject caused him to cease rowing, and Artie pulled the boat round so that it was headed to the shore.

"Pull away, Deck! What are you about? We don't want to stop here," said Artie with more than his usual vigor.

"I am about nothing; but when I talk with you I like to look you in the face, for that sometimes tells the story better than your words," replied Deck, as he gave way again with his oar. "As I said before, you have got something besides bones in your head, and I am in a hurry to know what it is all about. You can't talk it into me through the back of my head."

"But we don't want to stop here, Richard Cœur de Lyon!" protested Artie, rather vehemently for him. "Don't you see that we are still in sight of the bridge, and I would not have Uncle Titus see what we are about for all the world, with Venus and Mars thrown in. Besides, we have a long pull before us, and we have no time to spare."

"But I want to know what it is all about," Deck objected. "I am not going into any conspiracy with my eyes blinded."

"Pull away, Deck! I don't want that Secesher to see us stopping here. We shall come to the bend in five minutes; and then if you want to stop and talk I will agree to it, though we haven't any time to waste," suggested Artie as a compromise.

"One would think you were going to set the river on fire by your talk," replied Deck, profoundly mystified by the words, and more by the manner of his companion.

"We may set the creek on fire before we get through with this job," continued Artie, deepening the mystery every minute. "There's Levi Bedford," he added, as the manager, riding on a rather wild colt, in the road leading to the fields, came abreast of the boat.

He was too far off to talk to the boys; but he waved his hat to them, and the boatmen returned the salute, as he continued on his way.

"I wonder where Levi stands in the row that is brewing all over the country," said Deck. "I don't hear him say anything of any consequence, though he may have talked to father. He did not come from New England, and I don't know whether he is a Secesher or not; and it looks as though he did not mean anybody should know."

"He don't belong to the Home Guards any way," added Artie. "He is a Tennesseean, and it would not be strange if he had some Secesh notions."

"I don't believe he is going back on father," replied Deck, when the manager had disappeared and the boat had reached the bend. "Here we are; we can't see the bridge now, and the bridge can't see us."

"We will stop if you say so; but we may not get back to the house before to-morrow morning if we spend much time here," said Artie, as he rested on his oar, and seemed to be very unwilling to use any of the time in mere talk.

"If the time is so short, why didn't you start out this morning? and why didn't you let me know sooner that you were going to set the creek on fire? We might have brought our dinners with us, as we did when we went to school in Derry, and made a day of it," argued Deck.

"Things were not ready this morning, and I started just as soon as I saw the star in the east," replied Artie.

"You don't generally wait for the grass to grow under your feet when the lightning strikes near you."

"The lightning struck while we were at dinner," added Artie quietly.

"But I think we can fix things so that we can talk and keep moving at the same time," suggested Deck, as he rose from his seat with his oar in his hand, and stepped over his thwart to the aftermost one.

He seated himself on this thwart, facing the bow. The boys were not skilled boatmen, though they had practised rowing a good deal on the river and creek, and they had not trimmed the light craft to the best advantage for ease and speed, for it was down too much by the head. Deck asked his cousin to move one seat farther aft, and he complied readily, in spite of the fact that he was the more skilled of the two in rowing. In the smallest of the three boats at the lower pier he had often made long trips alone up the creek, besides those when his cousin was his companion.

"That lifts the bow higher out of the water," said Artie as he took his place.

"So much the better," replied Deck, proceeding to give philosophical and scientific reasons to explain what experienced boatman know by instinct, as it were. "Now take the stroke from me, and don't pull any faster than I do."

Placing himself in an angular position on the thwart, with his right hand hold of the seat, he began to row with his left. While pulling alone in the canoe, as the negro rowers called the smallest craft, he had been inclined to protest against the accepted custom of going backwards in rowing; and he would gladly have adopted the mechanical contrivance in use on some of the Northern waters which enabled the boatmen to pull while facing the bow. He wanted to see where he was going without turning around, and he had practised rowing in this position.

Deck was heavier and stronger than his cousin, though hardly as agile. Artie took the stroke from him, and it was quite as quick as he cared to row on a long pull. They kept good time, and the boat went along as rapidly as before.

"Now light your match, and start the fire, Artie. We shall lose no time by this arrangement, and we shall get back to the house before morning."

"Perhaps, after you understand the nature of the enterprise, you will not be willing to go with me," added Artie, looking earnestly into the face of his cousin.

"I can tell better about that after I know what it is," returned Deck, reciprocating the earnest gaze of the other. "But it is you who are wasting the time now. Why don't you come to the point without going around all the buildings on the plantation?"

"You heard the story mother told about the arms and ammunition Uncle Titus had bought for the Home Guards in order to make himself the captain of the company?"

"Of course I heard it," and Deck was unwilling to say another word to increase the preliminaries to the revelation.

"Did you believe it?"

"I did."

"Then you are satisfied that Uncle Titus has a lot of arms hid away somewhere in this region?" persisted Artie.

"I had my doubts, and I spoke to father about it on the bridge just before you came along in the boat. He thought that his brother was just crazy enough to do such a thing; but he thought whiskey had a good deal to do with the matter, especially in permitting him to tell his wife about it. Of course Sandy and Orly are mixed up in this business. But this is an old story by this time, Artie, and you have not told me yet what you are driving at," said Deck impatiently.

"We are going to look for the arms and ammunition, Deck!" exclaimed the originator of the enterprise. "Is that talking plainly enough?"

"To look for the arms and ammunition!" almost shouted the after oarsman, ceasing to use his oar in the astonishment of the moment.

"You insisted on my telling you all at once, and I have done so; you have stopped rowing."

"What you said was enough to throw a fellow off his base. Do you mean that you are going on a wild-goose chase all over the State of Kentucky to look for what may be a mere notion, conjured up by an overdose of whiskey?" demanded Deck, still resting on his oar.

"Don't get excited, Cœur de Lyon; cold steel cuts best," said Artie.

"And that's the reason father puts his razor into hot water when he is shaving."

"I don't think anybody is right down sure of anything in this world," continued the leader of the enterprise. "I think I am as sure as any fellow can be in this State of Kentucky, where no man or boy can tell which end he stands on, that I know where Uncle Titus's arms and ammunition are hidden."

"You know!" ejaculated Deck.

"I think I know."

"What are you doing up the creek, then? Didn't Aunt Amelia say that the arms were concealed near the river?" asked Deck, hardly able to breathe in his excitement.

"I think I know where they are hidden better than she did. If Uncle Titus told his wife that they were hidden on the river, — and that is just what aunt said, — her husband intended to cheat her," said Artie very confidently. "I should say that a dozen glasses of whiskey would not have made Uncle Titus fool enough to tell anybody where the arms were concealed, not even his wife; and they don't seem to be a very loving couple since they came to Kentucky."

"That's so," added Deck.

"Do you remember that time about a fortnight ago when father spoke to me about being out so late one night, Deck?"

"I remember it; it was on the bridge."

"That night I found out something I could not explain, but I can now, after what I heard at dinner to-day. But we have eight or ten miles to pull if we are going to find the arms to-day, and we must be moving," added Artie.

Deck rowed again, and they proceeded up the creek, Artie telling his night adventure by the way.

CHAPTER VII

A STORMY INTERVIEW ON THE BRIDGE

Probably Noah Lyon had never felt anything like the emotion of anger in his being against his brother until they met that day on the bridge. As one and another had said several times, no two men of the same blood and lineage could have been more differently constituted. Noah had been a diligent student as a boy, and a constant reader in his maturity; while Titus had been the black sheep of the family, had neglected his studies in his youth, and did not even read a newspaper in his manhood, unless for a special purpose.

Titus could read and write, and knew enough of arithmetic to enable him to keep the accounts of his business. Whatever he learned after he left school he gathered from the speech of people; and as his associates were not of the intelligent class in his native town any more than they were in his new home, his education was very limited.

and his moral aims, if he could be said to have any, were not elevated enough to keep him very far within the limits of the law, which were his principal tests between right and wrong.

Before he was twenty-one he obtained a position to drive a stage on a twenty-mile route, so that he spent every other night at a tavern; and this did not improve his manners or his morals. As a boy he had become disgusted with farming, and had learned the trade of a mason, working at it three years. Like his elder brother, he was a horse fancier, and was a skilful driver. An accident to the old stage-driver placed him on the box, and when the place became permanent he was only twenty years old.

With so little intellectual and moral foundation as he had laid for his future character, it was a misfortune for him that he was then a "good-looking fellow." He boarded at the tavern, and paid only two dollars a week in consideration of his position, for it was believed that he had some influence with his passengers. He was well supplied with money for one of his age in the country, and he spent all he had.

He was an agile dancer, which, with his good

looks, made him popular in the town, especially with the girls. Amelia Lenox was a pretty girl. She had a fancy for the handsome stage-driver; and, in spite of the earnest objections of her father and mother, she accepted him as her husband, and they were married. Titus took a cottage near the tavern, and for a year, with the help of his and her father, they got along very well.

All of a sudden a railroad shot through the town, and the business of the place was gone in the twinkling of an eye. The wages of Titus stopped, and he had a wife and child to support. He went to his father for advice. The mason, who had done a good business in the town and its vicinity, had grown old. Hopestill Lyon, the grandfather of the boys, was his best friend, and bought out his business for Titus.

For several years he worked well, made some money, and paid his grandfather for the investment made on his behalf. But he did not like the business. Unlike his brothers, he seemed to believe that fate, destiny, circumstances, or some other indefinable power that regulates the worldly condition of mortals, had misused and abused him;

for he ought to have been "born with a silver spoon in his mouth," with wealth at his command, so that he could live in luxury without work.

When he built chimneys, plastered rooms, or jobbed in filthy drains and smutty fireplaces, he labored with an active protest against his occupation in his soul, which extended down to his hands and feet, shutting out ambition, and making him lazy. He was always on the lookout for some other occupation, or for some change which would put more money in his pocket. He did a vast deal of grumbling and growling at his lot, occasionally taking home with him a gallon jug of New England rum, which did not improve his condition. He was not a drunkard, but he was unconsciously falling into a bad habit.

His wife was an intelligent woman, and was a good helpmate; but it did not require a prophetic vision to read the future, near or distant, of Titus Lyon. It was said by some of the old people in the town that he "took after" his grandmother, who had been a stylish woman in her younger days, though the solid character of Hopestill Lyon had controlled her inclinations so that she made him a good wife.

Mrs. Lyon reasoned kindly with Titus; but before she left her Northern home she had lost whatever influence she had ever exercised over him. He was eager to settle in Kentucky when the colonel's letter announcing an opening for him came, and she was utterly opposed to the plan. It was at least a change, and he was determined to make it, in spite of the fact that his brother could not advise him to do so; and the result proved the solidity of the colonel's judgment.

For seven years Titus fawned upon his wealthy brother. He was as obsequious in his presence as one of the field-hands of Riverlawn; but the colonel did not believe in him as he did in Noah, especially after his long visit to the latter. When the health of the planter began to be slightly impaired a couple of years before his death, Titus was sordid enough to think of what would become of his plantation, which seemed like a mine of wealth to him, at the decease of the owner.

He had talked planting, hemp, and horses to the colonel, and did all he could to impress him with the belief that he was competent to manage the plantation. It was his nature to believe in what he desired, and he was satisfied that Riverlawn would be bequeathed to him, as it ought to be. The reading of the will was a shock to him. The giving of ten thousand dollars more than his fair share to Noah, who lived far away, and had never even seen the plantation, in consideration for bringing up the two orphans of his brother, excited his wrath.

He regarded this gift as an absolute wrong to him, while he was compelled to pay the note out of his own share. He went home from Riverlawn that day choking down his anger; but he was furious in the presence of his wife, though she did all she could to console him. She pointed out the fact that he now owned his place clear of any debt, and had twenty thousand dollars in cash, stocks, and bonds; but he was not satisfied. He wanted Riverlawn, where he could live in style, with an abundant income without work.

As he brooded over his fancied wrong, it came to his mind that the colonel's *ante-mortem* inventory had not included the value of the negroes on the plantation. He hastened over to see Colonel Cosgrove, the executor. He exhibited a copy of the will, and Titus studied over it for half a day. Nothing was said about the slaves. Then he went to another lawyer with whom he had had some political dealings; but this gentleman assured him that he had no remedy; the colonel had an undoubted right to dispose of his property as he pleased, even if he had given the whole of it to Noah. He had bequeathed the plantation, the mansion, with all that was in or on them, or appertaining to them; and this included the negroes.

For nearly two years Titus had nursed his wrath, and was earnest in his belief that Noah ought to right the wrong the colonel had done him. Yet he had never had the courage to make this claim upon his brother, or even to mention to him the five thousand dollars which he insisted belonged to him. The law could do nothing for him, his own lawyer told him. Noah was his brother, now his only brother; and it was his duty, according to every principle of right and justice, to pay over to him half of the legacy of ten thousand dollars, and of the twenty-five thousand dollars which was a low valuation of the negro property.

The quantity of Kentucky whiskey which Titus consumed magnified his wrongs and made him more unreasonable than his natural discontent would have made him. When he learned from his younger son what his wife had told Mrs. Noah, he was more furious than he had ever been known to be before, and he descended to the brutality of striking her. He had taken more than his habitual potion of whiskey, and it made him ugly. His wife wept bitterly over the abuse she had been subjected to, both the words and the blow, and she had fled to her bedroom.

She was a high-spirited woman, and it seemed to her that the end of all things had come, at least so far as her domestic happiness was concerned. Her father was a well-to-do farmer; and neither he nor her brothers would permit her to be abused by any one, not even by her husband. A sudden and violent resolution came to her to return to her father's house. While she was thinking of this remedy and of the parting with her children, Titus rushed into the room. She must undo the mischief she had done, and he would drive her to Riverlawn for that purpose. He told her what to say, and she promised to say it; for she felt that she had been indiscreet in what she had said.

During the drive her husband had continued to abuse her with his unruly tongue, and she had wept all the way. They found Noah and Deck on the bridge, and Titus decided to pour out his grievances to his brother; for his drams had brought his courage up to the point where he felt like doing it. He was not intoxicated, but he had drunk enough to make him ugly. He descended from the vehicle, and Mrs. Titus drove over to the mansion.

Dexter was sent away as before related, and the father was somewhat moved by the rudeness with which the boy had been treated. He was a mild-spoken man; and though he was quiet in his manner, he had more real grit in his composition than Titus.

"You seem to be excited, Titus," said Noah, as he seated himself on the bench from which he had just risen.

"I have good reason to be excited," growled the angry man. "My wife has acted like a fool and a traitor to me!"

"I am sorry for that, Brother Titus; but I hope you don't hold me responsible for her conduct," said Noah in gentle and conciliatory tones.

"Not exactly; but you are responsible for enough without that, and I have made up my mind that it is time for you and me to have a reckoning, for you don't do by me as a brother should; and if father was living to-day he would be ashamed of you," returned the mason, with all the emphasis of a bad cause.

"I was not aware that I had been wanting in anything one brother ought to do for another. But we had better consider a subject of such importance when you are cooler than you seem to be just now, Titus. Your present complaint appears to be against Amelia, and not against me. What has she done? I have always looked upon her as a very good woman and good wife."

"You don't know her as well as I do. I don't know what bad advice Ruth has given her, or what influence she has over Meely, but she made her tell a ridiculous story about some arms and ammunition," said Titus in a milder manner; for he seemed to be intent upon counteracting the effect of her action. "I s'pose Ruth repeated to you the story Meely told."

"She said you had given five thousand dollars for the purchase of arms, ammunition, and uniforms for a company of Home Guards, of which you were to be the captain."

"I'll bet that wa'n't all she told you," added Titus.

"That was the substance of it."

"I suppose most folks in Barcreek know all that."

"I never knew it till to-day."

"You don't go about among folks in this county as I do."

"I don't associate much with Secessionists and Home Guards."

"I do! But that is my business, and I have a good right to give my money where it will do the most good; and I shall do so whether you like it or not," fumed Titus.

"I don't dispute your right; though I am surprised that a man brought up in the State of New Hampshire should become a Secessionist when more than half the people of Kentucky are in favor of the Union," added Noah.

"'Tain't so! I never was a Black Republican, as you were, and I don't begin on't now. If you want to steal the niggers, I don't help you do it! But Meely told your wife something more;" and Titus looked anxiously into the face of his brother, as if to read the extent of the mischief which had been done.

"I believe Ruth did tell me that the arms and

munitions had already been purchased, and were hidden somewhere on the river," added Noah. "But I did not pay much attention to this part of the story. The material part of it was that you had given so much money to assist in making war in the State."

"I give the money to keep the war out of Kentucky, and maintain the neutrality of the State," argued Titus.

"We had better not talk politics, brother, and I will not give my views of neutrality."

"The story my wife told about the arms was all a lie!" exclaimed the visitor with an oath which shocked the owner of the plantation. "No arms are hid on the river, or anywhere else. Meely understood what I said with her elbows; and she has come down now to take it all back."

"Very well; I don't care anything about the arms, though I should be sorry to have them go into the hands of the Secessionists or the Home Guards, for they are all in the same boat."

At this moment Levi Bedford rode over the bridge on the colt, and Titus was silent.

CHAPTER VIII

AN OVERWHELMING ARGUMENT

Levi Bedford had not come to the bridge to interfere with the conversation or to listen to what was said; but as he was returning from the distant fields of the plantation by the creek road, he could not help seeing that a stormy interview was in progress on the bridge. He believed that he understood Titus Lyon better than Noah did. He considered him capable of violence to his brother when under the influence of liquor, and he deemed it prudent for him to be within call if he was needed.

Noah would have scouted the idea of Titus raising his hand against him, even when he had been drinking; for in former years they had always lived together on the best of terms. Levi had seen more of the mason within a few years than Noah. While the colonel lay unburied in the mansion, he had spent most of the time at Riverlawn, and to some extent had assumed the control of the plantation.

The manager had not required the negroes to do anything but necessary work during the sad interval; but Titus had interfered, and sent the field-hands to their usual occupation. He had "bossed" Levi himself as though he were only a servant, and even meddled with the affairs of Diana in the house. The manager could not resent this interference at such a time, and he could not help seeing that Titus was taking more whiskey than usual; for he had even ordered Diana to bring out the choice stores of this article which the colonel had kept for his friends rather than for his own use.

He talked to Levi just as though the plantation would soon come into his hands, and had made himself as unnecessarily offensive to the overseer and all the petted servants as possible. It would not be overstating the truth to say that he was thoroughly hated at Riverlawn. Levi had packed his trunk in readiness to leave as soon as the tyrant took possession of the place; and even some of the people were thinking of making their way to the free State of Ohio.

Levi bowed and smiled as he passed the planter, but he only reined in his fiery steed, and did not stop. He did not even look at Titus, much less salute him, for he despised him; and pleasant as he was to all on the place, including the people, he was an honest man, and appeared to be just what he was. He rode over in the direction of the river, and when he reached a thicket of trees and bushes he stopped the colt and tied him to a tree. He remained there where he could see the bridge without being seen by those upon it.

"I wonder that you keep that fellow on the place," said Titus, as Levi rode off. "In my opinion, and I have seen more of him than you have, Noah, he is a rascal;" and the last remark was seasoned with an oath.

"I think he is a very useful man, and my family are already very much attached to him; for he is always good-natured, and kind and obliging to everybody," replied the planter.

"There ain't no accounting for tastes, as my wife says; but if I had this place that cuss would get kicked out before he had a chance to breathe twice more," said Titus with a look of disgust which caused him to twist his mouth and nose into such a snarl that Mrs. Titus would hardly have known him.

Levi had not told his employer in what manner the would-be owner of the plantation had conducted himself on the place after the death of the colonel; and Noah could not understand why his brother had such an antipathy to so genial a man as the manager, viewed from his own and his family's standpoint.

"I take Levi as I find him, and I have been very much pleased with him," added Noah.

"But I did not come over here to talk about that dirty shote," continued Titus, suddenly bracing himself up to attack the subject of the grievances which had gnawed like a live snake at his vitals for nearly two years. "In the fust place, I want you to understand, Noah Lyon, that there ain't a word of truth in the story Meely told this noon in your house."

"All right, Brother Titus," replied Noah. "I haven't looked for the arms and ammunition, and I know nothing about them."

"Do you believe what I say, Noah?" demanded Titus with a savage frown.

"I have no reason to doubt your statement."

"If you and your family want to make trouble over that statement, I s'pose you can do so. You 'n' I don't agree on politics."

"We are not disposed to make trouble. If there should be any difficulty it will come from your side of the house, Titus."

"You are an abolitionist, and folks on the right side in this county have found it out. They don't believe in no Lincoln shriekers, and the Union's already busted," said the Secessionist brother with a good deal of vim; and in this, as in other matters, he believed the popular sentiment was on the side he wished it to be.

"I voted for Lincoln, and I believe in the Union," added Noah quietly.

"Yes; and there is five hundred men in this county that would like to drive you out of the State, and burn your house over your head!" exclaimed Titus, becoming not a little excited. "I believe they'd done it before this time if I hadn't stood in their way."

"Then I am very much obliged to you for your friendly influence. I was not aware that I had been in any peril before," returned Noah with a smile, which was suggestive of a doubt in his mind. "Do you think I am in any danger from such an outrage as you suggest?"

"I know you are!" Titus belched out with

something like fury in his manner. "If it hadn't been for me they'd done it before now. You haven't been a bit keerful in your doings. You've got up a Union meeting at the Big Bend schoolhouse for to-morrow night; and if you go on with it, I'm almost sure you will get cleaned out; and the folks on the right side may come over here, after they have shut your mouths at the Bend, and see whether your house will burn or not. I have done all I could to keep our folks quiet, and advised them not to meddle with the meeting at the schoolhouse; but if you keep on the way you're going, I won't be responsible for what happens."

"Though I came from the North since you did, all the people I meet seem to be very friendly to me," answered Noah, the smile still playing upon his lips; a satirical smile which indicated that he did not believe more than a very small fraction of what his brother had been saying.

He had no doubt that the gang with whom Titus and his sons associated would do all and even more than he prophesied; but they did not form the public sentiment of the county.

"You don't meet all nor a tenth part of the

people, and you don't know what is running in their heads," protested the Secessionist. "You and your two boys keep on howling for the Union when the people round here are all dead set agin it. What can you expect? Seven States is out of the Union, and that busts the whole thing."

"I don't think a majority of the people about here are of your way of thinking, Brother Titus; but if I am in danger of mob violence, as you say I am, my house is my castle; I shall defend it as long as there is anything left of me," added Noah, the same smile resting on his lips as he uttered his strong words.

"Defend your house!" said Titus with a bitter sneer. "You hadn't better do anything of the sort. If you show fight, the crowd will hang you to one of them big trees. You ain't reasonable, Noah. Do you cal'late on fighting the whole county?"

"We differ considerably in regard to the state of feeling in this county. We are between two fires, and I think we had better not say anything more on that subject."

"That's so; but one fire is an alfired sight hotter than t'other; and that's the one that will burn up that big house of yourn."

"I shall defend my house, and I think I shall be able to hold my own. But I am not an abolitionist any more than you are, Brother Titus," mildly suggested Noah.

"You shriek for the Union, and it's all the same thing among honest folks down here," retorted the Secessionist.

"I hold about fifty slaves, and I had an idea that this made me a slaveholder," said Noah lightly.

"Don't you own 'em?" demanded Titus violently; for this subject touched upon one of his grievances. "I have done everything I could to save you from any hard usage on the part of our folks in spite of the way you've used me."

"I am not aware that I have used you badly, Brother Titus."

"You call me brother; but judging from your actions you ain't no brother of mine."

"I should like to have you tell me in what manner I have wronged you, Titus. I hear from others that I owe you five thousand dollars; but I am not aware that I owe you a nickel," replied the planter, who had by this time come to the conclusion that the quarrel his brother insisted upon fomenting might as well be brought to a head then as at any other time.

Titus was silent for a moment, and resumed his seat on the bench, from which he had risen a dozen times in his excitement as the interview proceeded. He looked as though he was gathering up his thoughts in order to present his argument, as he evidently intended it should be, in the most forcible manner.

"If a man has two brothers, and one of them goes back on him, is that any reason why the other should go back on him?" asked the dissatisfied one with more coolness and dignity than he had before exhibited.

Mrs. Amelia, years before, had tried to reform his language, picked up in the taverns and among coarse associates, and she had succeeded to some extent. He could talk with a fair degree of correctness; but he had two methods of expression, one of which he called his "Sunday lingo," used on state occasions, and his ordinary speech at home and among his chosen associates, enlarged by the addition of some Southern words and phrases. He began his argument in his best style, though he had never been able to banish his use of the milder slang.

"Decidedly not," replied Noah very promptly. "On the contrary, he ought to stand by the brother if he has been wronged."

"That is just exactly what you have not done, Noah Lyon!" exclaimed Titus, springing from his seat again. "And Nathan said unto David, 'Thou art the man!'"

"Which means that I am the man," answered Noah, his smile becoming almost a laugh. "I didn't know, Brother Titus, that I was the David, and I must ask you to explain."

"Dunk went back on me," continued the malcontent, recalling the name by which the colonel was known on the farm in his boyhood.

"I was not aware that Dunk did any such a thing. I suppose you mean in his will."

"That is just what I mean!" stormed Titus. "He gave you ten thousand dollars more than he gave me; and that was not fair or right."

"But the will explains why he did so."

"On account of fetching up them two children! I wouldn't have brought in any bill for taking care of my dead brother's children. I ain't one of them sort!" protested Titus.

"But you refused to take one of them into your

family when I proposed it to you," suggested Noah very gently.

"Because my wife was sick at the time," said Titus, wincing at the remark.

"You did not offer to take one of them afterwards. But I did not bring in any bill; I never even mentioned the matter to the colonel when I wrote to him. I boarded, clothed, and schooled them for ten years, and paid all their doctor's bills."

"But Dunk gave you ten thousand dollars for it; and it wasn't right. He spent a month with you in Derry not long before he died, and you smoothed his fur in the right way," snarled Titus.

"But the children were not mentioned. I am sure it cost me a thousand dollars a year to take care of the children; but I did not complain, and never asked you or Dunk to pay a cent of the cost. The colonel made his will to suit himself; and he never spoke or wrote of the matter to me."

"You got on the right side of him, and he cheated me out of what rightfully belonged to me. I ain't talking about law, but about right. Half of that ten thousand belongs to me, and you are keeping me out of it."

"It was right for you and Dunk to pay as much for supporting the orphans as I did. Then you and he owed me two-thirds of the sum bequeathed to me. At compound interest that would amount to more than I receive under the will. I will figure it up when I have time, and of course if you owe me anything on this account, you will pay me."

This argument completely overwhelmed Titus; but Levi had concluded there would be no violence, and dashed over the bridge on his fiery colt.

CHAPTER IX

A MOST UNREASONABLE BROTHER

Titus Lyon dropped into his seat once more when Levi approached. He scowled at the manager as he swept by with a bow to his employer. He had been talking very loud about what was fair and right, and he could not deny that the expense of supporting the orphans ought to be divided among the three brothers. According to Noah's calculation, the boot had been transferred to the other leg, and he owed his brother something on this account if the matter was to be equitably adjusted.

Titus could not gainsay the position of the planter, and he tried to choke down his wrath; and just then he would have vented it upon the innocent overseer if he had not flown like the wind across the bridge, making the planks dance a hornpipe under the feet of his steed. As the malcontent was silent for the want of an argument with which to combat that of his brother, Noah went over the subject, and clinched the nail he had driven in before.

"I'll look the thing over again when I go home, for I want to be fair and right in everything I do," said Titus, after he had sought in vain for an argument with which he could upset the theory of Noah. "I only claimed that you owed me half of the ten thousand; I didn't ask for the whole on't."

"You never asked for even half of it before; you only told others that I owed you that sum," replied Noah.

"Well, I believed it."

"In that case neither you nor the colonel would pay anything towards the support of the children for ten years, for the law would divide the property equally between us," replied Noah. "I can't tell exactly how the matter stands till I figure it up; but I think you will owe me something if we settle it on the basis you suggest."

"I guess we'd better drop the subject till we have both looked it over agin," added Titus, utterly disgusted with the result of the argument. "I don't say that Dunk hadn't a right to dispose of his property as he pleased; but jest s'pose'n he had left it all to me and gi'n you nothin' — would that been right?"

"If he had had any reason for doing so, it would have been his right to do so; but I should say I should not be in condition to be an impartial judge in the matter," said Noah with a smile.

"Did he have any reason for treating me any wus than he did you?" asked Titus sharply, as he sprang to his feet again. "Dunk wa'n't no abolitionist, and went with the folks round here on politics. He 'n' I agreed, and never had no dispute on these things."

"I don't think the colonel did treat you any worse than he did me. He chose to pay for supporting the orphans, though I never asked him to do so, or hinted at any such thing. We have talked that over, and nothing more need be said about it now. I have indicated how that thing might be fairly settled, and we will let it rest there."

"But I still say Dunk used me wus 'n he did you; and as a brother you are in duty bound to set me right, as you said one of the same blood should do."

"I don't understand you, Brother Titus; for I

am not aware that the colonel treated me any better in his will than he did you," replied Noah, wondering what further complaint his brother could make.

"Didn't he give five thousand dollars to that cuss that just rid over the bridge?" demanded Titus with a sort of triumphant tone and manner, as though he had the planter where no argument could avail him. "That was just the same as taking twenty-five hundred dollars out of my pocket, as well as out of yours."

"But you don't bear in mind, my dear brother, that the colonel was disposing of his own property, and not yours or mine," said Noah with a pronounced laugh at the absurdity of the other's position.

"Don't go to dearin' me, Noah; it will be time enough for that sort of thing when you've done me justice," snarled Titus.

"When I've done you justice!" exclaimed the planter, rising from his seat again to vent his mirth. "I must do you justice because your brother and mine gave Levi Bedford five thousand dollars! Must I pay you twenty-five hundred dollars on this account?"

"I didn't say so."

"But you implied it; for you were trying to prove that the colonel used me better than he did you It seems to me that you ought to make your claim on Levi, if anybody."

"You git ahead faster'n I do. I only meant to say that Dunk didn't use me right when he gave his money to this mean whelp; but he treated you as bad as he did me, Noah."

"I have no complaint whatever to make, and I am glad the colonel remembered Levi handsomely; he deserved it, for he had always been a useful and faithful overseer," added Noah very decidedly.

"Let that rest," said Titus when he found that he made no headway in the direction he had chosen. "I s'pose you won't agree with me, but I say Dunk ought to have left this place to me instid of you. I was his oldest brother, and I have lived here eight years, and know all about the plantation, while you never saw it till after Dunk was dead."

"I am inclined to think the colonel knew what he was about, and he made his will to suit himself," answered Noah.

"I should think he made it to suit you. Of

course I know it's law, but it wa'n't right," growled Titus.

"If you think it was not right, why don't you contest the will, and have it set aside?"

"Don't I say it was law; and I suppose it can't be helped now," and the injured man tried to put on an air of resignation. "But I ain't done."

"I should say you had said enough; for there seems to be no foundation for any of your complaints. I think the colonel meant to be fair and just, and make an equal distribution of his property between you and me. Taking out fifteen thousand dollars he gave to charity and his friends" —

"That was giving away what belonged to you and me," interposed the objector.

"You are as unreasonable as a pig in a cornfield, Brother Titus!" exclaimed Noah, whose abundant patience was on the verge of exhaustion. "Duncan was giving away his own property, and not yours or mine, as you appear to think he was, especially yours; for I believe he did just right. Taking out the fifteen thousand and the ten he paid for the support of the orphans, — which I suppose you mean to have settled up in another way,

— there was seventy-five thousand dollars left, which he divided equally among his brothers and the representatives of the one who died over ten years ago. That is according to the valuation annexed to the will."

"It's mighty strange, Noah, that you can't see nothin' when it's p'inted out to you," stormed Titus, his wrath rising to the boiling point at his repeated defeats; for, "though vanquished, he could argue still."

"I don't believe at all in your pointing, Brother Titus."

"You talk about that valuation; but it was a fraud, and it was meant to cheat me out of eight or ten thousand dollars!" roared the malcontent, gesticulating violently. "It ought to been thirty thousand dollars more'n 'twas! I say it out loud; and I know what I'm talkin' about!"

"I don't think you do, Brother Titus. I think you had better stop drinking whiskey for a week, and then we can talk this subject over more satisfactorily."

"Do you mean to accuse me of bein' drunk, Noah Lyon?" demanded Titus, shaking his fist in the face of his brother; and at this moment

"THEN YOU MEAN I AM DRUNK." Page 121.

that colt was dashing over the bridge at a dead run, with Levi on his back.

"I don't think you are drunk, Brother Titus, as tipplers understand the word, but you are under the influence of liquor, and it affects your judgment," replied Noah as gently as though he had been speaking in a prayer-meeting.

"Then you mean that I *am* drunk!"

Both of his fists were clinched, and he was shaking one in the face of the planter, when the bay colt dashed in between them, Noah falling back before the menacing demonstration of Titus. Levi had dismounted at the end of the bridge, and seated himself in the arbor where he could still see the two men. When Titus shook his fist in the face of the planter, he leaped upon the colt as though he had been fifty pounds lighter, and galloped to the scene of the wordy contest.

"What do you want here?" demanded the visitor, with a very unnecessary expletive.

"What is it, Levi?" asked Noah.

"I didn't know but you might want me," replied the manager; but the demonstrative person was his employer's brother, and he refrained from using the strong language that came to his tongue's end.

"I don't want you for anything just now, Levi," replied the planter, sorry that there should have been a witness to the stormy interview with his brother; and he wondered if he had not been too plain-spoken, mild and dignified as he had been.

"What do you mean, you scoundrel, by stickin' your nose in where you're not wanted?" demanded Titus savagely, as he shook his fist, relieved from duty before the planter, in the direction of the overseer.

Levi wheeled his horse so that he crowded the angry man out of his place, and made him spring to keep out of the way of the fiery animal; but he made no reply to the abuse cast upon him. Noah nodded his head in the direction of the mansion, and the manager rode off, though it was evident to his employer that he was itching to lay hands on the turbulent visitor.

"I hate that villain!" gasped Titus.

"And he despises you as thoroughly as you hate him; so there is no love lost. But I think you had better conduct yourself a little more peaceably, Titus; for I do not like to have the people on the plantation see that there is any difficulty between us, for we are brothers, I wish you to remember. Perhaps we had better drop the subject where it is, for it is almost supper-time," said Noah with the most conciliatory tone and manner.

"Not jest yet," returned Titus warmly. "I said that valuation was a fraud, meant to cheat me out of my rightful due; and you told me I was drunk, which ain't no kind of an argument."

"I did not say that exactly; but if it was an argument for anything, it was that we should talk this matter over some time when you had not drunk anything."

"I drink something every day; and I have a perfect right to do so."

"I don't dispute it."

"Dunk gave you all the niggers, and did not put them in the valuation. Wasn't that cheating me out of my share of the thirty thousand they would bring even in these shaky times?"

"I don't think it was. I repeat that the colonel had a perfect right, just as good a right as you have to drink whiskey, though I don't do so, to dispose of his property as he pleased," added Noah, looking down at the planks of the bridge, and remaining for a minute in deep thought.

"That ain't no argument!" blustered Titus. "The law gives a man's property to his brothers and sisters when he leaves no parents or children; and every honest and just man does the same thing."

"I did not mean to say anything to anybody about the servants on the place; but I feel obliged to speak to you about them so far as to tell the facts relating to them," said Noah when he had come to this conclusion.

"I cal'late you better speak out if you've got anything to say, or else pay me over fifteen thousand dollars for my share in the value of them niggers," replied Titus with a triumphant air, for he believed he had gained a point.

"When I was at Colonel Cosgrove's house on the day of our arrival, he handed me a letter, heavily sealed with red wax, from our deceased brother. This letter contained another. I have both of these letters in the safe in the library. Now, if you will go to the house with me, I will show you both of these letters," continued the planter, disregarding the tone and manner of his irate brother.

Titus was curious to know what the colonel

had to say in defence of his conduct, and he assented to the visit to the library. Noah produced the two letters, handing the opened one to his brother, and showing the heavily sealed one to him but not permitting it to pass out of his hands. The malcontent read the opened one.

"Not to sell one of the niggers for five years!" he exclaimed when he had finished it. "That is another outrage! And you are not to open that other letter for the same time. Give it to me, Noah, and I will open it now!"

"It shall not be opened till the five years have expired," answered the planter firmly, as he returned both of the epistles to the safe and locked the door of it.

Titus was more violent than ever, for he had been defeated in his last and most promising stronghold, as he regarded it. He stormed like a madman, and kept it up for nearly an hour. He made so much noise that Mrs. Noah knocked at the door to learn what was the matter. At the same time she called them to supper; but Titus was so angry that he rushed out of the house, called for his team, and left with his wife at once.

CHAPTER X

THE SINK-CAVERN NEAR BAR CREEK

THE supper at the mansion had waited till it was quite dark; and it was evident to Mrs. Noah that the brothers were engaged in important business, for they had been talking on the bridge all the afternoon, and Titus spoke so loud in the library that he could be heard all over the house, though he could not be understood. Something very exciting was passing between them; Mrs. Noah thought it was politics, but Mrs. Titus thought it was about "that story" she had repeated.

As the angry brother passed the door of the sitting-room he called his wife out, and bolted from the house. Noah followed, and rang the stable bell. Frank brought the team to the door; Titus pushed his suffering wife into it, and drove off without the formality of saying good-night. The planter ate his supper, and was as pleasant as usual. saying nothing of the business which had brought Titus to Riverlawn.

"It seems that story about the arms and ammunition has no truth at all in it," said Mrs. Noah.

"So Titus says," replied the husband.

"Meely was terribly excited about it, and said she ought not to have said a word about it. She begged me not to let any one in the house say anything about it to any one. Her husband abused her, and even struck her, for what she had done."

"I did not know but he would strike me this afternoon. I suppose the boys have had their supper," added Noah, looking over the table to their vacant places.

"No, they have not; I haven't seen anything of them since they went from dinner," answered Mrs. Lyon. "I wonder where they are?"

"They went up the creek together in one of the boats just after Titus came, and I haven't seen or heard anything of them since." said Noah. "I don't think they were going a-fishing. They have been gone about seven hours now, and it is time they were at home. Did you see anything of them, Levi?"

"I saw them rowing up the creek when I was riding up to the hill pasture; but I haven't seen them since," replied the overseer.

"I hope nothing has happened to them," continued Mrs. Lyon, looking quite anxious. "Perhaps the boat has been upset."

"I don't believe it did; but if it went over, both of the boys can swim like ducks," replied the planter.

The conversation in regard to the absentees was continued till the meal was finished, and all the party were very much troubled. Levi volunteered to ride up the creek road and look for them; and just as he was going to the stable, the absentees came into the house.

"Where in the world have you been, boys?" demanded Mrs. Lyon, delighted to find they were safe.

"We have been exploring the creek, and we have been a good ways up, as far as the rocky hills," replied Deck, as he seated himself at the table; and Diana went for the waffles she had kept hot for them.

"Did you catch any fish?" asked Levi.

"Not a fish; we did not put a line into the water."

They had no narrative to relate, or if they had they did not relate it, though they were questioned for some time, and they told what they had seen, or a portion of it.

"While you are here, boys, I want to tell you that your Aunt Amelia has been at the house all the afternoon," said Mrs. Lyon. "She came to take back that story she told me this morning in her own house about the arms and ammunition. She misunderstood your uncle, and there is not a word of truth in it. So you will understand, all of you, that not a word is to be said about it out of the house."

"Not a word of truth in it!" exclaimed Deck; and Artie dropped his hot waffle in astonishment, or under the influence of some other emotion.

"Your aunt says there are no arms hidden on the river, or anywhere else. You mustn't say a word about the matter, and I have cautioned all in the house not to whisper a sound of it," added Mrs. Lyon.

Deck looked at Artie, and Artie looked at Deck. A significant smile passed between them, but they said nothing. As soon as they had finished their supper they followed the planter into his library, which had been lighted before. It was an important conference which followed there, and it must be left in progress in order to return to the boat in which the boys were pursuing their adventure on the creek.

Artie had the floor on the boat, and he had just recalled the time when Noah had spoken to him about being out so late the night before. Deck remembered it very well, and also that his cousin had evaded an adequate explanation of his absence from the house when he ought to have been in bed.

"You never explained why you were out so late that night," said he.

"I wanted to look into the matter a little more before I said anything, for I didn't care to make a fool of myself," replied Artie.

"You have a habit of keeping your mouth shut pretty tight," said Deck with a smile.

"I don't believe in talking too much about things you don't understand, and I meant to have looked into the matter before this time, but somehow I haven't had the chance to do so," replied Artie, still pulling his oar. "I'm going to tell you about my night adventure now, and you can judge for yourself whether we are going on a wild-goose chase up the creek."

"All right; and I will keep my oar moving all the time, so that we shall be getting ahead while I listen," replied Deck.

"I was in the canoe, and I had gone farther up the creek than I had ever been before," Artie began. "You have been up the road that leads to Dripping Spring and the Mammouth Cave. It crosses the railroad about five miles before you get to the spring, and the creek flows within a quarter of a mile of this place."

"I remember the place very well; for Levi stopped his team there to let the girls get out and pick some flowers. I could see the creek from this spot," added Deck.

"Then you know the place. I had been up the creek three or four miles farther, and I was on my way home. I had been ashore just abreast of Dripping Spring, and I got interested in looking over a sink,—I believe that is what they call these holes in the ground down here,—and the sun went down before I thought how late it was getting. But I found the hole led into a cave; but it was too dark for me to explore it. I made a note of it, to bring a lantern up and survey the cavern when I had plenty of time to do so."

"That will be a good job for both of us some time," suggested Deck.

"I couldn't tell how far I was from home, but I knew it was a long distance, and I made tracks for the canoe as soon as I saw that it was getting dark. I hurried up till my arms ached so that I had to stop and rest. I made up my mind that I must take it moderately or I never should get home.

"While I was resting I saw three lights off to the south of me, and then I knew I was near that road. I could make out about half a dozen men or boys there, and I watched them for some time. I concluded that they were up to some mischief, and in my interest I forgot how late it was getting. I was possessed to know what iniquity was going on there, and I hauled the canoe up to the shore and made the painter fast to a bush. I landed, and made my way as near to the road as I dared to go. The ground was low, and covered with clumps of bushes, so I had no difficulty in hiding myself till I was within twenty feet of the party.

"I could hear every word they said; and the man who was bossing the job, whatever it was, satisfied me that he was Uncle Titus."

"Uncle Titus!" exclaimed Deck, ceasing to row in his astonishment.

"Not the least doubt of it; and more than this, I soon recognized the tones of Sandy and Orly; but I don't know who the other three were."

"But what were they doing?" asked Deck, absorbed in the narrative.

"You have stopped rowing, Deck, and we shall never get there at this rate."

The stroke oarsman turned his body so that he could change hands at the handle of the oar, and then resumed pulling.

"Well, this was an adventure; but you didn't tell me what they were doing," added Deck.

"I will tell you all about it, but don't stop rowing, or we shall not get home before midnight, and father will give us a lecture for being out late at night. The men were handling a lot of boxes. Some of them were long enough to hold coffins, and I wondered if they hadn't been killing Union men, and were getting rid of the bodies. Then they brought out a lot of haypoles or hand-barrows from the two big wagons in the road. I saw them put one of the boxes on the poles or barrow, and move towards the creek. I thought it was about time for me to be leaving, for I believed they would kill me if they caught me."

"They wouldn't have let you off with a whole skin, anyhow," said Deck. "Do you suppose the boxes contained bodies, Artie?"

"Hold on till I come to it, and I will tell you all about it," replied the narrator rather impatiently. "I wasn't safe where I was, and I crept back to the creek between the clumps of bushes without making a bit of noise on the soft ground. The box the first couple carried was heavy and the bushes were in their way, so that they could not get along very fast. As soon as I was out of hearing of the party, I ran with all my might."

"I don't blame you for being in a hurry, for if Uncle Titus had got hold of you he would have made you see more stars then were in the sky just then. I wonder if they had been killing Union men. The Seceshers have done that thing in this State. A Union man was murdered in his own house not far from here."

"Dry up, Deck, or I shall never get through with my story!" exclaimed Artie, who did not relish these repeated interruptions.

"Go on, Artie; I won't say another word," Deck promptly promised.

"I reached the creek, and cast off the canoe. I crossed over to the other side, and pulled down stream; for I knew that the two with the box could not be near the shore. I kept on towards home, but I was careful not to make any noise with my oars. Just below I saw a big flatboat, like the gundalow they used to have on the river to carry hay from the meadows. I drove the canoe into some bushes, and waited. The two men brought that long box to the shore, and loaded it into the flatboat, which was big enough to carry six cords of wood.

"The next load was brought by four men; and I could see by the way they handled it that it was very heavy. I stopped till they had brought down two more boxes, and then I thought it was time for me to be going. When the party had all left the shore I rowed along by the bushes that overhang the creek till I got round the bend. I didn't wait to see any more, but rowed as fast as I could; and when I got to the pier I was so tired I could hardly stand up. That is the end of the story, Deck, and you know as much about the affair as I do; and I will answer all of your questions as well as I can."

"You did not find out anything for certain?" added the listener, disappointed because his cousin had not ascertained what was in the boxes.

"I did not; but I have been able to guess at some things; and that is the privilege of a New England Yankee."

"Well, what do you guess was in those boxes?"

"I didn't guess on that question at the time of it; but I was satisfied that they concealed some sort of iniquity."

"What do you suppose they were putting them in the boat for?"

"Not to take them down the river, for they would have carried them to some place on its banks if they had wanted to do that. They wanted to take them up the creek, and this was the nearest point to it."

"What did they want to do with the boxes? Oh, I know! They were going to sink the bodies in the creek!" exclaimed Deck.

"That would have been a good enough guess a fortnight ago; but it isn't worth shucks now. I told you before that I could explain things better this afternoon than I could when I saw what the men were doing."

"How is that?" asked Deck with his mouth half open.

"The moment mother told that story from Aunt Amelia, I knew what was in the boxes; and they did not contain bodies, either."

"Oh, I see! They contained the arms and ammunition."

"A blind man could see that."

"Well, that was an adventure. You mean that they were going to put them in the cavern by the sink?"

"Precisely that, and nothing less; and now we are going up to the sink to see for ourselves what is in the boxes," replied Artie.

They had a long pull before them; but they reached the place by five o'clock, and explored the cavern. They found the boxes and two cannons with their carriages. They could not open the boxes for the want of any tools; but the labels assured them they contained muskets and revolvers. They hastened down the creek; but it was eight o'clock when they reached the mansion.

CHAPTER XI

AROUSED TO THE SOLEMN DUTY OF THE HOUR

It was more than two hours after supper-time when Deck and Artie arrived. They were very tired and very hungry after their long pull up the creek; but they felt better after they had taken a hearty supper. Deck sought the first opportunity to detail the operations of the afternoon to his father.

"Your Uncle Titus has been here this afternoon, and I have had a long talk with him on the bridge; but his first business here was to disclaim any knowledge of the arms and ammunition concealed on the river," said Mr. Lyon, before the boys had an opportunity to open with the story of their adventure. "He says your Aunt Amelia misunderstood him with her elbows, and it was a ridiculous story she told your mother without a word of truth in it."

"Without a word of truth in it," repeated Deck, who was more inclined than Artie to do the talking, though the latter was fluent enough of speech when the occasion required it.

The boys looked at each other; and they did something more than smile this time, for they laughed out loud. In view of the revelation they had to make, the affair became more exciting; but after the discovery they had made, they did not wonder that Titus had been so earnest in his purpose to contradict the statement their aunt had made.

"What are you laughing at, boys?" interposed their father. "This is a serious matter as your uncle looks upon it; and I suppose such a rumor circulated about the county might get him and his sons into trouble. The Unionists regard the Home Guards as precisely the same as Secessionists, and believe that they are armed, so far as they are armed, to help along the cause of the South."

"I should say that Uncle Titus might be a little shaken up about the story Aunt Amelia related," added Artie with a significant look at his cousin.

"I don't know but the Union people would mob him if they believed he had obtained arms for any Home Guards, especially for such ruffians as they say he has been gathering together for his company," said Mr. Lyon. "I have cautioned all who heard the story not to mention or hint at it in the strongest manner; for of course I don't want to get your uncle into trouble by repeating a false rumor."

"Suppose he gets himself into trouble?" suggested Deck. "He is an out-and-out Secesher, and he don't make any bones of saying so out loud. Sandy thinks they will break up the Union meeting at the schoolhouse to-morrow night."

"Titus says he has done his best to prevent anything of the kind being done," replied Mr. Lyon. "He thinks I should be mobbed and this house burned over our heads if he did not use his influence to prevent it. But your uncle believes what he wants to believe, and is certain a vast majority of the people of the county are Secessionists. I am very well satisfied that they are at least about equally divided. At any rate, the Secessionists are doing their best to overawe the Union people, and they might succeed to some extent if they could arm the villains they have enrolled."

"Then it is better not to let them be armed," suggested Deck, with a glance at his cousin.

"The story your mother told at dinner made it look as though they were to be provided with weapons and ammunition at once; but the statement is not true, and we appear to be safe for the present," said Mr. Lyon. "But where have you been all the afternoon, boys?"

"Deck will tell the story, father," replied Artie.

"You led off in this business, Artie, and I think you had better tell it," said Deck, though he was ready enough to relate the adventure.

"We will both tell it, then," added Artie. "I will begin and go as far as where you joined me this afternoon at the bridge, and you shall tell the rest of it."

"All right; fire away, Artie."

In accordance with this arrangement, the boys minutely narrated the events of the afternoon, to the great astonishment and indignation of Mr. Lyon. He occasionally interrupted his son to ask questions in regard to the boxes they had examined in the cavern. The boys described the cases, with the marks upon them, and the listener had no doubt they contained arms and ammunition. The two carriages for the field-pieces were the only portion of the warlike material not contained in boxes; and these were almost evidence enough to determine the character of the rest of the goods.

"Were the boxes all of the same kind?" asked

the father, deeply interested, and not a little disturbed by the revelation of the evening.

"They were not the same," replied Deck, taking a paper from his pocket, on which he had written down a list of the cases. "The lid of one of the two in which the cannon were boxed up had been split off in part, so that we could see what was in it. Twelve cases were labelled 'Breech-loading Rifles,' and the rest of the lot were marked with the kind of ammunition they contained. The smallest of them had cannon-balls and grape in them."

"There isn't any doubt about the matter now," replied Mr. Lyon. "This means war; and I have no doubt they are to be used in this county by your uncle's cut-throats; for that is what they are according to what Colonel Cosgrove said to me the other day. This is bad business," and the planter gazed at the floor, his wrinkled brow indicating the deep thought in which he was engaged.

"Sandy says the company of Home Guards is about full, and I suppose they will not leave the arms and ammunition in the cavern for any great length of time," suggested Deck.

"Something must be done," said Mr. Lyon.

"If that company get these weapons they will terrorize the whole county. There are some very strong Unionists in this vicinity. Colonel Cosgrove told me they had threatened to burn his house, though he is a very conservative man. He was in favor of neutrality; but he admits that the Home Guards in this county are about all Secessionists. Your Uncle Titus says I am looked upon as an abolitionist, and if it had not been for him they would have 'cleaned me out,' as he called it, before this time. It is time something was done," and the planter relapsed into a revery again.

The boys were silent. Fort Sumter had been bombarded, and its heroic garrison had marched out with the honors of war. The country was in a state of war. The call of the President for seventy-five thousand men had been made. Northern soldiers were marching South for the protection of Washington. Flags were flying, drums were beating, trumpets were blaring, and troops were organizing all over the loyal nation.

In Kentucky men were enlisting in both armies, though the majority of them clung to the flag of the Union, inspired by the traditions of the State. But large portions of it were subjected to a reign of terror. One party was struggling to carry the State out of the Union, and the other to keep it in the Union. The county in which Noah Lyon and his family were located was even more shaken by these discordant elements than most of the others; for it was not more than thirty miles from the southern boundary of the State.

"It almost breaks my heart to have my only living brother associated with, and even leading, these conspirators against the Union," Mr. Lyon resumed, as he wiped some tears from his eyes. "But when it comes to the defence of the old flag under which we have become the most enlightened and prosperous nation in the world, no true man can favor even his brother when he plots to ruin it. Something must be done!" he repeated with energy as he rose to his feet, and emphasized his remark with a vigorous stamp of his foot.

"What shall be done, father?" asked Deck, awed by the manner and the tears of his father; and he had never been so moved before in his life.

"We must defend the old flag, my boys! We must rally with those who are marching to the defence of the Union! The time for talking has gone by, and the time for action has come. I have

AROUSED TO THE DUTY OF THE HOUR

not passed the military age, and I shall not shirk the plain duty of the citizen, which is to become a soldier," replied Mr. Lyon impressively.

"Do you mean to say that you shall join the army, father?" asked Deck.

"Certainly; what else can I do at a time like this?" replied the father. "And that is not all, my son; you and Artemas are now sixteen years old, nearly seventeen. You are both stout boys; and not only the sire, but the sons, must shoulder the musket and march to the battle-field."

"I am ready for one!" exclaimed Deck with enthusiasm.

"I am ready for the other!" added Artie quite as earnestly.

"For some time I have seen that this was what we must come to; but I have put off saying anything about it, for it is a solemn and even an awful thing to engage in the strife of civil war, brother against brother, the son against his father, and the father against his son."

"In our own family, we shall all be on the same side," added Deck.

"But your uncle and his two sons will be with the enemies of the Union. It is not of our choosing, and God will be with us while we do our duty to our country," said the patriot father, as he solemnly lifted his eyes upward. "Now, my sons, for you both call me father, and I have always tried to be the same to both of you " —

"And you always have been! And Aunt Ruth has been a mother to me and my sister Dorcas!" interposed Artie, as he wiped the tears from his eyes. "I shall never again call either of you anything but father or mother. I am ready to enlist whenever you say the word, father."

"You are honest and true, and that is the kind of man you will make, my son; and I can say the same of Dexter. You will both make good soldiers."

Both the father and the sons shed tears as they realized, as they never had before, the solemn duty which the peril of the Union imposed upon them; and they were inspired to do that duty to the last drop of their life-blood.

"There, boys! I did not intend to make a scene like this; but the finding of the arms and ammunition convinces me that your Uncle Titus and his villanous associates mean to make war upon loyal men in this county. When you join the ranks of the Union army, you will find them all in the columns of the enemy. You have done good service to our cause in the discovery and ferreting out of this conspiracy against the true men of this locality."

"It was all by accident that I found out about it," added Artie modestly.

"I hope you will forgive me for scolding at you for being out so late that night," said Mr. Lyon.

"You didn't scold me; you only gave me some good advice, and I hope I shall always remember it. But I did not know then what I had discovered, or where they were storing the arms."

"You did exceedingly well, whether you knew what you were doing or not. Now it is driven into my very soul that I ought not to let the enemy profit by obtaining those arms. I have made up my mind that it would be treason, or next door to it, for me to let Titus and his gang have all these weapons; and with the blessing of God they never shall have them!"

"That is the talk, father!" exclaimed Deck.

"So say we all of us!" Artie chimed in. "But what can we do?"

"Before the light of to-morrow morning breaks upon Riverlawn, we must move all those boxes to the plantation," replied Mr. Lyon; and he proceeded to discuss the means by which this purpose could be accomplished.

"We have teams enough to haul the whole of them over here at one load," said Deck, boiling over with enthusiasm.

"Keep cool, my son, for we must be very prudent in our movements. Do you know what became of the flatboat with which the conspirators moved the cases up to the cavern?"

"Artie thought of that; and we found the gundalow in a little inlet at the mouth of a brook, covered up with bushes."

"Then we may use that," replied the planter. "But I am in doubt about one thing which may bother us."

"What's that, father?" asked Deck, who could not think of any impediment to the carrying out of the plan announced by his father.

"I don't know that we can depend upon every person about the plantation. A single one opposed to our scheme could ruin it. He might go to the village and tell Titus, or some of his fellow-conspirators, what we were about, and interfere with us before we got back."

"No one here would do such a thing," protested Deck. "All the servants believe in you."

"I was thinking of Levi Bedford."

"Levi!" exclaimed both of the loyal boys together.

"I have never spoken a word to him about politics, or he to me. Absolutely all I know about him is that he is a Tennesseean. But we must settle this point on the instant; you may go and find him, Dexter, and ask him to come into the library."

Deck left the room. He found the overseer in the sitting-room with the family, and he returned with him a minute later.

CHAPTER XII

THE NIGHT EXPEDITION IN THE MAGNOLIA

LEVI BEDFORD walked into the library not a little excited with curiosity; for Titus Lyon had spent the whole afternoon on the bridge with the planter, who had been closeted with the two boys for some time. It was evident to him that something unusual had occurred. Noah was seated in a great arm-chair which usually faced his desk, but he had turned it around. The overseer walked up to this chair, and planted himself in front of it with a respectful look of inquiry on his round face.

"I am in doubt, Levi, and I have sent for you," Mr. Lyon began. "As you are aware, I have never talked politics with you, and have not known to which party you belong."

"I don't belong to any party," replied Levi with a very broad smile on his face. "My party is the plantation and the family. I look out for them, and I don't bother my head much about anything else."

"I suppose you have relatives in Tennessee?" suggested the planter.

"Second or third cousins very likely; but I don't know anything about them, and I don't lie awake nights thinking of them. My father died before I was twenty-one; I had no sisters, and my only brother went to California twenty years ago, and I haven't heard from him in ten years."

"I don't mean to meddle with your affairs, Levi, but the time has come when every man must declare himself."

"I should think it had, Mr. Lyon; and this afternoon I thought I was going to have a chance to strike for your side of the house. I was ready to do it, for two or three times I thought you were in peril. I don't know what you were talking about, only it was something very stirring," replied Levi with his usual smile.

"I don't think I was in any danger, but I am very much obliged to you for looking out for me. Now things have come to such a pass that I must put a direct question to you: Are you a Union man or a Secessionist?"

"I am a Union man now from the crown of my foot to the sole of my head," laughed Levi.

"But it wouldn't be anything more than honest and square, Major Lyon, for me to say that I haven't been so many months. Colonel Lyon was a Union man; but he didn't have it half as bad as you have it. Some of his neighbors thought he was too tender with his people; but he and Colonel Cosgrove were pretty well matched on politics."

"He is a strong Union man, though he is in favor of neutrality if it can be carried out, which is utterly impossible," added the planter.

"About the only thing in the row that set me to thinking and made me mad was that such a set of reckless scallawags have run the machine on the other side. There is hardly a man of any standing among them. I know that your brother, who is nothing but a Northern doughface, is one of the principal leaders among them, and "—

"We haven't any time to talk about this matter now, Levi," interposed Noah Lyon, looking at his watch. "I see that you are all right, for you are a Union man, and you do not approve the course of the violent party in this county, and the time has come for the boys and me to do something."

The planter proceeded in rather hurried speech to state the situation, and to describe the discovery the boys had made that afternoon. The overseer evidently had a very strong desire to express his mind in regard to Titus Lyon; but with great effort he restrained himself, and listened almost in silence to the narrative of the speaker.

"I am with you in this matter, Major Lyon, on its merits, though I like to be on your side; but these ruffians who are trying to make civil war in the State of Kentucky must be checked." he replied, when the planter had hurried through his statement. "I am sorry that brother of yours used any of the money the colonel left him to buy arms and ammunition to help drag the State out of the Union. I will work day and night to euchre him and the rest of them."

"You are just the right man in the right place, Levi Bedford!" exclaimed Mr. Lyon. "We have no time now to decide what we will do with these warlike implements, only to get possession of them. It is quarter-past nine now, and I have my plan for the beginning. While we are carrying it out we can settle what is to be done with the arms."

"I know just where that sink-hole and cavern are, and all we have to do to get there is to follow the creek," added the manager.

"The flatboat is near the place, and we can move the boxes in that, as the conspirators conveyed them from the road," replied Mr. Lyon. "But there are only four of us, two men and two boys. The cannons must weigh six or seven hundred pounds apiece, and we shall want more help."

"Well, we have help enough, and we can take a dozen of the people with us, if we want as many as that;" added Levi. "I know something about these things, for when I kept stable in my State I used to belong to an artillery company."

"Can the negroes be trusted? We must keep our operations a profound secret."

"In this business you can trust them a great deal farther than you can a white man," said the overseer, as he took a piece of paper from the desk and wrote down the names of some of the hands. "How many do you want, Major Lyon?"

"Half a dozen; we can't accommodate more than that. Put in the boatmen, for there is a deal of boating to be done."

Levi revised his list and then handed it to the planter.

"General, Dummy, Rosebud, Woolly, Mose.

Faraway," Mr. Lyon read from the list. "I should say you had picked out just the men we need. They are all used to the boats, and they are among the toughest and strongest hands on the place. You must put them under oath, if need be, to be as secret as death itself. I will leave all that to you. Now, have them at the lower boat pier just as soon as possible, and we will be there."

"I will have them there in fifteen minutes," replied Levi, as he hastened to execute his mission.

"Now, boys, go to the pier, and get the Magnolia in condition to go up the creek," continued Mr. Lyon.

"The Magnolia!" exclaimed Deck. "Why, she " —

"We have no time to argue any question, Dexter," interposed the father. "Take your overcoats; and you are to be as secret as the rest of us. Ask your mother to come into the library, but don't stop to talk, my son."

The boys left the room, and Mrs. Lyon immediately presented herself in the library.

"What in the world is going on here to-night, Noah?" asked the good woman. "Ever since the boys came in you have been closeted in here as if you were planning something."

"So we are, Ruth, for the boys made a great discovery on their trip up the creek," answered the planter hurriedly. "That story about the arms and ammunition which Titus and Amelia came down here to disclaim and deny was all as true as gospel, for the boys have found them."

In five minutes more Mr. Lyon told his wife all that it was necessary for her to know, and charged her to be secret and silent. She seemed to be alarmed; but he assured her that there was no danger in the enterprise in which they were to engage. It was absolutely necessary that the arms and munitions should be removed beyond the reach of the conspirators. He asked her to bring him three lanterns without letting any one see them, which she did at once. With these in his hands, the planter left the house without going into the sitting-room.

Deck and Artie reached the boat-pier without speaking a word, and they ran half the way. The Magnolia was moored out in the creek; and taking the canoe, which was used as her tender when the sailboat was in service, as it had not been since the death of the colonel, she was towed alongside the pier. They went to work baling her out, of which she was in great need, though she had been well cared for in her idleness by the boatmen of the place.

The Magnolia had not been built for a sailboat. She was long and narrow for her length, about thirty feet, and was provided with rowlocks for six oars. Before they had finished baling her out the General and Dummy reached the wharf. They were great strapping negroes, fully six feet tall, and the weight of each could not have been much below two hundred pounds, though they were not of aldermanic build.

When they saw what the boys were doing, — for Levi had not given them even a hint as to the nature of the service in which they were to be employed, — they seized the buckets, and soon cleared the well of water. Levi was the next to put in an appearance, just as Deck was telling the two men to take the mast out of her, an order which the manager countermanded.

" We may want the mast and sail," interposed Levi ; " for the wind is fresh from the south-west to-night, and I don't believe in doing any more work with the oars than is necessary."

"But we have no boatman, and none of us know how to manage the sail," argued Deck. "It would be a bad time to get upset, and we have no time to indulge in fooling, Levi."

"The mast and sail are not in the way in the boat. I am no boatman, and I never tried to handle the Magnolia, for the colonel was the only person on the place who ever learned the trick of doing that; but I often sailed in her up and down the river, and I used to think I could do it if I tried," replied the manager, as the other four negroes came upon the pier.

"Oh, well, if you can handle her with a sail, that's another thing," answered Deck, yielding the point.

"Here, Rosebud, unlock the boathouse, and bring out six oars, the biggest ones, and all the boathooks you can find," said Levi, as he looked the boat over.

No one said a word about the mission upon which they were to embark, leaving the planter to do all the talking when he came. General and Dummy were the biggest of the six men who had been selected; but the other four were stalwart fellows. Their names were rather odd, the family thought when they first heard them; but not one of them bore the one his mother had given him in his babyhood, for the colonel had rechristened the whole of them on the plantation to suit his own fancy.

Some circumstance, or something in their appearance, had doubtless suggested the names; but after they were given they clung to their owners as though they had been recorded in a church. The General was a quick-witted fellow, which inclined him to take the lead when anything was to be done. Woolly had a tremendous mop of hair on his head. Dummy was a preacher in the shanty which served as a church at the Big Bend; and perhaps because he was always studying his sermons, he never spoke a word unless the occasion required it; but Levi, who had heard him preach, said he could talk fast enough in his pulpit, and delivered a more sensible sermon than some white clergymen to whom he had listened.

Rosebud, like the overseer, always had a smile on his face, and could hardly do or say anything without laughing. Mose did not swear profanely, but "by Moses;" and everything was as true, as high, as big, as handsome, as "Moses in de bulrushes." "Faraway" had been a pet word with the one to whom the planter had given this name. They were all reliable servants, and were devoted to their past and present masters. No king, prince, or potentate had ever been as big a man in their estimation as the colonel; and they had transferred this homage to the "major," as they were inclined to call Mr. Lyon after they heard the overseer use this title.

Levi placed the men in the boat, each with his oar, and then headed it up the creek. The boys took their places in the stern-sheets, and the overseer handled the tiller lines. These arrangements were no sooner completed than the planter appeared, and took his place with the boys. The rowers were sitting with the oars upright; for the General, who was the stroke oarsman, had learned either from pictures in the illustrated papers their former master used to give the hands when he had done with them, or from some person more experienced than himself, some of the forms used in boating.

"Drop your oars!" said Levi, and they all fell into the water together.

"Ought to say 'let fall,' Mars'r Levi," added General.

"No talk, General. Now gather up, and pull away!" continued Levi.

General would have given him the proper form, "Give way!" but Levi was not in the humor to be instructed, and the rower said no more. The men pulled their oars with a will, and the implements bent under their vigorous stroke. The planter had run all the way from the mansion, and was out of breath, so he was silent for a time.

CHAPTER XIII

AT THE HEAD WATERS OF BAR CREEK

It was quite dark when the Magnolia went out from the pier, though it was a starlight night. The crew pulled very well, for the colonel had taken no little pride in the appearance of his boat on the river. Before his health was impaired he occasionally went to the county town by water; for it was on a branch of the river, and was full thirty miles distant by the winding streams.

The crew were powerful men, and had had plenty of practice in former years. But the present planter preferred the vehicles, drawn by fine horses, and the boys used the smaller boats, so the Magnolia had not been manned under the new order of things. Under the vigorous stroke of the negroes she soon passed under the bridge, and headed up the creek.

"We are fairly started, and this boat seems to be making at least five miles an hour," said the planter, when he had fully recovered his breath.

"More than that, I should say, Major Lyon. I don't believe the hands can keep up this gait all the way; but we shall get to the sink about midnight," replied Levi.

"I don't know that there is anything to apprehend in the way of danger," added Mr. Lyon.

"I don't know whether there is or not; but I put my revolver and a box of cartridges into my pocket."

"I never owned a pistol of any kind, and have hardly fired a gun since I was a boy; but in the storeroom out of the library I found some very nice weapons,—a double-barrelled rifle and a fowling-piece."

"The colonel had two revolvers; and they must be somewhere about the library. A few years ago some horse-thieves were in this vicinity, and we kept a watch on the place every night for a couple of weeks," said Levi.

"If Uncle Titus put five thousand dollars into these guns and pistols, I should think he would be apt to keep a watch over them," suggested Deck.

"A watch would not amount to anything unless he put as many as half a dozen men on it," answered Levi. "But I think he depends upon the secrecy of his movements and the safety of the cavern for the security of the arms. He put the things away in the night, and I don't believe anybody ever goes over the spring road in the darkness. If he put a watch anywhere he would station it on that road at the place where they shifted the boxes from the wagon to the flatboat. But I reckon we can take care of the watch if there is any there."

"But the road is about a quarter of a mile from the creek," said Deck.

"All of that; and we may pass the place without much of any noise, and no one on the road would be likely to hear us," replied Levi.

"I don't think the watch, if there is one, will give us any trouble, for if they hear us, we can keep out of their way; and I don't think they would have any boat in the creek," added the planter. "Your revolver will keep them at a proper distance when we reach the cavern."

"I found a shingling hatchet in the boathouse, and I brought that along with me," said Artie.

"Are you going to fight with that?" asked Deck.

"Not exactly that; but we couldn't open one

of the boxes this afternoon for the want of a tool, and we can do so with this hatchet; then we shall have all the muskets, revolvers, and cartridges we can use," replied Artie.

"That is a good scheme, my boy," added Levi approvingly. "But I don't believe we shall have to do any fighting. If the conspirators have set a watch, it must be in the road; and I reckon we shall clean out the cavern before they can get there."

"We won't fight any battles before we get there," interposed the planter. "We have always been peaceable people, but I suppose we must get used to fighting, for we are going to have a terrible war; and I don't believe in Mr. Seward's prediction that it will all be over in a hundred days. I am ready to become a soldier, Levi, and so are the boys, in defence of the Union."

"I suppose I ought to do the same," added the overseer; "but I had not thought of it."

"You are fifty years old, and you will not be called upon to go into the army, Levi," replied Mr. Lyon.

"But I am ready to do my share of the fighting; and if I am over fifty, I reckon I am as tough and hearty as any of them that will shoulder a musket," said the overseer; and those near him could hear his chuckle, though they could not see his smile.

"I hope you will not go to the war, my friend," continued Mr. Lyon in a very serious tone. "I am only forty-two, and I believe it is not only my duty to send my boys into the army, but to go myself. I have thought a great deal of this subject within the last month, though I haven't said much. I believe a man's first duty is to his family, and I should hate to go off into the army, and leave my wife and the girls here; for I believe whoever stays in Barcreek will see some fighting here."

"And see some before a great while," added Levi. "Everything is boiling round here, and it will boil over before long. These Secession ruffians are not going to keep the peace much longer. They are itching to begin the work of driving the Union men into their cub pasture."

"That is my own opinion; and that is my only dread in joining the army. But I have comforted myself with the belief that Levi Bedford was over fifty, and he would remain on the plantation and take care of my family."

"I am very much obliged to you, Major Lyon, for the confidence you put in me, and I can assure you it shall not be abused," returned the manager, with more gravity in his tone and manner than usual. "If by staying here I can keep three good Union soldiers in the field, perhaps that will be doing my fair share of the work."

"We will talk this matter at another time, Levi; and I will only say I could not have found a man more to my mind to take charge of the plantation and the women-folks if I had hunted for him all over the nation."

"That's handsome, Major; and you may wager your life and all you have in the world that I will never go back on you or your family," protested the overseer warmly.

"We understand each other perfectly, Levi. But there is a more pressing question than that before the house just now," said Mr. Lyon, as he took Levi's offered hand, and gave it an earnest grasp. "What are we to do with all these arms and ammunition when we get them down to Riverlawn?"

"I haven't had much time to think of that; but I had an idea come across my head as I was running from the house down to the boat-pier. I passed by the ice-house, and it jumped into my noddle that it would make a good arsenal; but I haven't worked up the idea yet," replied the manager.

"That is a happy thought!" exclaimed the planter. "It never occurred to me. It is in just the right place; for my brother has given me warning that I was in danger of being mobbed as an abolitionist, and that nothing but his influence has prevented it from being done before."

"It is hard work for me to believe that doughface is a brother of yours and the late colonel; but if he dared to show his face in it, he would be the first man to get up such a demonstration. Excuse me, Major, if I am talking too plainly," said Levi, who had little patience with, or toleration for, Titus Lyon. "He may send his company of Home Guards over to clean out the mansion, but he won't come himself, for he is a poison snake."

"Perhaps you know my brother as he has developed himself in this locality better than I do, though he has even shown his fangs, under a mask, to me; but I shall keep the peace with him," replied Mr. Lyon very sadly.

"If he attempts anything of that sort, or any other border-ruffians do, I believe we can make them wish they had stayed at home," said Levi stoutly.

"We can make the ice-house into a fortress for the protection of the mansion," continued the planter. "It is near the creek, and commands the bridge and the road leading to it, which is the only practicable approach to the mansion. The swamp half a mile back of the house lies between the spring road and the creek, and extends all the way to the hills, not less than ten miles by water; and no body of men can get through that way."

Though he had had no military experience, Noah Lyon talked like an army engineer. He was a man of very decided general ability, and he readily comprehended the situation so far as his plantation was concerned. The ice-house was about twenty-five feet square. It was built of stone under the direction of Colonel Lyon, who had his own views, though they were not always scientific. To preserve the ice, which did not consist of great solid blocks as in New Hampshire, he believed that thick walls were necessary, and he had put two feet of solid masonry into them. The ice was generally not more than two inches thick in this latitude, though an exceptionally hard winter sometimes made it four. It was packed in solid, and then permitted to freeze by leaving the door and two windows open during the freezing weather.

"Stop rowing," said Levi, when they came to a bend five miles above the bridge. "Now rest yourselves for five minutes, boys."

"Don't need no rest, mars'r," said General, as he drew his arm over his forehead, from which the perspiration was dropping on the handle of his oar. "We done pulled dis boat twenty mile widout stoppin' once."

"A little rest will do you no harm, for you will be kept at work till morning," replied Levi.

"Whar we gwine, mars'r?" asked General.

"About five miles farther," replied the overseer evasively. "Have you brought your jackets or coats with you, boys?"

They had brought them. Levi had read of muffled oars, and he ordered each of the rowers to wind the garment not in use around the loom of his oar where it rested in the rowlock. They obeyed in silence, and no one asked any question; for this reason they would have made good sailors, for they must obey without asking the reason for the command. They had been well trained by the overseer.

"Now, not one of you must speak a loud word, or make any noise," continued Levi, when he had seen that the oars were all properly muffled. "You must excuse me, Major, if I request all in this part of the boat to keep still also; for we are coming to the nearest point to the spring road. If there is any one on watch there, we will fool him if we can."

"All right, Levi; we will keep as still as mice in a pantry."

"Pull away again, boys," he added, to the disgust of General, who wanted him to give his orders in "ship-shop" fashion.

The negroes obeyed the command just as well as though it had been "ship-shop;" and the Magnolia went ahead with renewed speed after the rest. A little later the overseer ordered them to pull more slowly and with less noise, for the oars could be heard in spite of the muffling. But they could not be heard at half the distance to the spring road, and no challenge came to them from that or any other direction.

"Now you may put your muscle into your oars, boys," said the overseer when the boat came to a bend which had carried it away farther from the road.

The men bent to their oars again, and the Magnolia flew over the dark water. Dark as it was, the pilot had no difficulty in keeping the boat in the middle of the creek. At the end of about an hour from the resting-place, Levi ordered the men to pull slowly again, for the boat was approaching its destination. The planter lighted a match and looked at his watch.

"Hold on, here, boys!" called the overseer. "We have gone too far, for here is the mouth of the brook, and I reckon the flatboat is under that heap of stuff;" and he pointed to a mound of branches by the shore of the inlet. "I reckon we want the lanterns now, Major Lyon. Did you light one of them?"

"No; I only looked at my watch. We are in good time, for it wants a quarter of twelve," replied the planter. "Get out the lanterns, boys, and we will light them."

Levi worked the boat into the little inlet, and alongside of the mound. The flatboat was found under it, precisely as Artie had described it in the library. Four of the hands were sent to the top of it, and ordered to clear away the branches, which they did by throwing them on shore and into the water. The gundalow was baled out, and then its painter was made fast to the stern of the Magnolia. Deck and Artie were sent ashore with one of the lanterns, and directed to find the sink.

The Magnolia towed the flatboat down the creek till Deck hailed her from the landing-place where they had gone ashore in the afternoon. By a little after midnight the gundalow was moored at a convenient point for loading it.

CHAPTER XIV

THE TRANSPORTATION OF THE ARMS

The three lanterns were lighted, and Levi Bedford lost not a moment in making the preparations for loading the boxes into the flatboat. The sink-hole was a tunnel in the ground, at the bottom of which could be heard the gurgling of waters. The overseer said the brook which flowed into the creek where they had found the gundalow had its source in this place, though it made a considerable circuit before it reached its outlet.

On the side of the inverted cone nearest to the creek there was an opening which led into the cavern, the bottom of which was at least twenty feet above the water, whose ripple they could hear. The descent was gradual, both in the tunnel and in the cavern; and with lanterns in their hands Deck and Artie led the way down, for they had made themselves familiar with the subterranean chamber in the afternoon, and it was years since Levi had been there.

Mr. Lyon followed his son, while the overseer, with a coil of small line on his arm, which he had taken from the boathouse, brought up the rear. The party were taking a survey of the entrance in order to determine the best way to move the cases. It looked as though the water had flowed through the cavern at some remote period of time, probably rising from the sink-hole below, for the limestone at the floor was worn tolerably smooth. Doubtless the extinct stream had found a new outlet, lowering the level of the water so that it had ceased to flow through the cave.

The boxes were piled up just as they had been found in the afternoon. The roof of the cavern was very irregular, and in some places it was not more than five feet above the floor, while in others it was from eight to ten. The arms were deposited in a recess about twenty feet from the entrance. When the boys visited the sink-hole they had found the opening of the cave partly filled up with branches of trees and other rubbish; but they had removed these obstructions, which formed only a very weak attempt to conceal the depository of the arms.

Levi studied the interior of the cavern and the situation of the cases, attended by the planter. The lanterns were sufficient to light it so that they had no difficulty in seeing to work. The apartment began to wind about just below them, and all was gloom and darkness in that direction.

"It is about twenty feet to the opening," said Levi, as he measured the distance with his eye. "The roof is not more than five feet high half the way; and, if their skulls are not harder than the limestone, General and Dummy will be likely to stave a hole in them."

"The rest of the hands are not so tall," suggested Mr. Lyon.

"I brought this rope with me without knowing that it would be of any use to us; but I find that it is just the thing we want," continued the overseer as he uncoiled the line. "Now, boys, all we will ask you to do is to hold the lanterns; but you must not go to sleep and let them fall on the stone floor."

"No danger of that," laughed Deck. "But we can work in the low place without smashing our heads."

"I am glad there is no hard work for you, boys,

for you must be tired after pulling a boat twenty miles this afternoon," added Mr. Lyon.

"I am not very tired, and I can do my share of the work," replied Artie.

"So can I," added Deck.

"But you can do the most good by holding the lights," replied Levi. "One of you stand down here; and the other, with two of the lanterns, near the opening."

The boys followed this direction, Deck placing himself at the entrance, where he could light a part of the cavern and the tunnel. The overseer uncoiled his rope, and with the help of the planter lifted one of the boxes down to the floor. He then made fast the rope to it with a slip-noose, the knot on the under side, so as to carry the case over any obstructions.

Walking up to the entrance, uncoiling the line as he proceeded, he passed out of the cavern into the tunnel. Calling General and Dummy from the place where they had been told to wait, he stationed them near the door, and then carried the line, which was not less than seventy-five feet in length, to the shore of the creek.

"Now, Rosebud, and the rest of you, take hold

of this rope, and when the word comes up to you from General, haul up the box which is made fast to the other end of it," continued Levi. "As soon as you get it up here, unhitch the line, and throw the end down to General. As soon as you have done that, load the case into the boat, then haul up another, and do the same thing over again."

"Gunnymunks!" exclaimed the laughing negro. "Whar all de boxes come from?"

"None of your business, Rosebud; mind your work, and don't ask questions," returned the manager, as he descended to the entrance to the cavern.

"W'at we gwine to do, Mars'r Bedford?" asked General.

"You are going to pull and haul; and you can begin now," replied Levi. "Take hold of that line, and draw that box up here. Pull steady, so as not to break it."

The two powerful negroes manned the rope, and dragged the case up to the opening without any difficulty, and without doing it any great injury. It was placed so that it could be readily hauled out of the sink.

"Above there!" called the overseer. "Now haul steady on the rope! Ease it out of the opening, General."

The two big men crowded it around the corner, and then it went up to the ground above without any obstruction or delay. The line was detached from the box, and thrown down to the entrance, General passing it down to the pile of boxes. Another had been prepared for the rope, and the planter made fast to it. Levi had gone up to superintend the loading of the box, and arranged a couple of planks he found in the boat, so that this part of the work could be conveniently done. He made Rosebud the "boss" for the time being, and then went down into the cavern to assist his employer.

"It won't take long to do the job at this rate," said Mr. Lyon when the overseer joined him. "Your plan of doing the work makes an easy thing of it."

"I could not tell how it was to be done till I saw the situation of things here; but we shall be back to Riverlawn before daylight," replied Levi, as they lifted down the third of the boxes.

When the method of moving the cases to the

boat had been adopted, and had been found to work so well, the task was practically accomplished. The ease and celerity with which they mounted to the upper regions astonished and delighted the planter and the boys, and they were filled with admiration at the skill displayed by Levi Bedford in the management of the business. He was accustomed to working the hands, and knew what each of them was good for; and no other person could have done so well.

The work proceeded with increased rapidity as the men became used to the operations. In less than an hour all but the two cases containing the cannon, which Levi said were twelve-pounders, had been removed. The "Seceshers" had evidently had a great deal of difficulty in handling them; for they had stove one of the cases in pieces, and the other was hardly in condition to hold the heavy piece. Levi made his rope fast to the cascabel, or but-end of the gun, and the word was passed for the men above to come down to the entrance.

The six negroes made easy work of hauling it up to the opening, while the overseer and the planter directed it with levers, split from the broken case, so as to prevent it from receiving any injury. The six men were then sent above the tunnel, and the gun was drawn up. Loading it into the boat was a more difficult matter; and the planter and the overseer were considering how it was to be done, when General interrupted them.

"Go 'way dar, niggers!" exclaimed General, waving his hand for the others to get out of the way. "Cotch hold ob de end ob de shooter, Dummy, and we uns will tote it in de boat!"

The big preacher seized the end of the piece at the vent end, and General did the same with the muzzle. They lifted the gun from the ground, though with a strain which brought out some grunts from them, and slowly marched to the boat with their burden. Levi ordered two more of the men to take hold with them, at the trunnions, and sent the other two into the boat, who assisted as they could obtain a hold on the load. It was safely deposited in the bottom of the craft.

The overseer opened the other case with the hatchet Artie had brought, and broke up the boards of which it was constructed. It was put into the boat in the same manner as the other.

The water was deep enough in the creek for the boat, and Levi gave his attention next to the trimming of the craft, while he sent some of the hands to bring up the pieces of board left in the cavern; but the cargo needed but little adjusting, and the party were ready to return to Riverlawn.

"When your precious brother visits that cavern next time, he will be likely to wonder what has become of his arms and ammunition," said Levi, wiping the perspiration from his brow. "Now, boys, go down into that hole again, and see that we have left nothing there, for I don't want Captain Titus to find anything to let him know who has done this job for him."

While they were gone upon this mission, the overseer placed the Magnolia ahead of the flat-boat, in readiness to tow it down the creek. The boys returned, and the hatchet was the only thing which had been left. To their astonishment they found that Levi had shaken out the sail of the Magnolia, and they had their doubts about his ability to manage it.

"I hope you won't tip the sailboat over, Levi," said Deck, as he stepped on board of her, followed by Artie.

"If I do I shall not spill you out, either of you; for I want you to take charge of the flatboat, with two of the hands," replied the overseer. "I shall keep four men in the Magnolia to row, and I think the sail will help us along a good deal."

"I should like to change that plan a little, Levi," interposed Mr. Lyon. "The boys and myself can take care of the flatboat, and you can have all the men at the oars."

"Just as you say, Major Lyon, and perhaps that will be the best scheme. I was thinking that you and the boys might sleep part of the way down," answered the overseer. "The wind is blowing pretty hard from the south-west, and I reckon we shall get some rain before a great many hours. The sail ought to help us a big piece."

The planter and the boys armed themselves with the long oars of the flatboat, which had been driven into the muddy bottom of the creek to hold her in place at the landing, and they were ready to keep her off the shore in going around a sharp bend. Mr. Lyon placed his between the pins in the stern to steer with.

With their oars in hand the six rowers were in their places, and Levi gave the word to shove off.

When the men had pulled a short distance, the skipper, a position which the overseer had assumed, hauled in the sheet, and made it fast at the cleat for the purpose. The sail filled with a vengeance as a sharp flaw struck it, and the Magnolia forged ahead with a dart, dragging her tow after her. As the creek widened the sail strained, and the Magnolia seemed to be struggling to get away from the gundalow astern of her.

As she proceeded on her course down the stream, she increased her speed, and appeared to make nothing of hauling the tow after her. The motion produced by the sail bothered the rowers, who were not used to this situation. Some of them "caught crabs," and the oars of all of them were lifted and thrown back by the water that rushed past them. They made such bad work of it that Levi ordered them to unship their oars.

The Magnolia was making something like six miles an hour, and would have made ten without the tow. He steered her so that she carried the gundalow safely around the bends of the stream; and the planter had little to do, the boys nothing. Deck and Artie stretched themselves on the boxes, and were soon fast asleep; for they were worn out with the exertion and excitement of the day and night.

The bends in the stream near the spring road perplexed the skipper at first; but his excellent common-sense helped him out, and he hauled in his sheet so as to bring the boat up closer to the wind. Above the most troublesome bend at this point, the general course of the creek was west north-west. He let off the sheet, and the Magnolia flew faster than ever.

When he came to the bridge by the mansion, he waked the negroes, who had all fallen asleep, to take down the mast, so that he could pass under it, for he had already lowered the sail. He ran the boat close to the bank off the ice-house, and the negroes secured it and the gundalow.

"Dexter, Artemas!" shouted the planter. "Wake up! The cruise is ended."

CHAPTER XV

THE ESTABLISHMENT OF FORT BEDFORD

THE two young voyagers of the night sprang to their feet on the pile of cases which filled the body of the gundalow, and looked about them. It was still dark, and they could not make out anything when just roused from their slumber.

"What are we stopping here for, father? Has anything broken?" asked Deck, discovering Mr. Lyon near him.

"Nothing but your slumbers, my son," replied the planter. "Haven't you got your eyes open yet? Can't you see that you have got home?"

"I believe I have been asleep," added Artie, rubbing his eyes.

"I know you have, my boy; for I spread your overcoats over you both before we reached the big bend, and I know you were sleeping as soundly as a pair of babies then. You must have slept an hour and a half," the father explained. "I am

THE ESTABLISHMENT OF FORT BEDFORD   187

glad you had some sleep, for we have more work to do before we can go to bed."

"I can see the bridge now," added Deck.

"And there is the house," said Artie.

The negroes were all wide awake by this time, and Levi had gone to the mansion for the key to the ice-house. Mr. Lyon lighted all of the lanterns, and sent the boys to the stone building with them, following himself soon after. The overseer came with the key, and it was opened with some difficulty. The ice with which it had been filled in the winter had been exhausted, and it contained nothing but rubbish. The hands were called, and the interior was soon cleaned out.

Though Levi had not closed his eyes during the night, and had been busy all the time, he was wide awake, and proceeded to drive things as he had done at the cavern. It was decided to move the cannons first, after a broad gang plank had been made of the material in the boat. A heavy cart-stake was procured, which was thrust into the first of the pieces, with room enough for three of the hands to get hold of it. Another was placed under the cascabel, which was supported by General and Dummy, with Rosebud at the jaws.

The gun was easily handled with this force, and the men walked briskly to the new arsenal. Three wheelbarrows were brought from the tool-house by the planter and the boys while Levi was superintending the removal of the cannons. Three wheelers were selected by the overseer, two placed in the gundalow to load the barrows, and one at the ice-house. In less than an hour, and when the daylight was appearing in the east, the job was finished.

"Now, boys, you can sleep all the rest of the day," said Mr. Lyons, and Levi sent the hands to their quarters.

"We haven't seen any men on the watch," said Levi, while he was placing some boards over the windows of the building, "but there may have been some on the lookout for all that."

"If they were in the road near the big bend, where you thought they would be, if anywhere, they could not have walked to the cavern in time to find us there, for we made quick work of loading the boat," added the planter.

"If there were any men there, they may have observed us; but they could not get round here to see what was done with the cases if they did,"

THE ESTABLISHMENT OF FORT BEDFORD

replied Levi. "They may possibly have recognized the Magnolia; and that is the only clew they could have obtained of the operations in this affair."

"It is time to go to bed, and I am inclined to think we shall do some sleeping to-day," added the planter, as he led the way to the mansion.

Levi was not willing to leave anything to chance; and before he went to his room in the house he had called up two of the servants and established a patrol along the bank of the creek from the bridge to the boat-house, with orders to call him if any persons were seen prowling about the vicinity.

All the operations of the night had been conducted with the most prudent regard to secrecy. Doubtless Levi Bedford knew more about the residents of the county than Noah Lyon, and probably more about Titus as he was and had been during the last few years. The disappearance of the arms and ammunition would make a tremendous sensation among the Southern sympathizers, though most of them were not yet aware of the existence of such a store of munitions in the vicinity; for the knowledge of them had probably been confined to the members of Titus's company of Home Guards. Even if the wrath and excitement occasioned by the loss of the war material was limited to these ruffians, there were enough of them to do a vast amount of mischief in the county.

The interview on the bridge with his brother had opened wide the eyes of Noah; but he had always lived in a peaceful community, and his overseer understood the situation better than he did. Levi had taken every precaution against the possible assaults of the "bushwackers," as he called the gang with whom the Northern "doughface" had cast his lot at the breaking out of the troubles in the State. The boys slept soundly till nearly noon, and the planter till the middle of the forenoon; but Levi appeared as usual at breakfast, having slept but about three hours.

Mr. Lyon had told his wife something about the events of the night, and assured her that the arms were safe in the ice-house, and nothing was said at the table about the proceedings of the party, though Levi was as good-natured as usual, and talked about other things. As soon as he had finished his morning meal with a most excellent appetite, he hastened to the ice-house with the

THE ESTABLISHMENT OF FORT BEDFORD 191

key in his hand. The field-hands had gone to their work, and all was quiet about the place.

The ice-house was near the creek, about half-way between the bridge and the boat-house, close to the stream. The door of it faced the water, and there was a small square window in either end. Levi walked around the building two or three times, closely examining the structure. Then he stopped at the door and cast his eyes all around him, especially at the lay of the land on the other side of the creek. He was not a military engineer any more than his employer; but he was a man of ideas, and he was evidently preparing for events in the future which he foresaw, and which the disturbed condition of the State rendered more than possible.

When he had completed his survey he unlocked the door of the building. The cases were all just as they had been piled up in the early morning. He bestowed only a glance at them, and then began a study of the two windows, from which he removed the boards that prevented any one from seeing what the building contained. Then he gave his attention to the doors, which were double, the thickness of the wall apart. He was evidently making a plan in his mind for some alterations to the structure; but he was alone, and of course he said nothing.

He appeared to have reached his conclusion. Closing and locking the outer door, he walked over to the boat-house, at the pier of which the Magnolia had been secured by the boatmen as soon as the work of the night was completed. Here again he stopped and made a survey of the neighboring swamp, which separated the lawn from the bank of the Green. Then he went over to the bank of the river, and followed it down stream.

At this point a bend of the river above forced the water of the stream over near the opposite shore, while half-way across from the bank on which he stood, the waters from the river and the creek had washed in the mud so that it formed a bar on a bed of rocks, and the descent here produced the rapids. The water for half a mile was considerably troubled when the streams were full, while it was deep enough on the other side to permit the passage of the steamboats that plied on the river.

Levi continued his walk in the road, with Green

River on one side and on the other the swamp which bordered the creek to a point near its source. The swamp was impassable on foot or by boat. It was better than a wall in the rear of the mansion, and the marauders of Titus Lyon could not approach from that direction. Farther along was a broad lagoon or pond, connected by a wide and sluggish inlet with Bar Creek. This could be crossed with a boat; but the approach to it from the spring road over the low ground was difficult and dangerous.

The overseer knew the whole region very well; but when he had viewed it again in the light of impending contingencies, he seemed to be entirely satisfied with the situation, for his chronic smile was on his round face, though no one was there to see it. He went to the shop, which formed part of the carriage-house, and began a survey of the lumber on hand there. A couple of three-inch oak planks were pulled out from the pile. He measured and marked them with a piece of chalk, and then left the shop.

Among the plantation hands were carpenters, masons, painters, and other mechanics, more or less skilful, though none of them had regularly learned a trade. Some of them had become quite expert in the use of tools, and could do a very respectable job, especially the carpenters. Levi was himself a "jack-of-all-trades," and he had trained some of them to the best of his ability.

When he came out of the shop he sent Frank the coachman to call the three carpenters, who worked in the field most of the time. The colonel had given these men names to suit himself, and they were proud of their cognomens. "Shavings" was the most skilful of them, and was the "boss" at any job to be done. "Gouge" and "Bitts" were only fair workmen, but they did very well under the direction of their foreman.

When they came, Levi ordered Shavings to make two doors of the three-inch planks, and described what he wanted very minutely. At the same time the two door-frames were ordered, and the mechanics went to work with a will, and without asking to what use the doors were to be applied.

By this time the planter came out from his late breakfast, and the overseer reported to him what he had been doing the last three hours. They visited the shop where the negro mechanics were sawing out the planks for the doors, and then went to the stables, where Frank remained on duty all the time when not out with one of the teams; and then one of the grooms took his place.

"How many horses are there on the place now, Frank?" asked the planter.

"Thirty-five in all, Major," answered the coachman.

"Are they all fit for service?" inquired the owner.

"No, sir; six of them are breeding mares, and nine are colts, two and three years old. We have fifteen horses and mares four years old and more, for sale, and I reckoned you would sell them about this time."

"That's all, Frank," added the planter as he left the stable.

"I don't know what you are driving at, Major Lyon, but we have twenty-seven horses over three years old, and fit for service, though the three year olds are rather young yet for hard work," said Levi, as they walked towards the ice-house.

"I have held my tongue about as long as necessary; but now all these sores in the State seem to be coming to a head, and I will tell you, between ourselves, that I have an idea of raising a company of Union cavalry to offset the Home Guards of this county," replied Mr. Lyon.

"That's a glorious idea!" exclaimed Levi with tremendous enthusiasm. "I wish I was ten years younger, and weighed thirty pounds less, for I should like to swing a sabre in that company."

"But you are to look out for the plantation and take care of my family while I am away, Levi. You can ride a colt better than any of us; but your work is here, and you may be called upon to do as much fighting as any of us," said Mr. Lyon.

"I will do my duty wherever you put me, Major; but I should rather enjoy a whack at those border ruffians who are making the whole county hot with outrages. Last night they burned out a Union man two miles above the village."

"The time for action is close at hand," added Mr. Lyon, as they came to the ice-house. "There have been talk and threats enough. My brother has told me that I am liable to be hung on one of the big trees after a mob has burned the house; but I think we are ready for such a gathering as he suggests. We may hear something about it to-night in the meeting at the Big Bend schoolhouse."

"I have looked the ice-house over this morning, and I have made up my mind what ought to be done," said Levi; and he proceeded to state his plan for turning the stone structure into a sort of fort. "I have ordered the doors already, and if you say the word, Major, I will make three or four embrasures in the walls for the two field-pieces; and we must have a magazine for the ammunition."

"I approve your plan; go ahead and do the work as you think best. You can use all the hands you need; and from this moment the ice-house will be known as Fort Bedford," replied Mr. Lyons.

"Thank you, Major, and I will endeavor to make the fortress worthy of a better name," returned Levi, as he hastened to the stable to send for the men he wanted.

CHAPTER XVI

THE UNION MEETING AT BIG BEND

In the afternoon Levi Bedford had half the hands on the plantation at work in and about the ice-house. Embrasures, or port-holes, were opened in the thick walls, one at each end and one on each side of the door, at the proper height for the twelve-pounders, which were mounted on the carriages, in order that everything should be correctly adjusted. Then the door which opened on the side next to the creek was filled up with stones taken from the quarry in the only hill on the plantation, so that it was as thick and as solid as the rest of the walls. Then a new door was made on the opposite side.

By sundown the carpenter had completed and hung the double doors; and they were secured with the heavy locks the colonel had purchased in the days of the horse-thieves. All this work was not completed when night came, and four trusty men were selected to patrol the creek from the bridge down to the boat-pier, two serving till midnight, and the other two till morning.

"I think we shall be in condition to stand a siege by to-morrow night," said the overseer, as he accompanied the planter and the boys to Fort Bedford, on the way to the schoolhouse at Big Bend.

"It looks so now," replied Mr. Lyon as he went into the building. "You have made remarkable progress for one day. But I want to open one of these boxes."

"Which one, Major?" asked Levi.

"The one which contains revolvers and cartridges, for some of the smaller ones are labelled with the names of these articles. I hardly expect any trouble at the meeting to-night; but I think it is best to be prepared for the worst. I have brought one of the colonel's pistols with me; but I want to put the boys in condition to defend themselves," added the planter.

"I think we can make good use of them, for we have had some experience with such tools," said Deck, who did not appear to be at all affected by the serious nature of the preparations they were making.

"Where have you had any such experience, Dexter?" inquired his father.

"Tom Bartlett and Ben Mason had revolvers at the time of the housebreaking scare in Derry, and Artie and I used to fire at a mark with them in the hill pasture," replied the enthusiastic boy. "Artie used to beat us all, and often put the ball through the centre of the target."

"Sometimes," suggested the other.

"Then you are both ahead of me, for I never fired a revolver or a pistol of any kind, though I used to go hunting with a fowling-piece when I was a boy," added Mr. Lyon.

"Then I think you had better practise a little, Major," said Levi, as he pulled out one of the smaller boxes from the top of the pile of cases. "This contains what you want, I reckon."

Deck brought the hatchet, and the case was opened. Most of the weapons were navy revolvers, wrapped in oiled paper to save them from rust. They were closely packed in the case, the spare space being filled in with packages of cartridges. They opened another box, and found half a dozen of smaller size, with the proper ammunition. The overseer selected two of them, handing one to each of the boys, with a box of cartridges.

"I should like to try this little persuader," said Deck, as he opened the box of ammunition, and proceeded to load the pistol.

Artie followed his example; and, setting up the cover of the case by the creek, they blazed away at it till the chambers of the revolvers were empty. They fired in turn, and the position of each bullet-hole was noted. Artie kept up his old reputation, for he hit near the centre of the board three times out of six. Deck fired the best shot, but his others were more scattering. They hit the board every time, and Levi said they " would do."

Then Mr. Lyon tried his hand with the revolver he had brought from the mansion; but his aim was less accurate than that of the boys. He put four of his six balls into the board, three of them outside of the punctures made by Deck and Artie.

"You will improve with more experience, Major; but I reckon you could hit a bushwhacker if he wasn't more than ten feet from you; and these tools generally come into use at short range. How were you going up to Big Bend, Major?"

"I thought we should walk," replied the planter; and he reloaded his revolver, as both of the boys had done by this time. "It is not more than three-quarters of a mile."

"I think you had better go in the Magnolia, with the crew that pulled us last night," suggested Levi. "If there should be any row at the schoolhouse, those boys will stand by you as long as there is anything left of you."

"I don't look for any row, Levi, but I suppose it is always best to be prepared for the worst," replied the planter. "You may send for the crew."

One of the watchmen happened to be near at the time, and he was despatched for the boatmen who had formed the regular crew of the Magnolia in the time of the deceased planter.

"I suppose, if there should be any trouble at the schoolhouse, and I should be protected by my negroes, it would tend to aggravate the charge against me of being an abolitionist; and that seems to be about the worst thing that can be said against a man in this county."

"But only among the border ruffians," the overseer amended the statement. "The man that owns fifty niggers cannot decently be accused of being an abolitionist. I advise you to go in the boat because the schoolhouse is right on the very bank of the river. The back windows over the platform look out upon the water. If the bushwhackers come down upon you, and things go against you, it will be easy to get out by one of these windows. A good general always keeps the line of retreat open behind him when he goes into battle; and you had better have the Magnolia under one of these windows."

"Why, Levi, you talk as though you were about sure an attempt would be made to break up the meeting," replied Mr. Lyon.

"To tell you the truth, I do feel almost sure of it," returned the overseer. "Captain Titus, as they call him up in the village so as not to mix him up with Major Noah Lyon, was about mad enough yesterday to do something desperate. You say he has threatened you, and " —

"I did not say that, Levi," interposed the planter. "Don't make my brother out any worse than he is, for conscience' sake."

"What did he say, then?"

"He told me the people on his side of the question would have mobbed me before this time if he had not prevented them from doing so."

"That's about the same thing. I don't like to say anything against your brother, Major, but I don't look on Captain Titus as a square man. He wants to keep his own head covered up because you are his brother; but I believe on my conscience that he would like to see your place burned to the ground, and it wouldn't break his heart to see you hanging by the neck to one of the big trees."

Mr. Lyon realized that the overseer understood the character of Titus better than he had supposed. His brother was terribly disappointed because the colonel had not left Riverlawn to him; and he had charged the deceased with unfairness and injustice in making his will. He was compelled to believe the claim of Titus that he had prevented the ruffians from destroying his property was a pretence, and nothing more. His brother was not only disappointed but revengeful.

"It is generally understood about here that you called this Union meeting," continued Levi.

"I suggested it, for we ought to know who's who; and it remains to be seen how many will have the pluck to attend the meeting. Titus believes that a large majority of the people in these parts are of his way of thinking, while I believe that they are about two to one the other way, though most of them are afraid to do or say much, and I want to bring them out if possible."

"You are right as to numbers, Major; and when a man is afraid that his house will be burned down over his head, or that he will get a bullet through his brains while he sits at his window, I don't much wonder that he is not inclined to speak out loud, and these bushwhackers have had it all their own way. I hope you will be able to bring out the prudent and timid ones."

"I talked the meeting over with others, and Colonel Cosgrove promised to come up and help us out with a speech. We all agreed that it was time to make a demonstration in favor of the Union," replied the planter as the boat's crew appeared on the ground.

"I should like to go with you, Major, but I don't think it is safe to leave the place alone," said the overseer. "Whether the ruffians had a watch on the spring road last night or not, I don't know. We haven't heard anything of them during the day; but I should be willing to wager a pair of my old shoes they have found out by this time that the arms and ammunition placed in the cavern have taken to themselves wings, like other riches, and flown away. If I am not much mistaken, Captain Titus finds himself some thousands poorer to-day than he was a week ago."

"Do you believe they have discovered the loss so soon?"

"I haven't much doubt of it. Captain Titus keeps three horses, and it was easy enough for him to send one of his boys over to the cavern to see that the arms were all right. He has missed them by this time; and if we do our duty they won't shoot any bullets into the heads and hearts of the Union army. Of course Captain Titus and his gang are boiling over with wrath. You won't see him at the meeting, perhaps; but there will be enough there to make a noise, if nothing more. I have been thinking of these things to-day, and that is the reason why I thought it best to take proper precautions."

"I am glad you have spoken out, Levi, for you have generally been very reticent," replied Mr. Lyon, as he led the way to the boat-pier, where the crew had manned the boat.

"I couldn't say much while I believed your brother was at the bottom of most of the mischief," pleaded Levi.

The planter and the boys seated themselves in the stern sheets of the Magnolia. Deck took the tiller lines with the consent of his father, and General was permitted to get under way as he pleased, giving all the orders in detail. None of the crew asked any questions, and in a short time Deck brought the boat up under one of the windows of the schoolhouse. Mr. Lyon charged General to keep the Magnolia just where they had placed her, and not to make any noise at all.

The building was already partly filled, and more were constantly arriving. Before the appointed time Colonel Cosgrove descended from his wagon at the door, and the planter welcomed him. At the hour named, Squire Truman, a young legal gentleman from a Northern county, who had settled in the village, called the meeting to order. It was said that he had not a very flourishing practice, but he was regarded as a young man of more than average ability. He had the credit of being a ready and able speaker; and Mr. Lyon had invited him to open the assemblage with a statement of the situation in the county, especially in the vicinity of Barcreek.

He was a decided and outspoken Union man. He began very moderately; but in a few minutes he became more earnest, and soon rose to the height of eloquence. He was warmly applauded by the audience, though there were some tokens of disapprobation, evidently proceeding from some of the individuals whom Levi called "bushwhackers." Titus Lyon was not there, but some of his representatives had already manifested themselves. The discordant elements soon became more demonstrative as the speaker waxed eloquent. They made noise enough to disturb the equanimity of Squire Truman; and he switched off from his line of remark, and proceeded to dress down the malcontents in the most vigorous language.

"I beg leave to inform those who are struggling to create a disturbance, that this is a Union meeting, called as such, and as such only," said the orator, shaking with indignation. "It was called for Union men only! It is a gathering of those who are loyal to the government at Washington, and not to decide between secession and fidelity to the old flag. Those who are not Union men are respectfully requested to retire from the meeting."

This request brought forth a torrent of yells from the ruffians, though there were apparently not more than a dozen of them. Squire Truman was defiant, and his handsome face looked as noble as that of a Roman senator.

"Has the time come when free speech in behalf of this glorious Union is to be put down?" And then the ruffians howled again. "Has it come to this in the State of Kentucky, the second to be admitted into the Union? and, with the help of God and all honest men, she shall be the last to leave it! Are we men to be badgered and silenced by half a score of blackguards and ruffians? I am one of half a dozen to put them out of the hall."

About a dozen rose from their seats, headed by Noah Lyon, and moved down the aisles of the schoolroom.

CHAPTER XVII.

THE EJECTION OF THE NOISY RUFFIANS

THE planter of Riverlawn was not a fighting character; he had always been one of the most peaceful of men. He had never raised a hand against one of his fellow-beings, and it required the stimulus of an occasion like the present to rouse a belligerent feeling in him, if the groundwork of any such emotion existed in his nature. It was hardly that, but rather a sense of his solemn duty, which he was called upon to perform, as a surgeon is required to amputate a limb to save life; and he was impelled to save the life of the Union.

Noah Lyon was not physically a large man, but one who weighed a hundred and a half; yet his frame was well knit, firmly compacted, and inured by hard labor from his boyhood. As he rose to his feet and marched down the middle aisle of the schoolroom, his face exhibited more strength than his form; for all the determination of his nature was concentrated in his eyes and the muscles of his countenance.

The fervid speech of the young orator had brought him to his bearings. Deck and Artie had been similarly affected; and with their fists clinched they followed the planter. Squire Truman leaped from the platform into the midst of them, as the dozen others sprang to their feet, some with their eyes flashing with indignation, and all of them with a fixed purpose not to submit to the outrage in which the ruffians were engaged.

When Mr. Lyon had proceeded as far as the middle of the room, one of the disturbers of the peace, whom the planter had spotted, rose to his feet and confronted him in the aisle. It was Buck Lagger, a pedler, who was one of the most virulent of the Secessionists, and who aspired to be a leader among the turbulent spirits of the county.

"What are you go'n' to do about it?" demanded he savagely.

"Are you a Union man?" asked Mr. Lyon with quiet determination.

"No, I'm not!" yelled the ruffian, who had the reputation in Barcreek of being a brute of the lowest order, with a whole volley of oaths.

"Then you were not invited here, and you will leave!" said the planter.

"This buildin' is public, and I have as much right here as you have!" answered Buck Lagger, with a coarse guffaw.

Noah Lyon did not wait for anything more, but grappled with the fellow as an eagle swoops down on his prey. Buck tried to get his right hand into his breast pocket, evidently to obtain a weapon of some kind; but his assailant understood his purpose, and crowded him over backwards upon one of the desks, choking him so hard that he soon lost all his pluck.

Colonel Cosgrove was close behind Mr. Lyon, and seized upon the boon companion of the pedler. He was an excellent specimen of a Kentucky gentleman, stalwart in form and determined in purpose. He bore his man down as the leader had done. The other ruffians rushed to the assistance of their leaders, and the *mêlée* became general.

There did not appear to be more than half a dozen active ruffians in the room; at least not more who were resolute enough to take part in these stormy proceedings. Mr. Lyon had choked

"HE GRAPPLED WITH THE FELLOW." Page 212.

so much of the energy out of Buck Laggar that he had ceased to feel for his weapon, and the planter took him by the collar of the coat with both hands, and dragged him to the door, where he pitched him on the ground all in a heap.

Colonel Cosgrove followed him with his man; and then came the orator with a fellow nearly twice his size, with whom he was having a hard tussle, when Deck leaped upon the back of this victim, and drawing his arms tightly under his throat, brought him to the floor, and then rolled him out at the door. The other Union men in the audience had tackled the remaining ruffians when they went to the assistance of those of their number who had been attacked, and hustled them out of the apartment.

"That will do for the present," said Squire Truman, as the resolute Unionists completed their active work, and stopped to catch their breath.

"I think we had better station a guard at the door, and challenge every man who wants to come in," suggested Mr. Lyon.

"That's a good idea, for it is the evident intention of the blackguards to break up the meeting; and I should be ashamed to have such a thing done, — a Union meeting dispersed by force in the State of Kentucky!" added the young lawyer.

"Precisely so!" exclaimed Colonel Cosgrove. "I will offer my services as one of the guard."

"Good!" shouted Colonel Belthorpe, a big Kentuckian whose plantation was near that of Major Lyon, "I will be another."

"Here are two more!" cried Deck Lyon, as he and Artie presented themselves.

"Lively boys," laughed Colonel Cosgrove. "Both of them took a hand in the skirmish we have had, and they will do very well for this duty."

The Union men in the assembly applauded warmly, and the young orator led the way back to the seats, mounting the platform himself. He resumed his speech with an allusion to the event which had just transpired, and roused his audience to the highest pitch of enthusiasm by his fiery eloquence. He spoke half an hour, and concluded by nominating Major Noah Lyon as the presiding officer of the evening; and the selection was heartily indorsed by the meeting.

Before he could reach the platform, a dozen men appeared at the door. The volunteer committee on admissions retired to the lobby so that they need not disturb the proceedings. Colonel Cosgrove took Artie by the arm, while Colonel Belthorpe did the same with Deck, each at one side of the door.

"Are you a Union man?" demanded Deck in a loud voice, for he felt that he must do or say something, boiling over with enthusiasm for the cause as he was; and perhaps the fact that he had a loaded revolver in his pocket was an inciting influence with him.

"I am!" exclaimed the person addressed, with emphasis.

"Pass in," replied Deck.

"Put the same question, Artie," added Colonel Cosgrove, amused at the earnestness of Deck.

Artie put the question with less pomposity than his cousin, and the answer was the same. The brace of colonels then took part in the challenging, and the dozen applicants were promptly admitted. One of the colonels then suggested to the other that the boys could remain in the lobby while they stood inside the door.

Noah Lyon had presided on several occasions in town meetings, and his modesty had been so far overcome that he could face an audience, especially in such a cause as the present. He was received with applause and cheers, and proceeded to make a speech in his usual quiet way. He said he could not make such a speech as the eloquent gentleman from Barcreek village had done; but he was a Union man in every fibre of his being, whether he was in New Hampshire or Kentucky.

This statement was received with tremendous applause. He proceeded to say that he was a peaceable man, and was in favor of peaceable measures; but he did not intend to be overridden and trodden down by the Secession element, which he believed was in a large minority in the State. He was ready to talk as long as talking did any good; but when he had talked enough he was ready to fight.

This was the popular sentiment in the meeting, and a tumult of applause followed, ending in nine rousing cheers. He was ready to shoulder a musket in any Kentucky regiment, and he was glad that some had already been organized. He had twenty-seven horses he would give " without money and without price," to the cause of the Union, with which to start a cavalry company;

THE EJECTION OF THE NOISY RUFFIANS 217

and "I think I can *find* arms for the men," he added.

This offer was greeted with yells of approval, and it was some time before he could say anything more.

"I will also contribute twenty horses," shouted Colonel Cosgrove.

"I will give the next twenty," Colonel Belthorpe cried out.

The clapping of hands and the cheering were renewed with more vigor than ever, if possible; and others offered to contribute from one to five each, till over a hundred horses were pledged for the company. In the midst of this enthusiasm the voice of Deck was heard in the lobby.

"Are you a Union man, sir?" he demanded in a voice loud enough to be heard in a momentary lull of the enthusiasm.

"No, I am not!" replied the applicant, with a volley of expletives.

"Then you can't go in," answered Deck.

"Who says I can't?" asked the intruder in fierce tones.

"This is a Union meeting, and none but Union men are admitted," replied Deck, loud enough to be heard on the platform; for the meeting had become silent, and all were turning around to see the door.

"Do you see that?" demanded the ruffian, as he drew a bowie-knife from his pocket, and threw it open with a jerk.

Deck had put his right hand on his hip pocket, which contained his revolver; and, the moment he saw the knife, he drew it, and pointed it at the part where the intruder carried what brains he had.

"And do you see that?" called the plucky boy.

"And that?" added Artie on the other side of the door.

"Take yourself off!" shouted Deck furiously, as he retreated a pace, to keep out of the reach of the wicked-looking blade of the knife.

"Isn't this a free building?" asked the ruffian, as he looked from one revolver to the other.

"Free to Union men to-night," answered Deck.

By this time half a dozen men from the interior were approaching the door, and the ruffian suddenly decamped. Deck followed him to the door, and saw the man disappear in the grove on the other side of the road. Then he heard a voice among the trees; and it was evident to him that there were more ruffians, perhaps biding their time to make an attack upon the Unionists when they went to their homes.

"Three cheers for the boys!" shouted one of the men who had come to the door, and observed the retreat of the ruffian.

They were lustily given, and then Deck announced to the meeting that there were more men in the grove, for some one had hailed the ruffian that had just left the door.

"No matter for them," said the chairman. "Let us go on with this meeting, and when they come in, if they do so, we will take care of them. The boys will keep watch, and let us know if they approach the schoolhouse."

A committee of three were appointed to attend to the enrolment of the company of cavalry. The two colonels and the major by courtesy were appointed on this committee. Then Colonel Cosgrove was called upon to make the speech he had promised. He was not so eloquent as his professional brother from the village; but he was more solid, and was as vigorously applauded as the other speakers had been.

He said there had been a sort of reign of terror

in the county, and it was because the Unionists had been less demonstrative than the Secessionists, and for that reason he believed in the present meeting. He was disposed to be peaceable, but he was ready to fight for the Union. He proceeded at considerable length. He was in favor of having it understood in the county that there were plenty of Unionists within its borders, and that they were not to be frowned or bullied down by the ruffians of the other side.

This remark seemed to be the sense of the assembly, which had now increased in numbers to over a hundred, and the applause was decided.

While the colonel from the county town was speaking, Deck and Artie had been over to the other side of the road, and penetrated the grove for a short distance. Probably those who had been ejected from the meeting were there; but the boys crept near enough to make out that there were not less than fifty men there, and possibly double that number.

As they retired from the grove they found that a single man was following them. They retreated to the lobby of the schoolhouse, with their revolvers in their hands. They had hardly resumed their stations at the door when the man presented himself before them. To the astonishment of his two nephews this person proved to be Titus Lyon.

"Are you a Union man?" demanded Deck.

"I am not," replied Titus.

"Then you can't go into this meeting," added Deck, as firmly as he had spoken at any time before.

The applicant could not fail to see that both of the boys had weapons in their hands. He looked earnest and determined, but he did not appear to be even angry. He halted and fixed his gaze upon the floor, apparently in deep thought.

CHAPTER XVIII

THE DEMAND OF CAPTAIN TITUS LYON

Revolvers are dangerous weapons; and Deck and Artie had used them enough in sport to realize this truth. They had not yet become accustomed to seeing bullets fired into the bodies of human beings; to the sight of strong men falling with a death-wound in the head or heart, which was afterwards almost an every-day spectacle in the battles of the Great Rebellion.

They had been brought up where human life was held to be more sacred than in the locality to which they had been transplanted; and if they had thought of discharging their weapons into the vital parts of even the ruffians who menaced the Union meeting with violence, they were certainly not ready to begin with one of their own flesh and blood, though Titus Lyon had proved himself to be one of the most virulent enemies of the public peace.

"I have no weapons, as you have, boys, and I

have something to say to this meeting," said Titus, after he had meditated for two or three minutes. "I want to go in; but I shall not stop there many minutes."

"We can't let you in, Uncle Titus," replied Deck decidedly; "that's the order of the meeting."

"But I'm going in if I'm shot for it," continued the applicant for admission very quietly, but with none of the bluster which had become almost a second nature to him.

Perhaps the interest he felt in the mission which brought him to the schoolhouse had induced him to refrain from his usual potations, for he appeared to be perfectly sober. He used none of the intemperate language which was generally on his tongue, so that the boys were not roused to indignation, even if they were tempted to use their weapons; but both of them placed themselves in the doorway as though they intended to dispute his passage into the room.

The meeting was proceeding with its business, though the orators had finished their speeches. A Union farmer was telling about one of his neighbors who had been threatened by the ruffians, as the Secessionists had come to be generally called by this time. He was quite earnest in his plea that something should be done to protect men who stood by the government.

The two colonels were interested, and they had moved forward where they could hear the farmer, who spoke in a low tone; and no one inside was aware of what was transpiring in the lobby, so that the boys were practically alone.

"We can't let you in, Uncle Titus, and we don't want to shoot you," interposed Artie. "I will call Colonel Cosgrove, and you can make your request to him;" and he went to the place where the colonel was standing.

"But I am going in," persisted Titus Lyon, attempting to push Deck aside.

"You can't go in!" said Deck, as he crowded his uncle back from the entrance. "Wait a moment, and you can tell Colonel Cosgrove what you want!"

"I don't want anything of Colonel Cosgrove; he is worse than your father," replied the applicant.

"Good-evening, Mr. Lyon," said the Kentuckian, presenting himself at the door at this moment.

"I have something to say to this meeting, Colonel, which it is important for the meeting to hear," added Titus.

"Come right in and say it, Mr. Lyon," replied the colonel, to the astonishment of the young guardians of the portal.

He was as polite as a Kentucky gentleman generally is; and he took the arm of the applicant, and marched with him to the space behind the desks, where he halted till the former had finished his remarks. Noah Lyon was taken " all back " by the appearance of his brother escorted by the most influential Kentuckian in the county. The entire audience turned and stared at the unexpected guest.

"Mr. Chairman, I have the honor to present Captain Titus Lyon of Barcreek to the meeting," said the colonel. " He claims to have something of importance to communicate. He is not a Union man, as is well known, but I trust no objection will be made to hearing him."

"I am not a Union man, as Colonel Cosgrove says," Titus began. "When I came to this State, I became a Kentuckian, and I go with the people of this section of the country. But I did not come here to talk politics. There is two sides to the question before the country, and each on 'em has its rights. I belong to the party that is tryin' to keep the peace in the State if we have to fight for it. As we had a perfect right to do, we bought about three thousand dollars worth of arms and ammernition to protect ourselves agin them that is tryin' to force the State into a war of subjergation agin our own flesh and blood.

"Them arms and ammernition has been stole," continued Titus, waxing indignant in spite of his effort to keep cool, and relapsing into his everyday speech. "I believe it was done by what you call Union men, and I cal'late I know jest who done it; and I cal'late, Mr. Chairman, you know jest as well or better'n I do who done it."

"Who was it?" demanded a person in the audience.

"I h'ain't got nothin' to say here about that," answered Captain Titus. "But if them arms and ammernition ain't given up right off, here and now, on the spot, or some plan agreed on for doin' so afore to-morrer noon, the blood will run in the low places round here, and the clouds in the sky will give back the light from the fires that is burnin' down some of the nicest houses in these parts. I hain't got nothin' more to say; but if any one wants to see me about settlin' up this matter, I can be found near the road in front of the school-house."

"But this is war, Captain Lyon," suggested Colonel Belthorpe.

"I know 'tis; and that's jest what I mean. We want the Union thieves to give up the property they stole; and that's all we ask now," replied Titus, whose wrath was beginning to be stirred to the boiling point.

"We are ready to meet you on that ground!" shouted Squire Truman, springing to his feet; for he knew that Captain Titus was the ringleader of the ruffians in the vicinity, and his threat roused him to a fiery indignation. "I know nothing about the arms and ammunition: but whoever took possession of them has done a noble and patriotic deed, and, Mr. Chairman, I move you that a vote of thanks be tendered to them for it."

This motion was hailed with thunders of applause; and when the presiding officer put it to the meeting, it was carried unanimously, and no one wished to delay it by making a speech.

Squire Truman then made another speech, in

which he pictured the result of permitting the arms to get into the hands of the ruffians for whose use they were evidently intended; and he magnified the prudence and forethought of the unknown persons who had taken the responsibility of such a forward step. This speech was received with cheers, in which the throats of the audience seemed to be strained to their utmost tension.

"Captain Lyon," said Colonel Cosgrove, when the tumult had subsided in a measure, "no formal answer seems to be necessary to your demand. The action of this meeting and the spirit with which it has been received are a sufficient reply. Personally, I can only say I heartily rejoice that the arms and ammunition have been turned aside from the purpose for which they were intended, and we will take care that they are not used against the government of the United States. We are loyal citizens, and we shall do our duty to the glorious flag under which we live. Have you any further communication to make to this meeting, Captain Lyon?"

"No, I haven't; I've said my say, and fire and blood is the next thing," replied Titus, as he rushed out of the schoolroom, furious with passion.

The business of the meeting was completed; but the boys informed the two colonels that the road was full of men. Then several of the Unionists drew revolvers from their pockets; for they had fully expected that the meeting would be disturbed, and that it would end in a fight. They had come prepared to defend themselves. The situation was discussed, but no one was inclined to avoid the issue. If there was to be a fight, it would be no new thing in the State.

Colonel Belthorpe, whose title was not one of mere courtesy, for he had served in the regular army in his younger days, and won his later spurs in the militia, advised that a procession be formed, with the armed men on the right, while the others were told to obtain clubs, or anything they could lay their hands upon. But before the column was formed Buck Lagger appeared at the door.

"We want Major Lyon and his two cubs!" shouted the ruffian, who appeared to be the right-hand man of Captain Titus.

The ruffians had held a meeting in the grove, privately notified by this Buck, — for Titus had not been inclined to show his hand, — and a delegation had been sent to try the temper of the assemblage in the schoolhouse. They had been defeated and ejected. It was plain by this time that the cavern had been visited and the loss of the munitions discovered.

The speech of Captain Titus indicated that he knew who had taken possession of the property, though Noah Lyon could not conjecture who had given the information. He was inclined to believe that his brother had jumped to his conclusion, though spies about the plantation might have obtained some clew to the night visit to the sinkhole of the Magnolia. The flatboat had been loaded with rocks and sunk in the deepest water of the river, so that it need not betray the planter and his people.

"We want Major Lyon and his cubs!" repeated Buck Lagger, in a voice loud enough to be heard all over the building. "We don't mean to meddle with nobody else, and all the rest o' you uns can go home without no trouble. Hand over Major Lyon and his cubs so we can get the property he stole, and we won't make no fuss."

"We shall not hand him over, but we will protect him to the last drop of our blood!" yelled Squire Truman, hoarse with the strain upon his voice. "Turn the ruffian out!"

But it was not necessary to turn him out, for he fled as soon as he had executed his mission. There was no great commotion outside, though the mob could be seen through the open door. The demand of Buck indicated the principal object of the ruffians, and the purpose for which they had assembled in the grove.

"My friends, I am grateful for your support and promise of protection to me and my boys," said Noah Lyon, who had descended from the platform to the floor, where the boys had joined him. "It appears from what the messenger of the ruffians has said that I am the sole object of their vengeance. I have the means here of taking good care of myself and my boys, and I need not involve you all in a fight to protect me."

To a few of the prominent men near him he stated in a low tone, so that he need not be heard by any ruffian lingering near the door, that his boat was under the south window, and he could escape without confronting the mob in the road. This course would save a fight, and the planter's friends decided to adopt it. The door was closed, and the boys passed out of the window first. They ordered the crew to be silent, and after Noah Lyon had shaken hands with the principal men, he followed them. The Magnolia was shoved out into the river. Deck headed it across the stream, so as to keep the schoolhouse between it and the ruffians.

Under the lead of Colonel Belthorpe, with his revolver ready for use, the Union men marched out of the building, forming four deep when they reached the foot of the steps. The ruffians had placed themselves so that the column passed through them, and they all scrutinized the faces by the light of a fire they had kindled at the side of the road. They did not see the victims for whom they were looking, and when the last of the procession had passed them they set up a furious howl.

"We have been fooled!" shouted Buck Lagger, as he started after the column. "Where is Major Lyon?" he demanded.

"He is not here," replied some one in the ranks.

"Where is he?"

"I don't know;" and he told the truth, for he

had not heard the planter's statement about the boat, and had not been near the window.

"Where is Major Lyon?" demanded Buck Lagger when he reached the head of the procession.

"He came in his boat, and he has returned by it," replied Colonel Belthorpe, with something like a chuckle at the discomfiture of the ruffian.

"This is treachery!" howled Buck. "You were to give him up to us."

"No, we were not," returned the doughty colonel. "Didn't you hear us say we would protect him to the last drop of our blood?"

"We will soon find him and his cubs!" growled the present leader, as he fell back into the grove, followed by the rest of the mob.

The Magnolia reached the boat-pier, and Levi Bedford was there to welcome the party.

CHAPTER XIX

THE CONFERENCE IN FORT BEDFORD

THE two windows in the rear of the school-house had been wide open all the evening, and the negroes of the boat's crew could not help hearing the excited speeches, and the thunders of applause in the meeting of the Unionists; but not one of them spoke a word about them to the planter and the boys. They pulled with all their might, and made a quick run to the boat-pier.

The first thing that attracted the attention of Major Lyon — we may as well call him so, as most of the people of Barcreek did — was the lights in Fort Bedford. Through the embrasures which had been made in the front and ends of the building it could be seen that the interior of the building was brilliantly illuminated.

"You have come back safe and sound, Major," said Levi, as he took the painter of the Magnolia.

"By the skin of our teeth we have," replied the planter.

"Then you have had trouble over there?" asked the overseer.

"Yes; some of the ruffians tried to break up the meeting, and we put them out without any ceremony."

"Good!" exclaimed Levi heartily. "I feel as though I were an inch taller. I was afraid our friends would let the ruffians bully you."

"Buck Lagger and about half a dozen others took places in the schoolhouse, and began to yell while Squire Truman was making his speech. He is a very smart young man, an eloquent orator, and full of vim. When he proposed to put the disturbers out, we went in with him and did it. The boys faced the music, and stood up to it like veteran policemen," said Major Lyon.

"Good, boys! I knew you would do it," added Levi.

"But why is the fort lighted up so late in the evening, Levi?" asked the planter.

"I have had a dozen hands at work there, all the carpenters and masons included, and we have the building about ready for business," replied the overseer. "The fact of it is, I am taking a more serious view of the state of things than you appear to be doing, and I thought I would have things ready for whatever comes, and as soon as it comes."

"I am glad you have done so; and I should have worked with you if I had not had to attend the meeting," added the major. "The situation looks decidedly serious to-night, and my eyes have been opened wide enough to see it."

The boatmen had been ordered by the planter to take all the boats out of the water; and while they were doing so the major informed the overseer more fully in regard to the meeting, especially of the demand for the restoration of the military supplies, and that he and the boys should be given up to the mob.

"I didn't think Captain Titus would show himself in the meeting," said Levi, as they walked up to the fort. "That Buck Lagger is one of the biggest villains that goes unhung; and hanging would do him good. I should say that the ball had opened."

The hands in the old ice-house were all hard at work, and it at once appeared to the planter that a great deal of labor had been done in the building during his absence. The cases had all been opened, the arms had been removed from them, and arranged conveniently about the interior. The two twelve-pounders had been mounted on their carriages, and the pieces were pointed out at the two front embrasures, from which they could be readily removed to those at the ends of the structure.

Two large chandeliers of three burners each had been removed from the drawing-room of the mansion, and were suspended from the roof; but these were for temporary use while the work was in progress. The ammunition had been arranged for the present in the boxes outside of the building.

Major Lyon and the boys had hardly taken a hasty survey of the premises in their changed aspect before the noise of carriage wheels was heard on the road leading from the bridge to the fort by the side of the creek. The vehicle was drawn by two horses, and was approaching at a rapid rate.

"Who can that be?" asked Levi with a troubled expression on his round face.

"It may be my brother coming to demand the arms," replied Noah Lyon, as he took one of the muskets from the wall. "Probably he has a load of his supporters with him if it is he."

"I think we are all ready for them," added the overseer; and he took a gun, and handed one to each of the boys. "I think we had better go out and meet them, for we don't care to have them see what we have been doing here;" and he led the way hastily up the road.

His employer and the boys followed him, and soon confronted the occupants of the wagon.

"Halt!" called Levi in a very decided tone, as he placed himself in front of the team; and the driver reined in his horses. "What is your business here?"

"Good-evening, Levi," came from the party in the wagon; and the challenger promptly recognized the voice of Colonel Cosgrove. "I wish to see Major Lyon at once."

"Here I am, Colonel; but I did not expect to see you again so soon," replied the planter, hastening to the carriage. "But drive on, and we will see you at Fort Bedford."

"Fort Bedford!" exclaimed the Kentuckian; and he told his coachman to drive on.

"This is Fort Bedford you see ahead of you; it

THE CONFERENCE IN FORT BEDFORD 239

is named after Levi, for he originated the idea. To what am I indebted for this unexpected visit to Riverlawn?" answered the planter.

"To the fact that we consider you in great danger, Major, and we thought you would be in pressing need of assistance from your friends even this very night."

"We are here to stand by you, Major," said one on the back seat of the wagon, who proved to be Colonel Belthorpe.

"And to show that we can fight as well as talk," added Squire Truman, who was seated at his side.

"I am very grateful to you for coming to my assistance, for you have all proved this evening that talking is not your only strength," said the planter, as he walked along at the side of the wagon.

"I see you are all armed and ready for business," continued Colonel Cosgrove.

"When I heard the sound of your vehicle on the bridge, I suspected that it might be my deluded brother and his supporters coming over here to execute the threat he made at the meeting."

"No; after we got away from the ruffians, we

talked the matter over," replied Colonel Cosgrove. "Buck Lagger demanded that the major and his cubs should be given up to them when they did not find you and the boys in the column. Then they swore that they would have you. I talked over the situation with our friends here, and we concluded that the ruffians would be over here before morning to capture their victims, and burn your mansion. We decided to come here for this reason,— to warn you of your danger, and help you beat them off if they came."

"I am very much obliged to you; but you will find everything in readiness for their reception," replied Major Lyon, as they reached the fort.

"You are lighted up here as though you were going to have a ball instead of a fight," suggested Colonel Belthorpe.

"There are plenty of balls in the fort, but they are all twelve-pounders," returned the major as the party alighted. "Levi has been at work here while we were at the meeting, and he will explain everything to you better than I can."

The trio of visitors entered the building, and were astonished at the nature and extent of the preparations to defend the mansion and its occupants from a hostile demonstration. Levi stated what he had done, and pointed out everything in detail.

"You think the ruffians are coming over here to-night, do you, Colonel Cosgrove?" asked the planter.

"I think they are on their way here now," replied the Kentuckian.

"Is there any other way they can get to your house than over that bridge?" asked Colonel Belthorpe, who was the only military man in the party who had seen real service, though Levi had been in the militia.

"There is no other way," replied Levi, when his employer nodded to him. "No mob could get through the swamp back of the mansion in the daytime, to say nothing of doing it in the night. The bridge is the only approach; and, if worse comes to worst, we can cut that away."

"You are in a very strong position, and I don't believe it will be necessary to cut away the bridge," added the military gentleman. "They can only cross the creek in boats."

"Our boats are all taken out of the water."

"With those twelve-pounders you can beat off

a regiment. You have everything for the defence except soldiers," added the authority of the party.

"Perhaps we can find them when they are needed," said Major Lyon.

The lawyer understood, but the planter did not. It was a delicate subject, and it could not be considered in that presence. The former realized this fact, and suggested that something ought to be done to give them notice of the coming of the hostile ruffians.

"That's so," added Colonel Belthorpe. "I think you had better station the two boys, who have proved that they have pluck enough for any duty, where they can give us early notice of the approach of the enemy."

"We shall want the boys here, and a couple of negroes will do for that duty just as well," replied Levi.

"All right," answered the military gentleman, who made no objection to the employment of the servants for this duty. "Give each of them a revolver, and tell them to fire three shots if any force approaches.

Rosebud and Mose were detailed for service

at the bridge; and perhaps this was the first time that negroes had ever been armed on the plantation. They were proud of the position assigned to them, and departed on the run, promising to be as faithful as white men could be.

"Where are you going to find your soldiers when you want them, Major Lyon?" inquired Colonel Belthorpe. "You hinted that you knew where to look for them."

"I think we had better not discuss that subject just now," interposed the lawyer, as he looked around him at the negroes, who had finished all the work given them to do, and were listening with their ears wide open to all that was said.

Levi solved the difficulty by sending all the negroes out of the building, and directing them to patrol the bank of the creek as far as the swamp.

"On the question of enlisting negroes in the army, either as regulars or volunteers, I have not yet come to a decision," said Major Lyon. "But in defence of my property and the protection of my family I should have no objection to using all my hands who were willing to be so employed."

. "Arm your negroes!" exclaimed Colonel Belthorpe.

"Not to fight the battles of the nation, but to protect my wife and children and my property," answered the Riverlawn planter. "We can muster but four white men, and two of them are boys. If a mob of fifty or a hundred or five hundred ruffians come over here to hang me and burn my house, shall I let them do so rather than employ the willing hands of men with black faces to defend myself?" demanded Noah Lyon, earnestly enough to mount almost to the height of eloquence.

"By the great Jehoshaphat, I believe you are right!" exclaimed Colonel Belthorpe, with a stamp of his foot. "I did not look at it in that way. But making soldiers of the niggers is another thing, and I'm not ready for that."

"We are all agreed so far as the situation on this place is concerned. If there were any State or national force at hand to call upon for protection against these reckless ruffians, I should invoke its aid; but there is none, and we must protect ourselves," added Colonel Cosgrove. "I heartily approve of Major Lyon's purpose to use his negroes to defend himself and his property."

"Then it is high time to get them in training

for this service," said the major with energy. "Levi, call in the hands you just sent away."

Two of them came back without any calling, for they burst into the fort in a state of high excitement.

"Well, Bitts, what's the matter now?" asked Levi very calmly.

"Gouge and me done went down to de rapids, whar we kin see de bridge ober de riber, and dar's more'n two tousand men comin' ober it!" gasped Bitts.

"Call it fifty or a hundred, Bitts. But no matter, boy; call in all the hands except the two on the creek bridge."

Both of the negroes rushed off on their mission.

CHAPTER XX

THE APPROACH OF THE RUFFIAN FORCES

If the negroes asked no questions, most of them were intelligent enough to interpret the preparations which had been made at Fort Bedford. The six boatmen who had remained half the night in the rear of the schoolhouse had had time enough to do some talking among the hands, though they had come in contact only with those who had been at work on the fort.

These men had listened to the tumult in the building and in the road, and through the open window near the boat had come to their ears the demand of Titus Lyon when admitted, and the reply of the meeting. They knew that Colonel Cosgrove, Colonel Belthorpe, and Squire Truman had taken an active part in the meeting, and they could understand for what purpose they had come to Riverlawn so late in the night.

The people on this plantation were doubtless better informed and more intelligent than upon most of the estates in this portion of the South, for they had always been treated with what other planters regarded as imprudent indulgence. In the time of Colonel Lyon, slavery had been a patriarchal institution, and the negroes regarded him as a father, guide, and friend rather than as a taskmaster.

Many of them had learned to read, and even carried their education several points farther. The planter had given them his illustrated papers, and others fell into their hands. Their usefulness increased with their intelligence; and to oblige his neighbors the colonel had occasionally sent his carpenters and masons to do jobs for them.

The more intelligent of them had kept their eyes and ears open to learn the "signs of the times" during the troubles which agitated the State; and there were those among them who were well informed in matters which were generally believed to be above their comprehension. They went about among the people of other plantations, and when they obtained any news in regard to the movements of either party, it was circulated among the whole of them.

Neither Noah Lyon nor Levi Bedford ever said anything about politics or the struggle between the contending parties for the mastery of the State; but the silence of the people indicated that they understood the situation. Though they were treated with what was considered extreme indulgence, and were entirely devoted to the planter and his family, the instinct of freedom doubtless existed in all of them.

In a short time about a dozen of the negroes had come to the fort in obedience to the order of the overseer. Half of them were mechanics who had been at work during the evening. They were collected in the building, and the white men present proceeded to interrogate them in regard to their qualifications.

"What is your name?" asked Colonel Belthorpe of the leader of the boat-crew.

"General, sar," replied he.

"You are a big fellow; did you ever fire a gun?" asked the planter.

"Yes, sar; Cunnel Lyon done send me often to shoot some ducks for de dinner."

"Are you a good shot?"

"De boys say I am," answered General modestly. "I done bring down tree quails out'n five on de wing, mars'r."

"Did you ever fire a rifle?"

"Yes, sar; Christmas time mars'r cunnel lend us his two rifles to shoot at a mark for a prize ob half a dollar; dis nigger won de prize," replied General, with a magnificent exhibition of ivory.

"Are you willing to fight for your master?" demanded Colonel Belthorpe sharply, as though he expected a negative response to the question.

"Yes, sar!" answered General with more energy than he had spoken before. "Ready to be killed for Mars'r Lyon; an' so's all de boys on de place."

"You will do," added the planter, as he handed him a breech-loader and a small package of ammunition. "Do you know how to use this piece?"

"Yes, sar; seen 'em before," replied the boatman, as he took the weapon and retired.

With the boys there were seven white men present, and each one of them had examined a servant in regard to his qualifications. The questions were similar, though not the same as those put by Colonel Belthorpe; and it appeared that all of them were more or less familiar with the use of firearms, for they were the best informed and most reliable hands on the estate. They were all provided with breech-loaders and cartridges. General and Dummy were sent with weapons to Rosebud and Mose at the bridge, and ordered to remain there; but they were not to fire upon the ruffians.

"Now we have a force of twenty-two men," said Colonel Belthorpe. "I don't know about these recruits with black faces, and I have my doubts about making soldiers of them. Fall in, and we will march up to the bridge."

All the white men were armed with revolvers as well as rifles. The men did not "fall in" in the military sense of the term, but simply followed their leader, as the experienced soldier, who had rendered most of his active service in fighting the Indians, was tacitly recognized to be.

"Don't you think we had better put out the lights in the fort, Colonel Belthorpe?" asked Levi.

"By no means. I have had fighting enough with cut-throat Indians to satisfy my tastes in that direction, and I am not anxious for any more of it," replied the planter. "Let the building remain lighted, and it will assure the ruffians that you are awake over here. If they will about wheel and go off, that will suit me better than a fight with them."

"Just my sentiments, Colonel," added Major Lyon.

"The creek is about fifty feet wide by the bridge," said Colonel Cosgrove. "It widens at its mouth to about a hundred. Is there any way by which the ruffians can get over at your boat-pier?"

"Without a boat there is no way to get across," replied Levi. "They must come across the bridge if they come at all."

"There they come!" exclaimed Major Lyon, as he pointed to the cross-roads where the creek road branched off from the others.

"They have provided themselves with lanterns and torches," said Levi. "We can see just what they are about."

As they came opposite the boat-pier the ruffians halted. They were not marching in any kind of order, but all of them were straggling along as though the Home Guard to which they belonged had not yet done any drilling.

"What have they stopped there for, Colonel Belthorpe?" asked Major Lyon.

"They can see your fort by this time, and the lights have attracted their attention," replied the military gentleman. "They can see that you are ready for them, and perhaps they will not deem it advisable to come any farther."

"I hope they will not," added the owner of Riverlawn.

The aggressive force remained a long time at this spot. In the stillness of the night the sounds which came up the creek indicated that a dispute was in progress in the ranks of the enemy. It looked as though the ruffians were divided among themselves in regard to the prudence of advancing any farther. If Titus Lyon was there, he could readily see that the stone ice-house had undergone some change. The brilliant light within it flashed out through the open door in the rear, and through the three embrasures in sight.

"Major Lyon, do those rascals know that you took possession of the military stores, or do they only guess at it?" asked Colonel Cosgrove.

"They know the arms they stored in a sink-hole

cavern are gone, and they appeared at the meeting to know that I had caused their removal; but I have no idea how or where they obtained their information," replied the planter; and while they were waiting the approach of the ruffians, he gave a full account of the discovery and removal of the ammunition.

"They don't know that three extra white men are with you, and I don't think they would believe you would arm your servants, or that they would be good for anything if you did so," added Colonel Belthorpe. "Perhaps it would be a good idea to return to the fort and send a twelve-pound shot over the heads of that crowd."

"It would let them know that we have the cannon, if nothing more," said Colonel Cosgrove.

"You are a lawyer, Colonel; can't Captain Titus recover these arms by process of law?" inquired the other colonel.

"There is no law in this part of the State at the present time. Men have been murdered within a few miles of this spot, and no notice has been taken of the fact. Those arms were brought here for the use of the Home Guards, which is the same as saying that they are for the use of the Secessionists.

The law won't touch the arms," replied the legal gentleman very deliberately.

"They have settled their dispute, whatever it was, and the ruffians are moving again," said Levi. "It is too late to send a twelve-pound shot over their heads, and if there is to be any fight, it will be at the bridge."

"You are right," replied Colonel Belthorpe, after a long look at the enemy; for as the road where they were was parallel to his line of vision, it was difficult to determine whether they were moving or not. "Let them come; and while they are doing so we will have a little drill of the forces."

He formed the six white men in one line, and the fifteen negroes in another, though some of the latter were only a shade or two darker than the former. Levi Bedford soon proved that he was familiar with the manual, and he was sent to drill the dark section of the army. But the exercise was confined to loading and firing. The men were drawn up in line across the bridge, and instructed as far as "shoulder arms," and then the drill officer explained how they were to conduct themselves.

"The ruffians are getting pretty near, Colonel," suggested Major Lyon.

THE APPROACH OF THE RUFFIAN FORCES

"We are all ready for them," replied he.

The men were then placed at "Order arms," and permitted to watch the approach of the enemy. Their torches, which had probably been made in a birch grove on the other side of the river, and must have been occasionally renewed with material brought for the purpose, blazed brightly, and lighted up the road, so that they could be plainly seen.

"There are at least a hundred of them," said the officer in command.

"And some of them have muskets," added Colonel Cosgrove.

"It looks as though some one or more of us might be shot," continued Major Lyon. "If there is any man here, black or white, who wants to leave and find a safer place than this may be in a few minutes, he is at liberty to do so. I don't want any man to render unwilling service on my account; and you can make peace with that gang by giving me and my boys up to them."

"Never! Never! Never!" yelled every one of the servants.

"Mars'r Lyon foreber!" shouted General.

"Glory to God! We all die for Mars'r Lyon!" cried Dummy the preacher.

"Now all hands give three cheers!" interposed Colonel Belthorpe; and they were given as vigorously as on the deck of a man-of-war. "That will convince the enemy that we are wide awake, and don't mean to run away."

"I reckon that squad is just a little astonished about this time," said Levi.

For this reason, or some other, the enemy suddenly made a halt, and the tumult of many voices came up the road. If Captain Titus was in command of the enemy, his force was not reduced to anything like discipline. From the sounds there appeared to be many commanders, each of whom wanted to have his own way. The defenders of the mansion waited full a quarter of an hour before the tumult subsided, indicating that some point had been carried, though enough of the shouts of the stormy ruffians indicated that they were in favor of going ahead and making the attack. It was plain to the listeners that some of the gang had cooler heads, and knew what prudence meant.

Presently four men were seen marching up the road towards the bridge, the two at the flanks carrying flaming torches, as if to illuminate a white flag borne on a pole, which had possibly cost some member of the troop his white shirt. The two in the middle were evidently the officers, or ambassadors, of the ruffians. They came up to their end of the bridge, and halted there.

CHAPTER XXI

THE BEGINNING OF HOSTILITIES

The representatives of the ruffians had halted about fifty feet from the line of the defenders of Riverlawn, and they could be distinctly seen. It was Buck Lagger who flaunted the flag of truce, and by his side stood Titus Lyon. The other two were simply torch-bearers. There the party stood, and there they seemed to be inclined to stand for an indefinite period of time. They could see the line of the defenders extended across the bridge, and the torches lent enough of their light to the scene to enable Captain Titus to discover that the men were all provided with muskets, though they probably could not make out the character of the weapons.

"This is all nonsense!" exclaimed Colonel Belthorpe, apparently disgusted with this peaceable display on the part of the enemy.

"Captain Titus wishes only to repeat the demand for the return of the arms," added Colonel Cosgrove. "But we can't spare them just yet."

"That is their ostensible purpose, but the real one is to see whether or not we are in condition to receive them," suggested Major Lyon.

"But I am not inclined to wait all night merely to be looked at," continued the commander of the forces impatiently.

"I think you had better speak to them, for they can hear you well enough at this distance," said Major Lyon.

"I am more inclined to march over the bridge and drive them away than to parley all night with them about nothing," replied Colonel Belthorpe. "In military matters I believe in vigorous action."

"According to the customs of civilized warfare we should respect a flag of truce, though we believe it is only an expedient to gain time," added Colonel Cosgrove.

"What do you want?" demanded the commander, adopting the suggestion of the planter of Riverlawn.

"We want to settle this business, and I want to see Major Lyon," replied Captain Titus.

"Come to the middle of the bridge, and he will meet you," shouted the officer in command.

Titus advanced with his three supporters, marching very slowly.

"I suppose I must see him," said Major Lyon, who would evidently have been glad to be spared the interview.

"Three of us will go with you, and make an even thing of it," added Colonel Belthorpe, as Noah Lyon stepped forward to discharge his disagreeable duty.

The commander placed Colonel Cosgrove on one side of him and Squire Truman on the other, taking position in front of them himself. He saw the planter of the estate did not like to meet his brother.

"Major Lyon, I think you had better let me do the talking, for the situation must be very annoying to you," suggested the leader.

"I shall be very glad to have you do so, Colonel," answered the planter. "I am extremely sorry that my own brother is the leader of the ruffians, and I did not expect to see him engaged in such a work. He warned me yesterday that my place might be burned, and that I might be hung to one of the big trees, though he had prevented such an outrage so far."

"I suppose the loss of the military stores has roused him to the highest pitch of wrath, which he manifested in his visit to the meeting. But if he can proceed so far as to bring a horde of ruffians to burn your house and hang you to a tree, you can't do less than defend yourself, even if he is your own brother," said the lawyer.

"I do not shrink from my duty," added Noah Lyon.

"March!" exclaimed the leader, as he advanced to the middle of the bridge, where the party from the other side had halted by this time.

Captain Titus was evidently surprised to find his brother supported by two of the most distinguished men of the county, to say nothing of the eloquent village lawyer. He could not help seeing that there was law enough on the other side, and that they knew what they were doing.

"What is your business here?" demanded Colonel Belthorpe in a very stern tone.

"I stated my position in the meet'n' you held to-night, and you heard what I had to say," Captain Titus began.

"We all heard you; and it is not necessary to repeat it," replied the commander. "What is your business here at this time of night?"

"We came here for the arms and ammunition that was stole from us last night. They were my property till they were given out to the company," Captain Titus explained.

"What company? Do you mean the ruffians you have led over here? They are a horde of lawless men. You have no authority to raise a company, and it does not appear in what service they are to be employed. They have made war upon the peaceable people of this county, as they did this evening at the schoolhouse."

"We hain't made war on nobody!" protested Titus, warming up to the occasion.

"You sent some of your force into the schoolroom to break up a Union meeting; and that was making war upon the people there assembled. The man at your side with the white flag was one that I assisted in putting out. We knew the arms were for the use of these ruffians in terrorizing the whole country," said Colonel Belthorpe in the most emphatic speech; and he used the "we" to shift the responsibility from the shoulders of Major

Lyon to those of himself and associates. "Captain Titus Lyon, you and your gang have been bullying and persecuting the Union citizens of this vicinity long enough; and from this time they intend to defend themselves in earnest. You have made war on them, and the arms and ammunition were simply the spoils of war."

"I come over here to talk with my brother, and not with you," Titus objected, upset by the logic and by the announcement of the intentions of the Unionists.

"Colonel Belthorpe represents me, as he does all the rest of us," interposed Major Lyon. "You threatened me yesterday to your heart's content, Brother Titus, to burn my house and hang me to a big tree; and I don't care to hear anything more of it."

"I have said all it is necessary to say," resumed the commander; "and we decline to hear anything more from you. We shall defend Major Lyon and his plantation from all enemies who may appear. The conference is ended."

"Defend him with niggers!" shouted Buck Lagger. "Are we white men to stand up and fight niggers in this war, as you call it? It is an outrage, and we won't stand it! We will hang every nigger we catch with arms in his possession!"

"Then a white ruffian will hang to the next tree! It will take two to play at that game," responded the commander vigorously. "When about a hundred ruffians, composed mostly of white trash, come over here to burn Major Lyon's mansion and hang him to a big tree, he is quite justified in calling in his servants to defend his property and himself."

The colonel had his doubts about the propriety of arming the negroes, and he wished to be understood even by the enemy; and he certainly made a plain case of it.

"We have had enough of your gabble!" continued the leader. "We decline any further communication with you under a flag of truce or otherwise. If you and your ruffians don't retire from this vicinity within five minutes, we shall open fire upon you! About face, march!"

The three men behind the colonel turned about, and deliberately marched back to the end of the bridge nearest to the mansion. The party of the flag hesitated a few moments, and then returned to the main body of the ruffians. At the end of the bridge the Riverlawn planter found his wife and the two girls. From the windows of the mansion they had seen the blazing torches of the ruffians, and the party who had marched from the fort to oppose them.

They found Deck and Artie in the ranks drawn up on the bridge; and they had explained the situation, including a brief account of the tumult at the meeting. Mrs. Lyon and her daughters were much alarmed for the safety of the male members of the family; but Levi succeeded in quieting them, so that they were quite calm when the major returned.

"We have been terribly frightened, Noah," said Mrs. Lyon. "When you and the boys did not come home from the meeting, I was afraid something had happened to you."

The two colonels and the village lawyer saluted the ladies, and assured them that there was no danger, and that they were amply able to defend the place from the assault of a thousand men.

"Now go home, Ruth, and go to bed," added Noah. "We will join you as soon as we have driven off these ruffians, and it won't take long to do it."

She accepted this advice, though she still appeared to have her doubts, and went back to the mansion. What she had seen looked like war to her; and though she had freely consented that her husband and the two boys should join the army of the Union, she and the girls had some of a woman's timidity in the face of the awful calamities of actual war.

"What are they about now?" asked Colonel Belthorpe, as his friends took their places in the ranks.

"They have sent a dozen men or more down the bank of the creek, and they are out of sight now," replied Levi.

"They are looking for a chance to get across the stream," added the commander. "They had better stay where they are if they don't intend to go home. Is there any boat on that side of the river?"

"No boat of any kind; but there is a lot of logs on the shore, about half-way to the river, and they might build a raft of them. I did not think of those logs before, or I should have rolled them into the creek," replied the overseer.

"It will be the worse for them if they attempt to

cross. Some one said you had served in an artillery company in Tennessee, Mr. Bedford; is that so?" inquired the commander.

"That is so, Colonel; and I know how to handle a twelve-pounder," replied Levi.

"How many men will it take to manage one of the guns in the fort?"

"If you will give me the two boys, I can send a shot across the creek every five minutes, and in less time when we get a little used to the piece."

"Then take the boys, if Major Lyon does not object, and go to the fort."

"Of course I don't object, Colonel," added the father.

"We don't want to kill any of the ruffians if we can help it; but I am decidedly in favor of driving them away. I saw plenty of broken lumber about the fort; and I think you had better kindle a big fire on the shore of the creek, so that you can see over on the other side. If they attempt to build a raft, give them a shot; but not otherwise," said Colonel Belthorpe, still straining his eyes to ascertain in the darkness what the squad were doing on the bank of the creek.

"Shall you remain here, Colonel?" asked Levi.

"Not at all; we shall march over the bridge. This is a neighborhood war, and I believe in carrying it on upon peace principles as far as possible, and the first shot must come from the other side," replied the planter from outside.

Levi departed for Fort Bedford, attended by Deck and Artie. The commander then arranged his men in ranks by fours, and taught them how to come in line again, using some technical terms which the negroes did not understand; but he succeeded in getting them to perform the manœuvre quite clumsily. They marched over the bridge by fours. The enemy still occupied the position where they had first halted, and the colonel continued the march till the force was within hail of the enemy.

Some of the ruffians had muskets; and whether in obedience to the orders of their leaders or not, three random shots were fired. This was enough to satisfy the conscience of Colonel Belthorpe, and he gave the command to halt, and the men came into line again across the road.

"Ready!" he shouted; and the men all brought themselves into position as they had before been instructed. "Aim!"

These orders and the movements of the men

THE BEGINNING OF HOSTILITIES

appeared to produce a decided sensation in the rabble in front of them; for they were simply a crowd, not formed in any order. Some of them took to their heels, and were seen running down the road at a breakneck speed.

"Fire!" added the commander.

A terrible yell came back as the men fired their rifles. That volley was enough for them, and they bolted before the smoke of the powder had blown aside. Two men were seen lying on the ground, killed or wounded, and the ruffians were too much shaken to give them any attention. Half-way to the river they halted again, as did the pursuing force. The enemy scattered at this point; but in a few moments the whizzing of bullets was heard over their heads by the defenders of the plantation.

CHAPTER XXII

THE FIRST SHOT FROM FORT BEDFORD

Levi Bedford had made all possible haste to reach the fort, and the boys had not lingered far behind him, though they could not help giving some of their attention to the enemy on the other side of the creek. The ruffians remained at the position they had taken; and certainly they had made no progress in the accomplishment of the purpose which had brought them to the vicinity of Riverlawn. Probably if the darkness had not concealed the artillery party, those with guns would have fired at them.

"Now, boys, the first order of Colonel Belthorpe was to build a fire, and we will attend to that," said the overseer, as he led the way to the rear of the stone building.

"Of course I obey orders," added Artie, "but I don't believe much in the fire. As soon as it blazes up it will give the ruffians light enough to see us. Some of them have guns, and they will fire at us then."

"What do you suppose these stone walls are for, Artie?" asked Levi with his usual smile.

"They were put up to keep the ice cool originally," replied Artie.

"Then they ought to keep us cool," said the overseer. "When the man with a big mouth opened it, the dentist told him he had opened it wide enough, for he proposed to stand outside. But we don't propose to stand outside, but inside, as soon as we have lighted the fire."

"But we have to see what the ruffians are about on the other side of the creek; for you are not to fire a shot unless they attempt to build a raft," suggested Artie.

"We can look through the port-holes, can't we?" asked Deck. "If they build a raft they will make a fire the first thing they do, and we can see what they are doing."

"We shall find a way to ascertain what they are doing," added Levi, as he led the way to obtain more armfuls of the broken boards; and they were the remains of the cases in which the arms and ammunition had been packed.

The wood was piled up a couple of rods from the fort, though a little at one side, so as not to obstruct the view of the party. Only a portion of the fuel was used, and the rest saved to replenish the fire. The match was applied, and in a short time the blaze mounted above the pile, and lighted the surrounding region.

"Now, boys, if you feel as though you might get a bullet through your heads, you can go into the fort, and you will be safe there," said Levi.

"Are you not going in, Levi?"

"I am when the occasion requires; but I want to see what they are about over there," replied the overseer.

As he was in no haste to put the stone walls between himself and a possible shot, the pride of the boys would not permit them to do so, and it became a sort of contention to see who would be the first to seek shelter.

"The Seceshers are firing at our people!" exclaimed Deck, quite excited as he realized that hostilities had actually begun.

"The ruffians are firing, each on his own hook, for there is no order among them," added Levi, as he heard several shots.

The plantation force could now be just seen, marching down the road, by the light of the enemy's torches. The random shots from the ruffians were continued, and it was evident that each man was his own commander.

"Colonel Belthorpe will not stand that sort of thing for any great length of time," Levi remarked, as his eyes and ears gave him further information in regard to the situation on the other side.

"They say chance shots sometimes do the most mischief, or I have read it in some story," said Deck. "I hope one of them will not hit father."

"Of course any one of us is liable to be hit while this game is going on. Perhaps you had better go into the fort, for this fire will soon attract the enemy's attention," suggested the overseer.

"When you get ready to go in we will go in with you," replied Artie.

"There is no need of exposing all three of us to the chances of a shot."

"Then one of us boys will stay out, for you are nearly twice as big as either one of us, and therefore twice as likely to get hit," laughed Deck.

"There!" exclaimed Levi, without noticing the remark, "now there will be music in the air!"

"What is it? I don't hear anything," added Deck.

"Don't you see that the colonel has halted his force? Now they have formed a line across the road," continued the overseer, as he closely watched the movements on the other side of the creek.

The fort party were silent with expectation and anxiety, and then they heard the orders of the commander, which ended in a volley from the fifteen breech-loaders. The birch torches still lighted up the ground, and the observers saw two men fall. This discharge produced a panic in the rabble, and they fled from the road to the shelter of a grove that lay beyond. From the fort it could be seen that a few of the ruffians, with guns in their hands, had taken refuge behind the trunks of the large trees, where they were reloading their pieces.

"That's Indian fighting," said Levi. "Our men, from their position, can't see these skulkers, who will have a good chance to pick off some of them at their leisure. We must attend to this matter."

The overseer elevated his rifle, and took deliberate aim at one of the ruffians behind a big tree, and fired. He saw his man fall. Deck and Artie followed his example, though they could not see any single individuals at whom they might direct their aim. They all continued to fire till the chambers of their weapons were empty.

"I don't believe we hit anybody with those last shots; for as soon as my man dropped and the others could see where the shot came from, they ran away or moved to the other side of the tree," said Levi, as he carefully observed the situation.

The retreat of the main body of the ruffians, taking the torches with them, left the scene in darkness. The number and direction of the last discharges assured those who had sought the shelter of the trees that they were flanked. Nothing could be seen in the gloom of the grove; and, as no more shots came from that quarter, it was supposed that the skulkers had retreated to the main body.

"There's a light down the creek, Levi!" exclaimed Deck, as a blaze flashed up at a point nearly opposite the boat-pier.

"That's where the logs lay," added the overseer. "The squad that was sent down the bank of the stream has got to work at last."

"Perhaps they have been at work for the last

half hour," suggested Artie. "They didn't need any light to enable them to roll the logs into the creek and build a raft."

"Quite right, my boy; you have hit the nail on the head. By the light of the fire I can now see the raft, though they haven't finished it," replied Levi.

"Hadn't we better fire at them?" asked Deck.

"You might as well fire at the moon, my boys," returned the overseer. "You haven't had much practice with these breech-loaders, and you couldn't hit anything at the distance they are from us."

"But where is our army?" asked Artie rather facetiously.

"Colonel Belthorpe don't seem to be following up the enemy," replied Levi. "Perhaps, as the ruffians are retreating, he is satisfied to let them go home and dream over their work of this evening. The torches of the main body of the enemy seem to be going out, and very likely their stock of birch bark is all gone. They are about half-way between our force and the raft."

"They are within rifle-shot of us, anyhow," suggested Deck. "We might give them a little more waking up."

"Don't be too enthusiastic, Mr. Lyon. We don't want to kill any more of them than is absolutely necessary," said the overseer rather more seriously than usual. "They have the raft in the water, and we will go in the fort and see what can be done for them."

Neither of the boys knew anything about artillery tactics, or of the process of loading a field-piece, and Levi proceeded to instruct them.

The creek bent a little to the south as it approached the river, and the chief gunner directed one of the pieces at the western embrasure, so that it covered the fire built near the logs. The inside of the opening was bevelled, so that he could bring the cannon to bear upon the objective point. It was then drawn in, and the charge, with a solid shot, was rammed home by the boys.

The cannon was run out again at the embrasure, and Levi pointed it, mindful of the instructions of the colonel commanding, so that the missile would go over the men at work on the raft.

"Now you may go outside, and see what you can see," continued Levi. "I don't mean to hit the men there, or even the raft; but I want you to notice what effect the shot produces upon the ruffians at the work."

"All right, Levi; sing out when you are going to pull the lock-string," replied Deck as he followed Artie out of the fort.

"Ready! Fire!" shouted the overseer when time enough for them to take a position had elapsed.

The discharge of the cannon gave forth a tremendous report, and the boys heard the whizzing of the shot as it flew like a flash through the air. The retreating army of the ruffians suddenly halted without any orders from Captain Titus or any one else as the echo of the report struck upon their ears. Doubtless they were astonished; but they were in darkness, for the last of the torches had gone out, and it could only be seen that they had halted as abruptly as though the shot from the piece had mowed its way through the mob.

The shot, as intended, passed over the heads of the men at work on the raft, and struck into a tree on the other side of the road, causing a heavy branch to fall to the ground. The raft-builders suddenly took to their heels, and disappeared in the grove.

THE FIRST SHOT FROM FORT BEDFORD

"Did it hit anything, boys?" asked Levi, coming out of the fort.

"Nothing but a big tree beyond the road, and a large branch fell to the ground," replied Deck.

"I had an idea that you had been fooling us at first, Levi," added Artie, "and had fired at the main body, for they stopped as short as though the cannon ball had gone through the crowd. All the men at work on the raft knocked off instantly, and ran away as though the shot were chasing them."

"I reckon we needn't fire another shot, for the ruffians won't go near that raft again," added Levi. "I fired over their heads, as I told you I should, and nobody was hurt by that shot. I dropped one man behind that tree, and that is all the mischief I have done."

"Are you sorry for that one?" asked Deck.

"I am sorry for him, but not that I hit him, for he might have killed two or three of our people from his hiding-place behind the tree. I don't believe in killing anybody as long as it can possibly be avoided; but the ruffians began the shooting, and they are responsible for the consequences. At least half a dozen Union men have been killed in this county by those ruffians, or those like them; and your father might have been swinging from a big tree by this time if we hadn't taken the bull by the horns. No, I am not sorry for anything I have done!"

"And the house would have been burnt down, and mother and the girls subjected to the insults of these miscreants," added Artie; and all three of them were much moved as they contemplated the possibilities before them.

"Can you see anything of our people over there, Deck?" asked Levi.

"Not a thing; it is too dark."

"I don't believe there will be anything more to do at the fort to-night, though the affair may not be over yet," continued Levi, after he had anxiously peered through the gloom to discover the rest of the defenders of Riverlawn. "I want you, Deck, to go up to the bridge, and down the creek road, and ascertain what our people are doing. You may report to Colonel Belthorpe that we have driven off the builders of the raft, and that the main body of the ruffians have fallen back from the road into the grove."

"All right, Levi," replied Deck, who was very

glad to be appointed to such a mission; and, with his breech-loader on his shoulder, he marched in the direction indicated at a lively pace, though he was so tired and sleepy that it required a determined effort to enable him to keep on his feet, for it was now two o'clock in the morning.

When he reached the bridge he found there, to his intense astonishment, a dozen horses, some of them with saddles and bridles on, and others with bridles, and blankets in place of saddles. They were in charge of Frank the coachman, with Woolly and Mose to assist him.

CHAPTER XXIII

THE PARTY ATTACKED IN THE CROSS-CUT

Deck Lyon could not imagine any possible use that could be made of the horses in charge of the boys, and it was not probable that those in care of them could afford him any information on the subject. It was evident that some new movement was contemplated, and it looked as though the commander of the forces intended to chase the ruffians with mounted men.

"Where is my father, Frank?" asked Deck.

"He's down the road with the rest of them; but I reckon they are all marching back to the bridge," replied the coachman.

"What are you going to do with all these horses?" asked Deck, as he began to move on.

"Dunno, Mars'r Deck, what they are for; but Mars'r Lyon sent us for them."

Frank knew nothing about the use to which the horses were to be put, and Deck continued on his way over the bridge. The fire from the blazing boards in front of Fort Bedford sent some of the light across the creek; but it did not reveal the presence of the defenders of the plantation, and the messenger could not see anything of the force. It could not be far away, and he continued to advance.

Just beyond the bridge he met a wagon coming towards him. When it came near enough for him to see it in the gloom, he found that it belonged to the plantation. Three men sat on the front seat, and were chattering at a lively rate as they drew near.

"Who is driving that team?" demanded Deck.

"Me, Mars'r Deck," replied the man who held the reins.

"Who's me?"

"Clinker, sar, wid Bitts and Filly," replied the driver, who was the blacksmith of the estate.

"What are you doing with the wagon over here?"

"Cart'n' off de wounded, mars'r."

"How many have you?"

"On'y two, sar."

These were the ruffians, doubtless, who had fallen when the volley was fired at the beginning of the affair.

"You haven't got them all, then," added Deck. "There is another opposite the fort, near a big tree, who was hit by Levi, firing from the other side of the creek."

"We go for him when we done unload dese we got," said Clinker.

"Can you tell me where my father and the rest of them are?" inquired Deck, who could see nothing of the main body.

"In de grove, Mars'r Deck. Wen de ruff'ns done runned off dat way Mars'r Belt'orpe lead de sodjers arter 'em."

Deck was afraid he might not find his father before morning if they pursued the retreating ruffians in that direction; for they would have to follow the river, when they reached it, about ten miles before they could come to a bridge by which they could cross. But he had a mission, and he bravely fought against the fatigue and sleepiness that beset him, and struck into the grove by a road some distance below the bridge over the creek.

He had not gone twenty rods in the gloom of the wood before he heard the sound of voices and the tramp of footsteps ahead of him, and he was confident the force was returning to the plantation. He soon confronted the little column, and placed himself by the side of the commander, who was leading the way.

"Levi sent me over to report what we have been doing," said he.

"I heard the report of one of your guns, and I concluded that you had work on your hands," replied Colonel Belthorpe, without slacking his speed or halting to listen to the report.

"Not much work, Colonel. The ruffians were building a raft at the pile of logs, and we fired over their heads, as ordered. The big branch of a tree came down, and all the men on the raft and near them ran into the woods. The road is all clear of them, and they are not going home by the Rapids Bridge."

"No, the villains!" exclaimed the commander. "They have other business on their hands. I am afraid we have been too tender with them."

"One thing more, Colonel, and I have done," continued Deck. "When the ruffians retreated before your fire, those who had guns stationed themselves behind the trees and began to fire at you. Then we three opened upon them with the rifles, and when Levi fired a man dropped. After that we saw nothing more of them."

"All right, my boy," added the colonel, hurrying his march. "I thought the villains were only making a detour, intending to reach the Rapids Bridge; but I find they are marching in the direction of my plantation."

Colonel Cosgrove and Major Lyon had been called forward to listen to the report of Deck, and it was decided that, so far as Riverlawn was concerned, the battle had been fought and won, inasmuch as the enemy had been driven away. By the time the report was finished and the result announced, the force had reached the bridge.

"Where are you going now, Clinker?" asked Major Lyon, when the wagon returned from the hospital, as the small building set apart for the sick of the plantation hands was called, and appeared on the bridge.

"Mars'r Deck done tell me a man dropped behind a tree down de creek, and I'm gwine for him," replied the blacksmith.

"Go over and get the small wagon for that; we want this one," added the planter.

"Where are you going, father?" asked Deck,

who saw that some expedition was in preparation.

"We are satisfied that the ruffians are going over to Colonel Belthorpe's plantation, to do there what they intended to do here, and we mean to get there before they do," replied Major Lyon. "We believe that everything here is safe for the present."

The party crossed the bridge and came to the saddle horses. By this time all the men on the plantation who had not before been called for duty had assembled by the horses, and the four white men mounted at once. The breech-loaders were provided with straps, and had been suspended at the backs of those who used them. Eight of the men who had already seen service were mounted and seven more were put into the wagon, provided with weapons which had been sent for.

"Filly!" called Major Lyon, addressing a mulatto who had the reputation of being a very intelligent fellow, "you will go to the fort and tell Levi we are going over to Lyndhall, for we are sure the ruffians mean to burn the house. Take the rest of the hands here with you, and tell him to keep a close watch over the place. I shall take Dexter with me."

The rest of the party had already ridden off at full gallop, fearful that they might be too late to protect the colonel's property.

"But I have no horse, father," said Deck, who had heard the planter tell Filly that he should take him with him.

"You will go in the wagon," replied his father. "I see that you are gaping, and you must be very tired. Get in; the body is filled with hay, and it will give you a chance to get rested."

Deck did not like the arrangement very well, tired as he was, but he obeyed the order. The negroes made way for him, and fixed him a nice place to lie down in the wagon. He dropped asleep almost instantly, for he had been up all the night before, and had worked hard and been intensely excited since he left his bed just before noon.

Major Lyon had his late brother's favorite animal, a blood horse that had won a small fortune for his master in the races, and he soon overtook the advance of the party. The wagon could not keep up with him, and was soon left far behind.

Near the east end of the Rapids Bridge over the river was a locality called the "Cross Roads," where four highways came together. At this point the one from the county town passing through Barcreek village crossed the stream. Another road branched off here, leading up the creek, from which the private way over the bridge led to Major Lyon's mansion. It continued half a mile farther up the creek, and then turned to the north-east. This was called the "New Road," and upon it, three miles from the creek bridge, was the plantation of Colonel Belthorpe.

From the Cross Roads also extended what was called the "Old Road," which was laid out nearer to the great river; and six miles distant by the later-built highway the two came together, though it was over eight by the older one. About half a mile of the new road was on the bank of Bar Creek, and upon it had transpired most of the events related.

The ruffians had been driven down this road towards Rapids Bridge. They had taken to the woods between the two highways; and by sending out the village lawyer to reconnoitre, Colonel Belthorpe had discovered that the enemy were marching, not to the bridge, but up the old road, which would take them, after a three miles' walk, to a point near his plantation, where they could easily cross to the new road. The distance by the new road was a mile less than by the other, and the fleet horses would carry the party to Lyndhall in abundant season to confront the marauders.

"I don't believe the villains can get there before we do," said Colonel Belthorpe, as Major Lyon galloped his horse to his side. "If I had anticipated the events of to-night, I should have been prepared for them. My overseer is not a Union man, and I am afraid he will not do his duty. My place is not so well situated for a defence as yours, Major."

"I believe we have force enough to drive the ruffians again, for they don't like the smell of gunpowder any better than other bullies," replied the Riverlawn planter.

"My son Tom is at home, and my nephew, Major Gadbury, is visiting at Lyndhall. But all of them, including my two daughters, have gone to a party at Rock Lodge. I suppose you know the place, Major?"

"Not by that name."

"It is over on the old road, close by Rock Hill, from which it takes its name. You must have met Captain Carms."

"I have met him, and we have called upon him, but I never heard the name of his place before."

"Just at the foot of Rock Hill there is a cart-path connecting the two roads, and the ruffians may come through by that passage, though it is very rough. Most of our stone comes from the quarry there, and the teams make bad work with the roads."

"The enemy can't be a great way behind us by this time," suggested Major Lyon.

"We haven't wasted any time, and it is some distance they had to travel round by the Cross Roads," replied the colonel, as he urged his steed to greater speed.

Though the road was anything but a smooth one, Deck Lyon slept like a log on the hay. His dusky companions did not speak a loud word for fear of waking him. Nearly half an hour after the horsemen had passed it, the wagon was approaching the cross-cut between the two roads at Rock Hill. Clinker the blacksmith, who had been excused from ambulance duty and another put in his place, was driving the horses.

"Cristofus! Wat's dat?" he exclaimed, as two very distinct female screams struck his ears, and he set his team into a dead run.

" 'Pears like it's women screeching," replied Mose, who was by his side on the front seat. "Dar's trouble dar!"

"I reckon de screeches comed out'n de cross-cut," added Clinker.

The screams were repeated several times, and as the wagon passed the hill the sounds of an encounter were heard. It was evident that a fight of some kind was in progress, and the men in the wagon unslung their breech-loaders ready for action; for they came to the conclusion at once that the ruffians were at the bottom of it. No shots were heard, and it did not appear that the marauders were armed.

"I reckon we mus' woke Mars'r Deck," said Clinker, as he reined in his horses at the cross-cut.

One of the men at his side shook the tired boy, and he sprang to his feet; for doubtless he was dreaming of the events of the night. Clinker explained the situation in as few words as his vocabulary would permit. Deck seized his musket and leaped from the wagon, followed by all but the driver, who drove the horses to a tree and fastened them there.

Deck ran with all his might into the passage, and presently came to a road wagon which had been "held up" by a gang of the ruffians. He ordered his six followers to have their arms ready, but not to fire till he gave them the word. With his revolver in his hand, which was a more convenient weapon than the gun, he rushed into the midst of the fight. The party attacked were the nephew and son of Colonel Belthorpe, with his two daughters, who had been to the party at Rock Lodge.

CHAPTER XXIV

THE ENCOUNTER WITH THE RUFFIANS

Deck Lyon rushed furiously down the lane which connected the two roads at this point. It was dark, and it was in vain that he tried to understand the situation from anything he could see. He was sure that the main body of the ruffians were not in the cross-cut, for there was not room enough for them. He had to depend chiefly upon his ears for information, for the trees on one side of the passage obscured his way.

The first sound that attracted his attention as he advanced, above the general din, was a half-suppressed scream quite near him. The lane was so rough that he was obliged to move more slowly than when he had left the wagon, and he halted when he heard the cry. A moment later he discovered a man bearing a form in his arms, whose cries he was evidently trying to suppress with one of his hands placed over her mouth.

An opening in the grove enabled him to see so

much, and to note the position of the ruffian. With his revolver in his hand he rushed forward; and, finding himself behind the assailant of the female, he threw himself upon him, and grasped him by the throat with both hands. He had done some of this kind of work at the schoolhouse in the evening, and the experience was useful to him.

He compelled the villain to release his hold upon his prisoner in order to defend himself. Deck wrenched and twisted him in an effort to throw him down, but his arms were not strong enough to accomplish his purpose, and he called upon Mose to assist him. The faithful servant was close by him; and perhaps he was desirous of striking a literal blow in defence of his young master, for he delivered one squarely on the head of the ruffian which knocked him six feet from the spot.

At this moment, and just as the captor of the lady went over backwards into a hole by the side of the cart-path, a bright light was flashed upon the scene, and Deck could see where he was and where the ruffian he had encountered was. When Clinker had secured the horses at the end of the lane, he realized the necessity of more light on the subject before the party; for though he heard much he saw little.

Taking a quantity of the hay from the wagon, he hastened to the scene of the conflict just as Deck had closed with the ruffian who was bearing the lady away. Putting it on the ground, he lighted it with a match, and then heaped on sticks and bits of board and plank scattered about by those who had loaded stone in the passage. The blaze revealed the entire situation to Deck and his companions, and it made a weird picture.

"Good, Clinker!" shouted Deck, as he saw the blacksmith standing with his musket in his hand, busy doing what he had undertaken. "Keep the fire up!"

The ruffian whom Mose, who was not much inferior to General and Dummy in bulk and strength, had knocked both literally and slangily " in a hole," lay perfectly still. Some five rods ahead of him Deck discovered a road wagon in the lane. Two horses were harnessed to it, and at the head of each of them was a ruffian, doing his best to restrain the spirited animals, frightened by the cries and the movements of the assailants. Behind the wagon were two white men engaged in a terrible struggle with half a dozen of the soldiers of the ruffian army. They were getting the worst of it, though they fought with desperate energy.

From their appearance and the fact that they were defending themselves, it was plain enough to Deck that they were in charge of the two females. They were unarmed, though one of them had procured a piece of board, and was doing good service with it. Just beyond the scene of the fight stood Buck Lagger, holding a female by the arm. She evidently realized that resistance was useless, and she had ceased to struggle or scream.

"Now follow me, boys!" shouted Deck. "You had better walk over to the fire, miss," he added to the young lady redeemed from the hands of the ruffian. Clinker will see that no harm comes to you."

The six men who had followed the young man in advance of them, marched close to him, with their muskets in readiness for use. Deck could not order them to fire, for they were as likely to hit friends as enemies; but he rushed to the scene of the conflict, where the two white men had just been forced back by the marauders.

"Both fall back this way, gentlemen!" called the young leader.

Major Gadbury and Tom Belthorpe, as the colonel had given the names of those who attended his two daughters to the party, could not help realizing that assistance was at hand, though they saw only a stout boy and half a dozen negroes, and they promptly detached themselves from their assailants, and retreated behind the wagon.

"Now fire at them, one at a time!" shouted Deck, when it was safe to do so.

Mose was nearest to him, and instantly discharged his musket at the foremost assailants of the gentlemen. One of them dropped to the ground. The ruffians had not bargained for this sort of discipline, and they fled on the instant; for they had heard Deck's order, and saw that there were more bullets where the first one came from. They ran into the woods, and disappeared behind the trunks of the great trees.

"Don't fire again, but follow me!" said Deck, as he started at his best speed towards the spot where Buck Lagger stood with his prisoner.

This ruffian perceived the defeat of his party, and he attempted to force the lady in the direction taken by his infamous comrades. He led the

"I HAD TO BE CAREFUL NOT TO HIT THE LADY." Page 299.

way, dragging his prisoner after him; but she resisted now, hanging back so that he could not move at anything more than a snail's pace. She screamed again, and Major Gadbury and Tom Belthorpe started to assist her.

Deck had accomplished half the distance to the ruffian when he saw that the strength of the lady was failing her, and Buck was advancing more rapidly. He raised his revolver, and, aiming the weapon with all possible care, he fired. Clinker had kept the fire blazing freely, and he had plenty of light. The ruffian released his hold upon his prisoner, and swung his right hand over to his left shoulder. Deck believed his bullet had struck him there, though he continued his retreat to the wood.

"I am sorry you didn't kill him!" exclaimed one of the two gentlemen, as they halted at Deck's side.

"I had to be careful not to hit the lady," replied Deck. "But we have driven them off. "Now, boys, in line!" shouted the young leader to his men. "Face the woods!"

The six men came into line very promptly, though the movement would hardly have been satisfactory to a drill officer.

"Ready!" he continued. "Aim! Fire!"

That was about the extent of the recruits' knowledge of the drill; but they fired their weapons, and each of them sent two more shots after the first as the command was given. One of the gentlemen suggested that none of the ruffians were hit by the volley, and Deck explained that the last discharges were for their moral effect, though not in these words.

"I don't know you, sir, but we are under ten thousand obligations to you for this timely assistance," said the gentleman who remained with Deck, for the other had hastened to the lady Buck had abandoned.

"My name is Dexter Lyon," replied the young defender. "What is yours?"

"Tom Belthorpe," returned the other, who appeared to be something over twenty years of age. "We have been to a party with the girls at Rock Lodge, and were on our way home."

"Then you are the son of Colonel Belthorpe. Who is the other gentleman?"

"That is Major Gadbury, who is spending a week at my father's plantation," replied Tom, rubbing his head and some of his limbs, for he

THE ENCOUNTER WITH THE RUFFIANS 301

was rather the worse for the wear in his conflict with the ruffians, as the other gentleman conducted the terrified lady to the spot.

"I never was so frightened in all my life," gasped the lady, as they stopped in front of Deck.

"It is all over now, and I would not mind any more about it," added the Major cheerfully, though he was considerably battered after the fight through which he had passed.

"This is Mr. Dexter Lyon, Major, the son of our neighbor," said Tom, presenting the leader of the colored battalion, though Deck was somewhat abashed at the formality, and to hear himself "mistered" was a new experience to him.

"I am glad to know you, Captain Lyon," replied the Major, grasping his hand and wringing it till the boy winced. "You have rendered us noble and brave service, and we shall all be grateful to you as long as we live. This is Miss Margie Belthorpe."

"I am delighted to see you, Mr. Lyon!" exclaimed the young lady, who was only nineteen years old, as she sprang to the hero of the night, grasped his hand, and then kissed him as though he had been a baby.

Deck was seventeen years old, and rather large of his age, as well as somewhat forward for his years; and he felt as though he had tumbled into a sugar-bowl at that moment. The blaze of Clinker's fire lighted up his blushing face, and possibly he was sorry there were no more ruffians at hand for him to shoot if such was to be his reward. He forgot that he was tired and sleepy in the pleasurable excitement which followed the encounter.

"If you please, we will go over to the fire where the other lady is waiting for you," said he, as he started for the point indicated. "Fall in behind and follow us, boys," he added to the recruits.

"I have never happened to meet any negroes in arms before," said Tom Belthorpe, as he walked along with Deck. "But they seem to be ready for business."

"They are indeed; and these boys are as brave as any white men could be," added Deck, loud enough for the subject of his remark to hear it.

The two ruffians who had been left at the heads of the horses had fled into the woods as soon as they saw that the assault was repulsed, and the animals had become restive. Clinker had rushed over to secure them, and he had quieted them down so they were quite reasonable by this time. The young lady committed to his charge had followed him.

"This is my sister, Miss Kate Belthorpe," said Margie, when the party reached the spot.

"Oh, I am so glad you came when you did, Mr. —— "

"Dexter Lyon," added Tom.

"Mr. Lyon; and you were as brave as a lion!" exclaimed Kate, as she took the hand of Deck; and either because she had witnessed the reception her sister had given the hero, or as an inspiration of her own, she promptly kissed him on both cheeks, and Deck felt as though he had fallen into a barrel of sugar. "You grappled with that villain just as though you had been as big as he was, and held on to him till one of your boys knocked him into the hole with his fist. You are a brave fellow, and I shall remember you as long as I live."

"And 'none but the brave deserve the fair,'" added Major Gadbury.

"How did you happen to get into this scrape, Mr. Belthorpe?" asked Deck.

"We were all invited to a party at Rock Lodge, and we went. The governor couldn't go, for he insisted upon attending a Union meeting at the Big Bend schoolhouse," replied Tom. "But he promised to call for us on his way home, for he drove us to the Lodge himself. Most of the guests left by midnight, but father did not come, and we could not walk home. But at three o'clock Captain Carms volunteered to send us home when we became impatient."

"My father and I went to that meeting, and so did some of these ruffians that committed this outrage," added Deck.

"But these scoundrels are not Union men," objected Tom.

"But some of them were there, all the same, and some of them got put out. But it is a long story, and we had better be moving before we tell it."

The ladies agreed to this last proposition, for they were in evening dresses, and the chill air of the night made them shiver. The driver of Captain Carms's wagon had come out of the quarry, whither he had retreated, as soon as the danger was passed, and his team was ready to proceed. Deck sent Clinker for his wagon, and he drew it up at the end of the cross-cut.

The ladies were assisted to their seats again, while the two gentlemen took the seat in front of them. Miss Kate insisted that Deck should ride with them, for she wanted to hear the story about the meeting. More than this, she insisted that he should sit on the back seat between her sister and herself. Margie did not object, and the major and Tom only laughed. Deck had his doubts about his ability to tell his story in the midst of such delightful surroundings.

The team started, and at the corner Deck directed Clinker to follow closely after him. But his story was interesting and exciting, and he did not suffer from cold or embarrassment during his recital. When he had disposed of the Union meeting, he described the battle fought at Riverlawn, and the preparations which had been made for the onslaught, including the discovery and removal of the arms and ammunition. He had hardly finished before the wagon stopped at the plantation of Colonel Belthorpe.

CHAPTER XXV

THE GRATITUDE OF TWO FAIR MAIDENS

The mansion house of Colonel Belthorpe was quite near the road. The force under his command must have arrived some time before, for several of the windows were lighted. The four white men were not to be seen, but the eight boys who had been mounted stood near the house, apparently waiting for orders.

Though the encounter of the wagon party with the ruffians has required a considerable time for its recital, they had not been detained over half an hour, if as long as that; but no one took account of time in the exciting event of the night. The ladies were handed out of the wagon, and Deck perceived that Major Gadbury was very attentive to Miss Margie, while he waited upon Miss Kate, the younger, and, in his judgment, the prettier of the two daughters of the colonel.

When the hero of the occasion had attended the young lady to the door of the house, he excused himself, and hastened to the mounted men who stood in front of the mansion. They were astonished at the arrival of two wagons instead of one, and were discussing the matter among themselves.

"Where is Colonel Belthorpe, General?" inquired Deck, after he had saluted the boys in his usual familiar manner; for he had none of the haughtiness of those who were "to the manner born."

"Don't know, Mars'r Deck; he and the oder gen'lemen done went ober dat way," replied General. "De ole road's ober dat way, and I 'spect dey went to look out for de ruffi'ns."

"They won't be here for half an hour or more," added Deck, as Captain Carms's man drove up to the party with the wagon.

"You done see 'em on de road, mars'r Deck?"

"I have seen some of them, General."

"Dey was ober on de ole road, mars'r, I t'ought."

But Deck did not stop to give them any information, for both wagons had stopped near the party. The driver from Rock Lodge had run away as soon as his vehicle was beset by the ruffians; yet he could tell his portion of the story, while those from Riverlawn could relate the rest of it. The hero went into the mansion, and a mulatto in a white jacket, who was gaping with all his might, showed him to the sitting-room, where he found the wagon party. There was no Mrs. Belthorpe, for she had passed away years before.

"I was afraid you had run away and left us, Mr. Lyon," said Miss Kate, rushing up to him as he entered.

"Please don't 'mister' me," replied Deck, laughing. "It makes me feel just as though I was a dude."

"Well, you are not a dude," added the fair daughter of the planter, as indignantly as though some person besides herself had called him by the opprobrious name.

"And I don't run away, either."

"That's so!" exclaimed Major Gadbury with decided emphasis. "But I really wonder that you did not run away instead of pitching into that scoundrel who was carrying off Miss Kate."

"I couldn't have done that if I had tried while the lady seemed to be in such a dangerous situation," answered Deck, as he seated himself as near Miss Kate as he could find a place. "But

I have been talking myself all the time since we started from the cross-cut, and I don't know yet how you happened to get into this scrape."

"We don't know much more about it than you do, Mr. ―― "

"Deck," interposed the hero.

"Deck, if you insist upon it, Mr. Lyon," laughed the major. "We left Rock Lodge, and Tom told the driver to go by that cross road. It was a terribly rough passage we had of it, and I think we went over rocks a foot high."

"As I told you in my account of the troubles of the night, the ruffians, after they had been driven off from Riverlawn, took the old road, and Squire Truman found that they were going to this mansion," said Deck. "Didn't you see anything of them before you turned into the cut-off?"

"We neither saw nor heard anything."

"The main body of the ruffians could not have been very far down the road. I don't see how Buck Lagger happened to be where he was with the rest of his gang," added Deck.

"He appears to have had six men with him as nearly as I can make it out," said Tom Belthorpe.

"I don't know what he was doing there, but I can guess," continued Deck.

"But which was the fellow you call Buck Lagger?" asked the major.

"He was the one who captured Miss Margie, and whom I wounded with the shot from my revolver," replied Deck. "I am sorry to say that my Uncle Titus is a Northern doughface, and is the leader of these ruffians. He bought the arms and ammunition of which we took possession at the sink-hole. I believe he hates my father on account of his Unionism and his taking of the arms worse than any man who is not his brother."

"I have heard something about him since I have been at Lyndhall," said Major Gadbury.

"Buck Lagger is his lieutenant and supporter, and I have no doubt Captain Titus sent him to the schoolhouse to disturb the meeting. He carried the flag of truce to-night at the bridge over the creek when his leader demanded the return of the arms," Deck explained. "Though I don't know any more about it than you do, I have no doubt Captain Titus sent this scalliwag ahead of the main body to see that all was clear."

"As scouts," suggested the major.

"Yes, sir; as scouts. As the ruffians had been severely punished in the fight from the bridge, and by the shots from Fort Bedford, they were likely to be more cautious than they had been before. They were whipped out at every approach to Riverlawn. Captain Titus may have found out that Colonel Belthorpe was on the way to his plantation to protect it with force enough to do his ruffians a good deal of mischief. I think Buck Lagger was sent out to obtain information."

"That is a reasonable supposition," the major acquiesced.

"Of course he could not expect to find the colonel and his force on the old road, and he was going by the cross-cut to the new road, which passes by the bridge over Bar Creek," Deck proceeded, perhaps feeling that he had an inspiration of wisdom as well as of heroism. "When he came to the cross-cut he must have seen that the Lodge was lighted."

"What you say reminds me that our party stood for some time on the portico talking with Captain Carms and his family about an excursion up the river which Tom suggested as we came out of the house. The wagon was standing before the door waiting for us."

"I haven't any doubt Buck was near enough to hear what you said," interposed Deck. "Probably he had sent his scouts up the cross-cut, and wanted to see why the mansion was lighted up at three o'clock in the morning. He understood that those who were to go in the wagon belonged to Colonel Belthorpe's family."

"The house is close by the road, and he could easily have seen who we were," said Tom.

"He had been on the creek bridge when the colonel talked with Captain Titus, and he saw that he was in command of the forces there. Very likely he knew it was he who gave the order to fire upon his party below the bridge. He must have been as hard down on your father as he was on mine, Mr. Belthorpe. When he saw your two sisters ready to get into the wagon, he had some trick in his head to obtain a hold upon your father. The two ladies were to be hostages in the hands of the ruffians for the conduct of your father."

"I think you have solved the problem, Deck, and only your bravery and skill saved the girls," said Major Gadbury.

"My father would have burned his buildings himself to recover my sisters, for no man was ever more devoted to his children than he is," added Tom. "If Buck had carried off the girls he would have had a tremendous hold on him."

"I suppose the villain would have confined us in some hovel, under guard of these miscreants, while he negotiated with my father with all the odds in his favor," Miss Margie commented. "Perhaps that was his way to have the arms returned to Captain Titus."

"You have saved us!" cried the younger and more impulsive Miss Kate, as she rushed forward to grasp the hand of Deck; and perhaps she would have kissed him again if Colonel Belthorpe had not entered the apartment at this moment, and she retreated to the chair she had before occupied.

"I see you have arrived," said the devoted father. "I have been worrying about you the last hour; but I concluded Captain Carms would send you home. I left my wagon at the stable of a friend near the schoolhouse, and I have been so busy all night that I have hardly thought of you, for I knew that you would be safe at Captain Carms's."

"But we haven't been safe, papa," said Miss Kate, rushing into her father's arms.

"Why, what has been the trouble, Kate?" asked the colonel, with his arms around the beautiful girl.

Before she could answer, Colonel Cosgrove, followed by Major Lyon and Squire Truman, entered the room.

"It seems that a fight has already come off in the cross-cut," said Colonel Cosgrove, with some excitement in his manner. "Major Lyon's man tells us you had a stormy time in the road, Deck. We did not wait to hear the particulars."

Colonel Belthorpe presented his guest and the members of his family to the party. Major Gadbury stated what had happened to them in the cross-cut, and then asked Deck to describe the fight. But Deck, who was not a bully or a blusterer, and was well ballasted with innate modesty in spite of the great amount of talking he had done, declined to do so, and the guest of the mansion described the fight with the marauders, giving the young hero at least all the credit that was due to him.

Deck blushed up to the eyes at the praise bestowed upon him, and was rather sorry he had not told the story, for he could have spared himself the crimson on his cheeks.

"It is all true, every word of it, papa!" exclaimed Miss Kate.

"Deck, I am your debtor for life!" exclaimed Colonel Belthorpe, detaching himself from the twining arms of his daughter, and rushing to the hero of the night with both hands extended. "You are a noble and brave fellow, Deck, and you will make your mark in the world!" And he pressed both the hands of the boy.

"Upon my word, I think he has made his mark already!" added Major Gadbury. "At any rate, he made it on the shoulder of Buck Lagger."

"My son, you have done well," said Major Lyon very quietly, as he took the boy's hand. "I am glad I brought you with me."

"But, father, I was beaten by the ruffian who was holding Miss Kate; he was too much for me, and he would have shaken me off if Mose had not come up and given the fellow a sledge-hammer blow with his fist which knocked him into a hole," Deck explained.

"Where is Mose?" demanded the father of the girl, as he took a gold piece of money from his pocket. "Send for him, and let" —

"Excuse me, Colonel," interposed Major Lyon,

placing his hand on his arm. "I see what you mean, and I must beg you not to reward him, for Mose did no more than every one of the faithful boys would have done if he had had the opportunity, though all of them have not so hard a fist as he."

"Just as you say, Major; but I feel grateful to Mose, as I do to Deck, for the hard hit he made for the safety of my daughter," replied the planter of Lyndhall. "We shall talk of this affair for the next week; but just now perhaps we ought to attend to the duty of the present moment. I sent the mounted men from Riverlawn down the old road for a mile to reconnoitre, and those who came in the wagon over to the new road to notify us of the approach of the enemy. We went over there on our arrival to arrange a plan for the defence of the place."

"After hearing what transpired at the cross-cut, I doubt whether Captain Titus will march his army up here," suggested Major Lyon.

"I think he will," added Colonel Cosgrove. "He is the maddest man I ever met in my life, and he is determined to recover the arms."

"But the — I mean Captain Titus will try to

THE GRATITUDE OF TWO FAIR MAIDENS

gain his point by some infamous trickery such as his lieutenant attempted at the cross road," said Major Gadbury, who was on the verge of calling him by some harsh epithet.

"Your mansion is safe for the present, Colonel Belthorpe," said Major Lyon, rising from the seat he had taken. "We might as well fight the battle, if there is to be one, on the road near your house. I suggest that we send our whole force down the new road, and drive the ruffians across the river."

Before the others could express an opinion on this policy, the mulatto in a white jacket announced that the horsemen were at the door, and wanted to see "de ossifer."

CHAPTER XXVI

THE SKIRMISH ON THE NEW ROAD

The officer whom the riders wished to see was evidently Colonel Belthorpe, as he had been in command from the beginning. He hastened to the hall, and found General there, who was rather more excited than usual, simply because he had something to communicate. In about every assemblage of men, white or black, there is generally one who naturally becomes the leader, though there may be a number of others who think they could do better. General was this single man, and had thus won his name.

"What is the matter, General?" asked the Colonel, as he confronted the bulky form of the black leader.

"Not'in' de matter, Mars'r Cunnel, but de rebels is on de road, comin' dis way," replied the self-appointed captain of cavalry.

"How far off are they?" asked the commander.

"About a mile, mars'r; but I reckon some ob

'em done went home, for dar isn't more'n half as many as we done see near de creek bridge."

"I should think they might have got enough of it by this time," replied the colonel. "What do you want now, Sam?" he said, turning to the mulatto in a white jacket, who appeared to be the man-servant of the house.

"Another man here wants to see you, mars'r," replied Sam, as he presented Mose, who had just come to the front door, where a servant does not usually come in the South. "He's a footman, an' not a hossman, mars'r."

"What is your name, my boy?" asked the colonel, turning to the new-comer.

"Mose is w'at dey all calls me, sar, but my truly name is 'Zekel. De ruffins is stopped half a mile from whar we com'd out on de ole road, mars'r," replied Mose, clinging to his old hat, which he pressed to his chest, as he bowed low, trying to be as respectful and deferential as possible.

"Did you go near them, Mose?" asked the commander.

"Not berry near, mars'r; but dey done make a fire, so we see 'em plain nuff."

"The main body of the ruffians cannot very well be on both roads," said the colonel.

"No, sar; but I reck'n Cap'n Titus done dewide his army, and he's gwine to take de place on de front and on de back," suggested Mose.

"Quite right, my boy; you have a head on your shoulders, and we shall not soon forget the hit you gave the fellow that was carrying off my daughter," added the colonel, surveying the leader of the foot party, as he proved to be. "How far off is this party at the fire?"

"About half a mile, mars'r. I reckon de fire is a signal to dem as is on de new road," replied Mose, bowing low and hugging his old hat again.

"All right, my boys; now return to your men, and we will be with you soon," said the commander as he returned to the party in the sitting-room.

All the party in the apartment fixed their gaze earnestly on Colonel Belthorpe as he entered, and there was an expression of fear and anxiety on the fair faces of the two daughters. By this time they all understood the situation perfectly. A gang of ruffians were approaching the mansion to revenge their defeat at Riverlawn upon the owner of this plantation, for he had been the chief man of the defence. It was evident that the commander had been put in possession of additional information in regard to the enemy.

He lost no time, but proceeded to state the facts which had just been reported to him by the scouts he had sent out. It was plain to all the defenders that another battle, if such a name could be properly applied to the skirmish near the creek bridge, was imminent.

"I think we are ready for the enemy," said Major Lyon; "and it will not be a difficult matter to drive the ruffians off. But I am not a military man, and we leave the defence entirely in your hands, Colonel Belthorpe."

"As I have said before, my place is not as favorable for a defence as yours is, Major Lyon," replied the commander. "We have no stream or swamp to cover our position, and we must act on open ground. Now, what force can we take into the field?"

"We have all that we had at the bridge," replied Squire Truman.

"Including Dexter, we have five white men here," added Major Lyon. "Eight of my boys are mounted, and seven came over in the wagon, and all of these are armed with breech-loaders, so that they can fire seven shots apiece. That makes twenty."

"And here we add to our number," said Colonel Cosgrove, glancing at Major Gadbury and Tom Belthorpe.

"Certainly; we expect to take part in any fight that is to come off," added the major.

"We have three repeating rifles in the house, two double-barrelled bucking guns, and four revolvers. We laid in a stock of arms when the horse-stealers were at work in this county," said the commander. "But I have never put arms in the hands of my negroes."

"I never did till to-night, and I found that all mine were as willing to fight as to work for me," the major explained. "You have an overseer, of course."

"I have; but I have my doubts about him. Tilford is rather a brutal fellow, and I believe he is a Secessionist at heart, though he has never said anything to commit himself. The worst thing I know about him is that he associates with Buck Lagger."

"Make him face the music, governor," added Tom. "If he is not willing to stand by you at such a time as this, he ought to be fired off the place."

Sam was sent for the overseer. Everybody about the mansion had been roused from his slumbers, and Tilford had been sulking about the space in front of the house, evidently disgusted to see the negroes from Riverlawn mounted on fine horses with breech-loaders slung at their backs. He obeyed the order of his employer, and stalked into the sitting-room with a defiant expression on his face.

"Tilford, something like a hundred ruffians are coming up the two roads for the purpose of burning my mansion and hanging me to the nearest tree," Colonel Belthorpe began in a mild tone. "With the aid of my friends here, I intend to defend myself, my family, and my property."

"Are them niggers with guns strapped on their backs your friends?" demanded the overseer, with a cynical smile on his ill-favored face.

"They are brave men, who have this night defended their master from an attack of the reprobates who are marching upon my place; and I honor them for their bravery and fidelity, for not one of them has flinched!" returned the colonel vigorously. "I want to know now upon whom I can depend to defend me from the violence of these villains who are coming down upon me."

"I reckon you can depend upon your niggers, but you can't depend on me!" replied the overseer, edging towards the door. "You have fotched all this on yourself by turning abolitionist!"

"If assisting my neighbor and friend to defend himself and his family from the attacks of a pack of ruffians is being an abolitionist, then I am one with all my mind, heart, and soul!" replied the planter with a vehemence that brought down the applause of his associates, even including the ladies.

"Them gentlemen you call ruffi'ns is my friends, Colonel Belthorpe, and I don't never go back on my friends, not unless they turn abolitionists, and I ain't go'n' to fight ag'in 'em," added Tilford, working nearer to the door. "I reckon my time's about done on this place."

"Quite done!" said the colonel, taking a revolver from his pocket.

"Go and join your friends! I will order every

man with a gun to shoot you if you are seen about the place in five minutes!"

The overseer did not like the looks of the revolver in the hands of his employer, and he fled from the house. The commander had sent all the Riverlawn force back to the two roads to observe the movements of the ruffians, or he would have given the faithless fellow an escort from the vicinity of the mansion.

"The boys will all stand by you, mars'r," said Sam in the white jacket as the colonel followed the renegade to the front door.

"Then call two of them" —

"They're all right here, mars'r," interposed the servant.

The commander sent two of them to follow Tilford. He found, somewhat to his astonishment, that all the servants on the place, even to the old men, had armed themselves with clubs, pitchforks, shovels, or whatever they could lay their hands upon, ready to defend their master, who had always been kinder to them than the overseer. Besides, the armed negroes from Riverlawn had remained some little time on the premises, and had very fully informed them in regard to the events of the night, including the capture of the two daughters of their master, which had roused them to the highest pitch of indignation, for they looked upon Margie and Kate as a pair of angels, and wondered they had no wings.

When Colonel Belthorpe returned to the sitting-room, he found that Tom had collected all the arms and ammunition in the mansion, taking a repeating rifle for himself, and giving another to the guest of the house. Each of them took a revolver, and they were loading these weapons for immediate use. The rest of the arms were given to a few of the most trusty of the servants.

The commander led the way to the large court-yard in front of the mansion, where he divided the force into two parties, one to meet the enemy on each of the two roads. Before this could be done, the scouts on the new road returned, with the two Lyndhall boys who had followed Tilford. They had passed him through the ranks of the mounted men when they were in sight of the ruffians, and some of them had stoned him as a farewell salute.

The commander made Major Lyon the officer of the old road force. He objected, and suggested Major Gadbury for the position; but it was found that the visitor held his title only by courtesy, and was not a military man, and then the Riverlawn planter accepted the position. Tom Belthorpe, Squire Truman, Deck, and four of the eight mounted men, with about twenty of the Lyndhall boys, were placed under his command.

The commander had endeavored to make a fair division of the force, and Colonel Cosgrove, Major Gadbury, four Riverlawn horsemen, and a score of his own people composed his own force. The ruffians were within fifty rods of the mansion on the new road, and the division for this service marched at once. The cavalry were sent out ahead, with orders not to fire unless the ruffians opened upon them.

General was at the head of the horsemen, and he galloped his horse up to the front of the ruffians. He and his men had loosened the slings of their weapons, and brought them in front of them, so that they were ready for immediate use. The ruffians had halted as soon as they discovered the riders in front of them. Then they built a fire, and as soon as its light shone upon them, General discovered a flag of truce.

The leader ventured to approach a little nearer

to the enemy, when he was saluted with a volley of oaths, and some one of them, not Captain Titus, demanded where his master was.

"Ober on de ole road," replied General, almost as savagely as he had been addressed.

"Do you know what this flag means, you nigger?" interrogated the speaker with an oath.

"Yes, sar! Mars'r Belthorpe won't hab no more ob dat nonsense," answered General.

"Tell him I want to see him under a flag of truce!" shouted the one who appeared to be in command.

The horseman was afraid of making some mistake, and he sent one of his boys back to the commander with this message. Colonel Belthorpe had sent Sam back for his saddle horse, and presently he galloped to the front.

"Take in your flag of truce, or I will fire upon it!" shouted the colonel. "No more fooling! I don't parley with ruffians!"

The flag immediately disappeared. By the light of the fire it could be seen that about half a dozen men at the front of the column were armed with muskets, which, with or without a command from the officer, they brought to their shoulders and fired. Colonel Belthorpe put his hand on his left arm, as though a ball had struck him there.

"Now, my boys, fire at them at will, just as you please," continued the commander, as he began to blaze away with his heavy revolver.

The four mounted men began to use their repeaters; but their horses were restive, and they could not fire at the best advantage, though several of the ruffians were seen to fall, while the main body of them fled into the adjoining fields.

CHAPTER XXVII

AN UNEXPLAINED GATHERING ON THE ROAD

The ruffians were a mere mob, entirely devoid of any semblance of discipline; and it was again made manifest that they could not stand up against a continuous fire such as the mounted boys and those on foot were beginning to pour into them, scattered though it was at first by the restiveness of the untrained horses. Titus Lyon was not a military man, and he did not appear to appreciate the advantage of order in the handling of his force.

It is true that the negroes that confronted him were not organized to any adequate extent for military purposes, though the little training Colonel Belthorpe had given them on the bridge had been of very great service to them. It was absolutely astonishing to the commander that the boys did not drop their weapons and run when the random shots from the enemy were discharged at them; for this idea was in accordance with his estimate of negro character.

It was a new revelation to him, the manner in which the men conducted themselves under fire, hurried as they had been, without any training, into the ranks; and the same number of white men of average ability could hardly have done better under similar circumstances. But the negro was strong in his affections, and the feeling that they were fighting for the family who had used them kindly, and treated them with more consideration than they had been in the habit of receiving, even under the mild sway of Colonel Lyon, was the stimulus that strengthened their souls and nerved their arms.

The "people" of Lyndhall were inspired by the example of those from Riverlawn, and they were filled with admiration when they saw those of their own kind bearing arms, some of them well mounted, and learned that they had actually done duty during the night as soldiers. General, Dummy, and Mose had talked to them, and roused their spirit of emulation. Besides, they had been moved by the same devotion to the members of the planter's family; and their indignation at the conduct of the overseer, who had been their tyrant, had done not a little to develop their belligerent feelings.

The ruffians had taken to their heels, and fled into the open country between the old and the new road. There were some trees upon the tract, and the fugitives proceeded to utilize them as far as they were available to shelter them from the balls of the horsemen. At this point the negroes of Lyndhall, unexpectedly to their owner, manifested their presence in a very decided manner. The sight of the four stout boys on the horses, undismayed by the random shots which had been fired at them, had a tremendous influence upon them, and they became exceedingly excited, not to say crazed; and, without any orders from the commander, they rushed into the fields after the ruffians.

Doubtless they would have obeyed from instinct the order to return if the colonel had given it; but he allowed them to have their own way. With the various weapons with which they had armed themselves, they fell upon the helpless fugitives, pounded, punched, and hammered them till they begged for mercy. They, in turn, were confronted by an infuriated mob. Those who were able to do so fled with all the speed they could command towards the old road, which was nearly a mile distant at this point. Not a few of them had been so beaten that they could not run, and they dropped upon the ground. The victors were not cruel, and they did not meddle with those who no longer made any resistance.

The Lyndhall boys had gone into the fight with no leader of their own number; but as soon as they left the road one developed himself in the person of the preacher of the plantation, a white-haired negro of over seventy years of age, whom the family called "Uncle Dave." He had always been a mild, gentle, and very religious man, and he was always treated with respect.

Uncle Dave seemed to become a giant in strength, his voice that of a stentor, and his manner fierce, as soon as his flock went into action. He called upon his people not to kill the ruffians, for their souls were black with unrepented sins; and when one of the marauders sunk to the earth, he commanded them not to touch him again. The fleeing ruffians were indebted to him for their lives, while he ordered his flock to punish them severely as they deserved.

Colonel Belthorpe regarded this man with wonder; for he had always been as gentle as a lamb, obedient in all things, and anxious to minister to the people in sickness and death. Now he seemed to be the most terrible fighting character he had ever met. He saw his volunteers, as he called them, chase the ruffians till they disappeared in the distance and the darkness. The mounted men had ceased firing, for there was no enemy near, and they were fearful of hitting those who were fighting on their own side.

"We have made a clean sweep here," said the commander, as Colonel Cosgrove and Major Gadbury joined him in the road; for they had been in the fields south of the road, engaged in a flank movement.

"It has been an easy victory," replied the gentleman from the county town. "But they were nothing but a mob; and your boys seem to be lunatics. They are likely to kill the whole of them before they get through."

"They will not kill one of them unless it is by accident, for I heard Uncle Dave order them as they took to the fields not to do so; and I notice that when a man drops on the ground they let him alone," added the Lyndhall planter.

"We have nothing more to do here, unless we go down the road and pick up the wounded, for I see half a dozen of them in front of us, though they are all sitting up and looking about them, so that none of them have been killed," said Major Gadbury.

"Our occupation here appears to be gone," continued Colonel Belthorpe, as he looked over the fields from which the combatants had disappeared, with the exception of those who were unable to run away. "Major Lyon over on the old road may not have been as fortunate as we have been, and we must go over and re-enforce him. General!"

"Here, sar!" replied that worthy.

"We are going over to the old road to help out Major Lyon. You will leave two of your men here, one mounted, and the other on foot, to watch the enemy; the others will go with me," added the planter.

"Yes, sar," answered General, as he detailed the two scouts. "I reckon we done finished 'em ober here, Mars'r Cunnel."

"No doubt of it, General; and I hope Major Lyon has done as well over on the old road."

The commander started off at a gallop, and the mounted men closely followed him. They passed through the deserted courtyard of the mansion, where the planter was accosted by his two daughters, who had been observing the movements of the combatants from the elevated veranda of the house.

"Where are you going now, papa?" asked Miss Kate.

"We have driven off the ruffians from this side, and we are going over to assist Major Lyon," replied the colonel. "Sam, you will remain here, and look out for the house," he added to the man with the white jacket, to whom this duty had been before assigned, and then rode on towards the old road.

"Don't shoot, Colonel Belthorpe!" called a voice from behind the stable, as the horsemen advanced, and a man came out into the roadway.

It was Tilford, the overseer, who had retreated from the mansion, and joined the ruffians, whom he called his friends. At the first discharge of the mounted men which followed the revolver practice of the commander, he had been hit in the thigh with a bullet; and at the general stampede of the enemy he had made his way into the field. Realizing that there was no safety for him among "his friends," he had limped all the way back to the mansion.

His wound was not a bad one, though it was painful, and partially disabled him. As he had detached himself from the ruffians there was no one to dispute his passage, and he had reached the stable, behind which he had concealed himself when he heard the approach of the horsemen. But, dark as it was, the colonel perceived and recognized him.

"What are you doing here, Tilford?" demanded the commander.

"I am wounded and in great pain," replied the overseer in weak and submissive tones.

"Then why don't you join your friends?" asked the colonel.

"I made a mistake to-night, and I did not know who my friends were," pleaded the wounded man.

"Sam!" shouted the planter to the house servant, who had followed the party nearly to the stable; and the boy immediately presented himself before his master. "Take the overseer to his room, and do what you can for him."

"Thank you, Colonel!" exclaimed Tilford; and his wound seemed to have made another man of him.

Sam took the sufferer by the arm, wondering at the magnanimity of his master, who had ordered all the people to shoot him if he was seen again on the premises, and conducted him towards the mansion, where he had a chamber back of the dining-room. As he led him up the steps, Margie and Kate came to him; and they proved to be as forgiving as their father, for they did everything they could to make him comfortable. One of the old "aunties," skilled in nursing, was sent to him, and his wound was dressed.

The mounted men, led by the commander, galloped over to the old road, which was deserted at the place where they came out. On a slight elevation in the highway a great fire was blazing brilliantly, and near it was an assemblage of people, the nature of which the commander could not make out.

"I don't understand that gathering," said he, as Major Gadbury rode up to his side.

"It looks as though the enemy were using the flag of truce ruse over here," replied the major.

"I don't believe Major Lyon would fool with them. They are marauders and disturbers of the peace, and I think he is as disposed to deal summarily with them as I am," added the commander. "But we will ride up to the place, and we shall soon know what is going on."

"Who are these men coming into the road just ahead of us?" asked Major Gadbury, pointing to three men who were making their way through the field to the road. "The fire on the hill don't give quite light enough to enable me to make them out; but I suppose they are ruffians who have made their way from the new road."

"I don't know what they are, but we will go and see;" and they rode forward about a dozen rods to the point where the men were emerging from the field. "Who goes there?" demanded Colonel Belthorpe.

"Is that you, Mars'r Cunnel?" asked one of them.

"Uncle Dave!" exclaimed the planter.

"That's the parson," added Colonel Cosgrove.

"What are you doing over here, Uncle?" asked the commander.

"We done have nothin' more to do over yonder," replied the preacher. "The boys are all movin' over this way."

"But where are the ruffians that retreated from the new road?"

"The boys fell upon 'em and drove 'em over to the west, sar," the parson explained. "We don't kill any of 'em; but we bang 'em so they hold still on the ground. We think they was comin' over here to help the ruffians on this side, and we come over to 'tend to 'em."

"All right, venerable Uncle," laughed the colonel. "But can you tell me what is going on upon the hill yonder?"

"I don't know, Mars'r Cunnel. I don't see 'em till now."

Uncle Dave had a pitchfork in his hand, and it was plain enough just now that he was of the church militant, for he was in fighting condition. It was said that he could read and write; but from motives of policy he never allowed a white man to see him do either. He was a sensible old man in spite of his condition, and was employed about the stable and carriage-house, and was favored by his master and all the family. He had learned to speak without using the negro dialect, though his sentences were not rhetorical models, and from the force of habit he retained some of the old forms to avoid the imputation of "putting on airs."

"There seems to be no fighting going on up there," said the commander after he had studied the situation some time, though he could not understand it. "If the ruffians are moving over here, as Uncle Dave says, we shall be needed in that quarter."

"I don't think so, Mars'r Cunnel, for we maul the ruffians so that they won't want to fight no more for two weeks and a half," added the preacher, who heard the remark.

"You may stay here, and if your flock come to this road, send them up to the hill where we are going," ordered the commander, as he dashed off, followed by the other horsemen.

The gathering on the hill was not a parley under a flag of truce, as Colonel Belthorpe feared it might be; but to explain its nature it will be necessary to go back to the time when Major Lyon, followed by his command, had marched over to the old road.

CHAPTER XXVIII

THE RESULT OF THE FLANK MOVEMENT

EVEN the title of major which had been thrust upon him could not make the planter of Riverlawn feel like a military commander as he led his battalion of foot and mounted volunteers to the old road, which might prove to be a battle-field. His force consisted of only four white men, — himself, his son, Tom Belthorpe, and Squire Truman. Deck had been provided with a saddle horse from the stable of the Lyndhall planter, so that all of them were well mounted.

Four of the mounted boys from Riverlawn, four of them on foot, and about twenty of the colonel's ablest hands formed the rest of his force. The latter were as emulous to fight the battle of their master as those who had been sent to the new road. Major Lyon's boys had already been under fire, and they were exceedingly proud of the experience. They talked rather large, perhaps, to the Lyndhall volunteers, and told them they must stand up to it when the enemy fired, and must not run away though they were sure they would be shot. They were earnestly counselled not " to disgrace the race."

At that time a negro soldier was unknown, and most white men, especially at the South, would as soon have thought of arming and drilling a lot of baboons and monkeys; and even those in Barcreek who were willing to accept their services in defence of their families and their property had never dreamed of such a thing as making soldiers of the negroes. Their steadiness under fire, though they had been subjected to only a discharge of random shots, filled the slaveholders present with astonishment, if not with admiration.

When the force reached the old road, there was nothing to be seen of the ruffians, for it was quite dark, and they were beyond the hill, which obstructed their view. But the scouts had reported them as approaching, and the major in command was not inclined to await their coming. He gave the order to march; but they had gone only a few rods before the column was seen at the top of the hill. A halt was called in order to enable the prudent commander to prepare a plan for the assault.

The advance of the force was evidently perceived by the ruffians, for they also halted, and in a few moments more a great fire was blazing up at the side of the road. On the march so far, Tom and Deck had done a good deal of talking together. Since his brave and determined defence of Miss Kate in the cross-cut, and his strategy in disposing of Buck Lagger, Tom had a very high respect and regard for Deck.

"My father isn't much of a soldier, any more than the rest of us," said Deck, as the major gave the order to halt. "If we fire at those scalliwags, they will scatter and run away, as they did at the creek bridge, and be all ready to burn a house or run off with a girl as soon as they get the chance. I believe we ought to punish them so that they will remember it till to-morrow or next day."

"Just my idea," replied Tom. "These niggers stand up to the fight like white men. I believed they would all run away at the first shot from an enemy."

"Not one of them flinched on the bridge or in the road when the ruffians fired into them, my father says, for I was not there then; I was in the artillery service just at that time."

"In the artillery service!" exclaimed Tom, laughing at the magnificent speech of his companion in arms.

"Exactly so; you have heard the story of the capture of the arms at the sink-hole; the cannon are mounted in the ice-house. If you see one of our darkeys flinch when the firing begins, I wish you would let me know, and we will cut down his hominy ration," rattled Deck, as enthusiastic as though he had slept all night instead of half an hour. "But I have got an idea."

"You seem to have one in tow all the time."

"I want you to mention it to my father if you believe in it, and he will think more of it than if I put it forward."

"Your father seems to think a good deal of what you say and do."

"He will think I am too old for my years; but he is the best father I ever had, and I want him to come out of this scrape with flying colors."

"But what is your idea, Deck?" asked Tom curiously.

"I think my father is waked up to the bottom of his boots; he won't fool with any flags of truce, and he will order us all to fire as soon as the time comes, though his own brother is in the gang ahead of us, or in the one over on the other road."

"I am sure he won't wince."

"And the moment we fire, the ruffians will all run away, which the darkeys won't do. That is just what I have seen them do twice to-night. I wonder what they came over here for if they didn't mean to fight."

"They came over here to burn your father's house and that of mine; but I reckon they didn't expect to get the reception Major Lyon had prepared for them."

"They will run away, Tom," repeated Deck; "and that is just what I don't want them to be allowed to do."

"Not if we can prevent it; for I believe that hanging would do good to some of them."

"We can prevent it if my father will adopt your suggestion," added Deck.

"My suggestion! I haven't got any suggestion, and I don't know what you are talking about, Deck," replied Tom, puzzled with the remark. "All the way I can see to manage this affair is to rush at the ruffians and drive them off."

"We don't want to drive them off till we have given them a little wholesome discipline. I suppose you know what a flank movement is, fellow-soldier?"

"I have an idea what it is."

"We used to practise it when we were snowballing on sides away up in the glorious State of New Hampshire, if we got a chance to do it."

"We don't practise snowballing much down here, and I never was engaged in a flank movement at a snowball match. But I have an idea that it is getting around the enemy, whether in a battle or a game, and taking them on the side or in the rear."

"You could not have stated it any better if you had been studying the art of war or the science of snowballing all your lifetime," added Deck.

"Be a little more serious, Mr. Lyon, and I shall understand you better," said Tom, looking very grave himself.

"I will be as serious as the parson at a funeral, Mr. Belthorpe. We have plenty of men to flank them handsomely; for it don't take a great crowd with seven-shooters in their hands to hold that gang where they are."

"I see what you mean now."

"What kind of ground is it over on the left of this road, Tom?"

"It is one of our best fields."

"Can horses travel on it?"

"Just as well as on this road."

"Then your suggestion to the commander-in-chief of the forces is that he send a detachment of six men, mounted and armed with repeating rifles, through the field on the left, with orders to fire on the ruffians when the fight opens," continued Deck earnestly.

"It is a brilliant idea, and I will do it at once," replied Tom.

"Hold on a minute, and suggest that the detachment be under the command of Captain Tom Belthorpe," added Deck.

"I shall amend that by substituting the name of Captain Deck Lyon," replied Tom, as he started ahead to overtake the commander.

"Don't do that!" shouted Deck.

Everything seemed to be at a standstill; but the blazing fire revealed a flag of truce flying in front of the enemy. Tom delivered his suggestion to Major Lyon without mentioning the fact that it came from his son; and the commander promptly approved it. He believed that there must surely be fighting this time, and that if the defenders, as he called them, were defeated, Colonel Belthorpe's mansion would soon be in flames, and perhaps his lovely daughters would fall into the hands of the vicious wretches composing the mob.

"How many men do you need?"

"The four mounted men from your place, Deck, and myself," replied the bearer of the suggestion.

"Very well, I give you the order to that effect; but don't you think some older person than Dexter had better be in command?"

"Decidedly not, Major!" answered Tom with emphasis. "I believe Deck is the smartest fellow in the crowd, except yourself."

"All right; have your own way, then," replied the commander. "But can you tell me the nature of the land on the right hand side of the road?"

"The creek runs from above the mansion in that direction to the river, and it is swampy on both sides of it," replied Tom, as he hurried away to rejoin Deck.

During the absence of Tom Belthorpe, the young hero had been carefully studying the position of the enemy and the surroundings. He could see the brook, or creek as such streams are called in that region, by the light of the fire on the hill, hardly deserving that appellation. for it was only a very slight elevation. The bushes were like those he had seen near the spring road, and several pools or ponds reflected the light of the fire. He was satisfied that the ruffians could not retreat in that direction.

Before Tom joined him the flag of truce with four men began to advance towards Major Lyon's force. The commander's "infantry," consisting of four Riverlawn negroes, were drawn up in front. The twenty Lyndhall hands, miscellaneously armed with clubs and such implements as they had been able to obtain, had also been formed across the road; and they were as eager to "pitch into" the marauders as their fellows on the new road had been; but the commander restrained them.

"Here you are, Captain Lyon, and my mission has been a success," said Tom, as he rode up to the "cavalry" posted in the rear, where that arm is not usually placed. "You are to command the flanking party, and Squire Truman is requested to join the commander at the front."

The lawyer, who had not been informed of the intended movement, immediately hastened to the front. Tom reported what had passed between the major and himself, and a few minutes later the squire was seen riding towards the hill. He had been directed by the major to inform the ruffians that no flag of truce would be respected, and that he would open fire very soon.

Deck objected to taking command of the cavalry; but Tom insisted, for he really believed his companion was better qualified for the position than himself, and the young man finally yielded the point. Captain Lyon, as he had been called more than once during the night, proceeded to address the four cavalrymen, informing them what was to be done, and what was expected of them.

He did not put on any airs, though he could hardly help "feeling his oats;" but he was too much absorbed in the success of his enterprise to think much of his personal self. There were no fences at the side of the road; and, giving the command to march, he started his spirited horse, and dashed at full gallop into the field, with Tom at his side, and the four riders from Riverlawn in rank behind them.

Deck passed beyond the range of the firelight, so that the enemy could not see his force, and in less than ten minutes they were abreast of them. By this time the message of the major had been delivered by the squire; and the result was a manifestation on the part of the ruffians. Those who were armed with muskets or other firearms appeared to have been placed in front, and they delivered what was intended for a volley, though it was a very shaky one.

As the cavalry were passing over a knoll, Deck saw that his father was marching his force up the road; for the combatants were too far apart to do each other much mischief by their fire. The enemy kept up a desultory discharge of their guns, but they were evidently not repeating-rifles. When he had reduced the distance by one-half between them, he ordered a halt. At this point he unslung his breech-loader, as the squire had done before, and ordered the front rank to fire.

But Deck did not halt; on the contrary, he

urged his horse forward at a more rapid rate, and was closely followed by his command. The infantry in the road continued to fire at will after the first volley, and it was evident to Captain Lyon that the enemy were breaking under this hot work. Those in the rear had already taken to their heels; but the cavalry dashed in ahead of them, and the young commander drew up his little force in front of them. As soon as he had given the order to halt, and the six men in line faced the enemy, he gave the command to fire in detail. In the case of Major Lyon and his son, both officers did duty as privates as well as commanders. The retreat was instantly checked; and this was the situation when Colonel Belthorpe appeared upon the field.

CHAPTER XXIX

THE HUMILIATING RETREAT OF THE RUFFIANS

The situation on the rising ground was a puzzle to Colonel Belthorpe and his companions. They could plainly see the little force of Captain Deck in the rear of the enemy, and realized that it prevented the ruffians from running away, as they had done on the new road. The commander was inclined to laugh; for taking into account the fury with which the mob had followed up their purpose, it was rather ludicrous to see them penned in, as it were, on the hill.

As it was the policy of Major Lyon and his son to kill or wound as few as possible of the ruffians, the firing had entirely ceased on the part of the defenders, though an occasional shot came from the unorganized mob. The negroes from the new road were coming in all the time; but Uncle Dave had been studying the situation as well as his master, and his flock obeyed him as implicitly as they did the colonel himself.

The preacher saw that the enemy were surrounded so far as the old road was concerned, and could not retreat in the direction of the creek. The field by which Captain Deck had reached his present position was still open to them, and without orders or suggestions from any one he proceeded to occupy it with the few of his people who had come with him. He intercepted the others as they approached, and led them to a point where they could fall upon the ruffians if they attempted to escape in that direction.

The firing had ceased, and Captain Titus Lyon could not help seeing the movement of the negroes under the lead of Uncle Dave. Probably a few of the refugees from the skirmish on the new road succeeded in reaching the hill where his advance had been checked, and had informed him of the disaster to his other division. Even the desultory firing of his men was discontinued very soon when they saw that they were hemmed in on all sides, and that they were at the mercy of the victors.

"Well, Major Lyon, you seem to have brought everything to a standstill on this portion of the field," said Colonel Belthorpe as he rode up to the planter from Riverlawn after he had taken a full view of the situation. "I see that you have made a flank movement, and placed a portion of your force in the rear of the enemy."

"My son is in command of that detachment, and the movement was made at his suggestion," replied the major, who could not help laughing in sympathy with the colonel. "The movement was made at his suggestion, and I think there is a great deal more military in Dexter's composition than in mine."

"Captain Deck has skill as well as pluck, and he has put the enemy in a tight place," added the commander-in-chief. "There they are like a flock of sheep in a pen, and they cannot get out. What are you going to do next, Major Lyon?"

"That is for you to say, for you command all the forces," answered the major.

"You have brought this sore to a head, my friend, and probably you can suggest in what manner the wound may be healed," returned the colonel, still laughing; for to a military man like him the whole affair appeared to be rather in the nature of a farce. "You have proved to be an able commander, and I need your advice."

"You seem to look very lightly upon the whole

matter, Colonel Belthorpe," said the major, who could not understand why his superior officer indulged in his continued laugh.

"Not at all, my dear sir; I have looked upon it, up to the present stage of affairs, as a very serious matter; and I am confident that both your mansion and mine would have been in ashes before this time if we had not taken the bull by the horns as we did."

" You appear to be amused."

"I am amused at the present situation; and perhaps the victory we have achieved puts me in condition to be amused. My property and my daughters have been saved, and we have the ruffians pinched up in a tight place. I think you have as much reason to rejoice as I have, Major Lyon."

"Certainly I have; but, not being a military man, it looks more serious to me than to you. I thought you were inclined to make fun of the whole affair."

"Not at all. For a civilian you have done wonders. As we have won we can afford to laugh. But it is about daylight now, and this operation must be finished. What is your counsel, Major?"

"I think we had better get a little nearer to the enemy," replied the major. "I see a good many of your people in the field on our left."

"From mild, peaceable, and even timid people, they suddenly became as brave as lions, and as ferocious as fiends, and they have severely punished the ruffians who fled in this direction. I never supposed there was anything like fight in them before."

"If you are ready we will advance, Colonel," added Major Lyon, as he gave the order to march.

The commander took his place by the side of the planter of Riverlawn, and the column moved up the declivity. The fire was still burning brightly, and lighted up the whole of the surrounding region. It was evidently replenished with fuel frequently, in order to enable the entrapped foe to observe the movements of the visitors. The approach of the forces appeared to cause a decided sensation in the ranks of the ruffians, and presently a white flag was displayed in front of them.

"Captain Titus seems to have a passion for white flags," said the colonel. "He tried that dodge for the second time over on the new road."

"And for the third time on this road," added

the major. "But there appears to be some reason for showing it this time."

The major did not give an order to halt this time; but the force marched to a point within twenty-five feet of the front rank of the ruffians, if there could be said to be anything like a rank in the mob. Then the command to halt was given.

"I shall leave you to do all the talking, Colonel Belthorpe," said the major, as he backed his horse so as to leave the commander alone at the front.

"I am quite willing to do the talking, but I may need your advice," replied the colonel.

The planter of Riverlawn could distinctly make out his brother at this distance, and he was glad that he had not been shot dead, or apparently wounded. Two men came from the direction of the fire, bearing lighted torches, and placed themselves one on each side of Captain Titus and another person at his side, who carried the white flag.

"Do you know that man with the flag, Squire Truman?" asked Major Lyon, as he observed the proceedings on the other side.

"I ought to know him, for I prosecuted him for an assault not long ago," replied the lawyer.

"That is Swin Pickford, a bully and a ruffian of the vilest sort."

"My brother is not very particular in the selection of his associates," added Noah Lyon very sadly.

Captain Titus advanced with the flag and the torches at a stately pace, as though he were the victor instead of the vanquished in the several conflicts of the night, and halted in the middle of the space between the contestants.

"I desire to meet Noah Lyon," said he.

"I decline to meet him," called the owner of the name.

"He declines to meet you on the present occasion," replied the commander sternly. "This is not exactly a fraternal meeting, and there is only one question which is in order: Do you surrender?"

"Surrender? No! not as long as there is a breath left in my body!" replied the leader of the ruffians, as fiercely as though he expected to have all his own way in spite of his disastrous defeat.

"What do you want, then?" demanded the colonel.

"I want justice!" stormed Captain Titus.

"If you got it you would be swinging to one of these trees; and that is where you would be if you were not the brother of Major Lyon."

"Major Lyon, as you call him, is a thief and a robber!" yelled Titus. "The very guns and cannon you have turned against us to-night were stolen from me by him!"

"At a meeting of the Union men of this vicinity last night, a vote of thanks was passed to Major Lyon for taking possession of the arms and ammunition found in a cavern; and we all stand by that vote," replied the colonel with dignity.

"What do we care for the vote of a set of traitors to the State!"

"This is not the time or the place to discuss the subject. I desire only to know what you and your mob are going to do about it."

"We are going to have justice if there is any such thing left in the State."

"It is your next move, Captain Titus."

"I wish to be fair and reasonable," continued Titus, moderating his speech and manner. "I have done my best to keep the gentlemen with me from doing violence to them that stole our property, and"—

"And for that reason you became their leader and captain-general in an attempt to burn your brother's house and mine!" interjected the colonel.

"No matter what we came out for; I have a plan to state that will settle the difficulty," Titus proceeded, struggling to keep cool.

"State your plan, and be quick about it!"

"If the stolen arms and things are returned to us at once, we will go to our several homes and let the matter end here," said Titus.

"That's enough!" exclaimed Colonel Belthorpe indignantly. "Have you come over here under a flag of truce to say that?"

"That is what I come here for; and I insist on't that the things be given up!" replied Titus, waxing wrathful.

"Now you can retire with your flag of truce."

"I won't do no such thing!"

"If you won't I shall be obliged to open fire upon you and your mob; and you will be the first to fall," added the commander quietly.

"Do you mean to murder us?" demanded Titus, aghast at the determined policy of the commander. "You have hemmed us in so that we can't get out, and now you mean to fire on us!

I cal'late you've got a bone to pick with your feller-citizens for armin' niggers."

"I can pick it without any help from you. Now, do you surrender, or shall I order my men to fire?" demanded the colonel so sternly that Titus was silenced. "I give you five minutes to consider my offer."

"I don't want to be shot like a mule with a broken leg," said Swin Pickford, loud enough to be heard in the front rank.

"Can't we make terms?" asked Titus, who was terribly alarmed.

"No terms with a mob," replied the colonel.

Half a dozen of the ruffians came forward to their leader, and it was evident that they were quite as much frightened as he was himself. Enough was heard from those in the front rank of the defenders to assure them they pleaded for surrender. Some of them farther back even shouted, "We surrender!"

"I s'pose we can't do nothin' but surrender or be shot," resumed Titus.

"That's all; and you may thank your stars that some of you are not swinging by the neck from the trees at the side of the road."

"Then we surrender, for we can't do nothin' else," said Captain Titus. "But I want to tell you, Colonel Belthorpe and Noah Lyon, that you haven't seen the end of this thing yet. If the whole country don't howl ag'in you within twenty-four hours, I lose my guess."

"You had better fall back on your ruffians and guess again," added the colonel, as he placed himself at the side of Major Lyon.

"What does the surrender amount to, Colonel?" asked the planter of Riverlawn.

"It really amounts to nothing but a way to get rid of these fellows. We have had enough of them for to-night," replied the commander. "Captain Gadbury, will you ride around through the fields to Captain Deck, and ask him to let the mob move down the road toward the bridge? If any of them have guns, take them from them."

Captain Gadbury started on his mission. Four mounted negroes were sent after him to assist in disarming those who had weapons if needed. In a short time the captain and his followers arrived at their destination, as could be seen from the position of the main body. It was light enough by this time to see the force there place themselves on each side of the road.

Then the commander ordered his men to march, shouting to the mob to do the same. The ruffians began their humiliating retreat, and the defenders followed them as far as the bridge. The planters and their attendants then returned to their homes.

CHAPTER XXX

LEVI BEDFORD AND HIS PRISONER

Colonel Cosgrove and Squire Truman returned to Riverlawn with Major Lyon and his son. Colonel Belthorpe and Tom renewed their expressions of gratitude to Deck for the important service he had rendered to the family in the protection of Margie and Kate, and insisted that he should visit Lyndhall as soon as possible. They parted at the cross roads, and both parties received a warm welcome at their homes.

Levi Bedford and Artie Lyon had remained on watch in the fort, while a sufficient number of the hands patrolled the bridge and the creek; but the ruffians had found enough to do in the direction they had gone, and there was no alarm during the rest of the night. The major took his guests to the mansion, while Deck related to Levi and Artie the events of the visit to Lyndhall.

"Captain Titus and the mob have really been thoroughly whipped out of their boots," said the overseer, when Deck had finished his narrative. "But, as the leader of the ruffians said, we haven't seen the end of this thing yet."

"Do you think they will make another attack upon Riverlawn, Levi?" asked Deck with a long gape.

"I don't reckon they will try it in the same way they did before; at least not till they are fully provided with arms and ammunition," replied Levi. "That attempt to capture the two daughters of Colonel Belthorpe looks like one of Buck Lagger's schemes. If he had obtained possession of the two girls, very likely he would have confined them in one of the caverns like the one where they put the arms, with a guard over them."

"That would have been awful," added Artie.

"I reckon they didn't mean to hurt the girls, and wouldn't if they had got possession of them," continued Levi. "But you can see for yourselves, boys, that they would have had the key to the fortress in their own hands if they had obtained the girls."

"That's so!" exclaimed Deck, who had seen the point before without any help from the overseer.

"I don't see what good the girls could have done them," said Artie, who had been asleep most of the time during the absence of the planter and his son.

"It is as plain as the nose on a monkey's face," added Deck. "With the two girls as prisoners, Captain Titus would have demanded the return of the arms and ammunition of Colonel Belthorpe."

"I see!" exclaimed Artie, as the object of the capture dawned upon him. "But the colonel did not have the arms, and he could not have given them up."

"But father would have made common cause with him, and he could not well have helped giving up the arms to get back his neighbor's daughters," Deck explained.

"But I wonder they didn't try to take our girls," suggested Artie.

"That is what they may try to do next; and I shall advise your mother not to permit Miss Dorcas or Miss Hope to go outside of the plantation unless they are well guarded," added Levi. "If Captain Titus could get away with your two sisters, and hide them, he could have things all his own way with your father."

"We must keep a sharp lookout for the girls," said Artie.

"Buck Lagger, with his gang, must have gone ahead of the main body of the ruffians," continued the overseer thoughtfully, "or he could not have been in the cross-cut. He must have known about the party, and that the colonel's daughters were there."

"Where does this Buck live?" asked Deck.

"He has a shanty on the road to the village, just above the schoolhouse. He is a pedler when he does anything like work, and I suppose he knows about every family in the county," replied Levi. "He could easily have found out all about the party, and who were to be there."

"There is the breakfast-bell," said Deck, who was quite prepared by his night's work for the summons.

At the table the story of the night's adventures was repeated for the information of Mrs. Lyons and her daughters, and they wanted to hug Deck; first, because he had been so brave and vigorous in the rescue of Margie and Kate Belthorpe, and second, because he had not been killed or severely wounded in the encounter of which he had been the hero.

After the meal Major Lyon and his two guests retired to the library, while the boys went to bed. Before the former separated, they had arranged a plan for the enlistment of a company of cavalry which had been discussed at the meeting the evening before. But all concerned were tired out after the labors of the night. Colonel Cosgrove was sent to the place where he had left his team, and Squire Truman was driven to the village by Levi, who had chosen this duty himself, in order to " see what was going on," as he expressed it.

The ruffians who had formed the mob had been gathered from the region around Barcreek, and not a few of them lived in the village. There appeared to be no excitement there, and the overseer started for home. On his way he had to pass the shanty of Buck Lagger, where he lived alone when he was at home, which was not much of the time. His worldly wealth, consisting of his stock of miscellaneous goods, was contained in a couple of tin trunks, with which he tramped all over the county.

As Levi drove by the hovel a bullet whistled past his head ; and, removing his soft hat, he found that the missile had passed through it, and within a couple of inches of the top of his head. It required no reasoning to convince him that Buck Lagger had fired the shot which had narrowly failed to send him to his long home. This particular kind of outrage was not an uncommon occurrence in Kentucky during the exciting period which followed the bombardment of Fort Sumter. Not a few who had enlisted in the armies of the Union were killed in this cowardly manner.

Levi Bedford reined in his horses, and then secured them to a tree. He was not a man to permit such a dastardly deed to remain unpunished a moment longer than was necessary. The ruffian, who had appeared to be the lieutenant of Captain Titus the night before, could not be far off. Passing to the rear of the shanty, Levi discovered him running for the woods a short distance from the road. In his hand he carried an old flint-lock musket, from which he had doubtless fired the shot intended to deprive Major Lyon of the services of his valuable overseer.

Buck turned to look at his pursuer, though he hardly abated his speed in doing so. His left arm was hung in a sling, the material of which looked as though it might have been a part of the flag of truce displayed on the creek bridge the night before. Levi had the heavy revolver with which he had armed himself still in his pocket; and it had even occurred to him that he might have occasion to use it before he returned from his present visit to the village.

Though he was a heavy man, Levi was agile in his movements, and the ruffian could not help seeing that his pursuer was gaining upon him. Before he reached the woods, he realized that he had no chance to escape, and he halted. Elevating his gun, he took aim at the overseer. But Levi knew that the weapon could not be loaded, for he had fired its only charge at him, and had not had time to reload it.

"It won't go off again till you load it," said the overseer, as he rushed up to him, and wrenched the musket from his hand, thinking he might try to use it as a club. "It's no fault of yours, except in your aim, that you are not a murderer, Buck Lagger!"

"I'm only sorry I missed my aim," replied Buck. "You have a revolver in your hand, and you can shoot me as soon as you please."

"Shooting is too good for a ruffian like you. If

"It won't go off again until you load it." Page 372.

I had a rope I would hang you to one of the beams of your own shanty," replied Levi, as he grasped the ruffian by the collar of his coat.

"Oh, I'll lend you a rope if you will come to the house," replied the obliging ruffian. "But hold your hand! You hurt me! You can see for yourself that I am wounded. One of Lyon's cubs put a ball through my shoulder last night."

"It's a pity he did not put it through your brains, if you've got anything of that sort in the top of your head," added Levi, as he proceeded to lead his prisoner to his wagon.

"You hurt me, Bedford!" pleaded Buck. "If you want to hang me, I'll help you do the job in proper fashion; but you needn't torture me before you do it. When we lynch a fellow we don't do that."

Levi released his hold upon the prisoner.

"My aim is better than yours; walk to my wagon, and if you attempt to run away, I won't kill you, but I will put two or three balls through your legs, so that it won't be convenient for you to run," said he, as he drove the villain before him towards the road.

"What are you go'n' to do with me, Bedford?" asked Buck.

"That's my business," replied Levi.

"Well, I think it rayther consarns me too."

"If you live long enough you will find out in time. Now get into the wagon."

"Are you go'n' to take me down to Lyon's place?" asked Buck, looking his captor in the face as they stopped at the side of the vehicle.

"Get in quick, or I may hurt you again!" said Levi impatiently. "You won't get killed by a ball from my shooter, but you may have another wound."

Probably the ruffian preferred shooting to hanging, and the remark of the overseer did not please him. If he had told his whole story, he would have said that he had been unable to sleep on account of the wound in his shoulder, and for that reason he had been up early enough to see Levi drive past his shanty with Squire Truman. The suffering made him angry, stimulated his desire for revenge; and he had tried to put the overseer out of the way.

He pretended to be more afraid of wounds than of death; and with the assistance of Levi he climbed into the wagon, taking his place on the front seat as directed. His captor put the gun he had brought with him into the wagon, and then seated himself beside his prisoner. The spirited horses went off at a lively pace, and Buck immediately complained that the motion increased his pain.

"That wasn't a bad scheme of yours to get possession of Colonel Belthorpe's girls, Buck. You meant to trade them off for the arms, I suppose," said Levi, as he reduced the pace of his horses to a walk; for he desired, if he could, to obtain some information from his prisoner.

"That was just it, Bedford; and if that cub of Lyon's hadn't interfered, we should have had the arms before this time," replied Buck, with both a chuckle and a groan.

"Why didn't you try it on Major Lyon's girls first, for that would have brought the matter nearer home?"

"That's just what we meant to do," replied Buck, with refreshing confidence in his custodian. "That was my plan; but Cap'n Titus was obstinate, and wouldn't hear to me. He ain't much of a cap'n; and I'd had the arms and the rest o' the things if he had left it to me."

"What was your plan, Buck?" asked Levi quietly.

"That's tellin'; we may try it on some other time, if I live long enough. Our folks are fightin' this thing on principle, and we ain't go'n' to see the good old State of Kaintuck turned over to the Abolitionists."

"What do you mean by Abolitionists, Buck?"

"Such fellers as Lyon, Cosgrove, Belthorpe."

"They are all slaveholders."

"They're all Lincolnites, and gave arms to their niggers to shoot down white Kaintuckians last night," replied Buck bitterly.

"Only when a mob of ruffians came down upon them to burn their property and carry off their daughters!" added Levi. "They are Union men, and they will stand by the old flag as long as there is anything left of them."

"The Union's busted!"

"Not much! Why don't you enlist in the Confederate army, and carry out your principles? You are a cowardly ruffian, Buck!"

"We can do more good to the cause by stoppin' here, Bedford; and when I git command of that Home Guard, as I shall afore long, I'll clean out the Abolitionists in less'n a week," said Buck boastfully.

"If you live long enough," suggested Levi.

"If I don't I'm willin' to be a martyr to the good cause!" protested the reprobate.

As before suspected by Levi and his employer, "that Home Guard" was composed of the ruffians who had been the assailants the night before. Levi drove to the fort, where a guard of a dozen negroes, under the command of General, had been placed over the arms and ammunition. The prisoner was taken from the wagon, and permitted to lie on one of the beds which had been brought from the mansion the night before for the use of the defenders of the plantation. General and his men were charged to shoot the captive if he attempted to escape.

CHAPTER XXXI

DR. FALKIRK VISITS RIVERLAWN

LEVI BEDFORD, in spite of his threats to hang his prisoner, was a kind-hearted man, and he did what he could for the comfort of Buck Lagger. He had often been called upon to prescribe for the sick or injured among the hands on the plantation. He examined the wound of the ruffian; but it was beyond his skill, and he did not attempt to treat the patient.

During the absence of the expedition for the defence of Lyndhall he had done what he could for those who had been wounded on the creek road; but he was not an expert in the treatment of gunshot wounds. There was little he could do for them; and early in the morning he had sent Frank to procure the attendance of Dr. Falkirk, who resided near the village. He had been called to a case on a plantation several miles from Barcreek. He had not returned when Levi went to his bed.

Major Lyon and the boys had taken to their beds as soon as the guests departed, and the overseer was in condition to follow their example. The premises were well guarded along the creek, and two men with breech-loaders in their hands were in charge of the wounded prisoner. In the mansion Mrs. Lyon and her daughters, who had been up most of the night, for they could not sleep while the major and his sons were in danger, had gone to bed to obtain needed rest.

Even the hands who had been on service the whole or a part of the eventful night were asleep, and the guard at Fort Bedford had been relieved. Levi slept soundly on the bed he had taken within the works, in spite of the groans mingled with curses of the wounded ruffian. There was no white person awake on the plantation to wonder what was to be the outcome of the events of the night. Doubtless Colonel Cosgrove and Squire Truman were also sleeping off the fatigues of the night. The aggressive ruffians had fled to their several homes, defeated, exhausted, and disgusted with the result of their labors in the cause of Secession. There was a calm after the storm.

Dr. Falkirk appeared about the middle of the

forenoon. He was of Scotch descent; but his father had settled in New Orleans, and the son became as violent a "fire-eater" as though he had been the possessor of half a thousand slaves. He had made a fortune in the practice of his profession, and had purchased a plantation in Kentucky, on the outskirts of Barcreek, where he intended to end his days in peace and quiet. But some of his investments had been unfortunate, and he had been compelled to resume practice.

His skill as a physician and surgeon had brought to him an abundant practice, though his patients were widely scattered, and he was obliged to pass much of his time in his gig. When the troubles of the nation began, he developed into a Secessionist of the most ultra stripe. He was a highly educated man and a fluent speaker in public and private. In the Lyceum of the village he and Squire Truman were often pitted against each other, and one was quite as outspoken as the other.

But Dr. Falkirk was faithful to his patients, poor or rich, and without regard to their creed or politics. Though his fortune had been impaired, he was still in comfortable circumstances, and never refused to visit any sick person to whom he was called, with no regard to color or the expectation of payment for his services. In fact, he was the beau-ideal of a good physician, and held the honor of his profession above every other consideration.

The men on patrol at the bridge conducted the doctor to the fort as soon as he appeared, in obedience to the orders of the overseer. When he reached Fort Bedford he manifested no little astonishment at the appearance of the old icehouse, with its four embrasures, through which the twelve-pounders could be seen. The negroes with breech-loaders in their hands were a disgusting exhibition to him, and he turned up his nose, though he made no remark.

The sentinel at the door politely ushered him into the presence of his patient. Without asking any questions in regard to the manner in which the sufferer had received his wound, Dr. Falkirk proceeded to examine him. Buck Lagger was still in great pain, and had kept up a continual groaning all the forenoon. The doctor immediately gave him a couple of little pills, intended to ease the pain. The skilful surgeon discovered that a bullet was embedded in the shoulder, and he took from the handbag the instruments for its extraction.

Then he called upon a couple of the guards to assist him. There were but two sentinels in charge of the fort, who were faithfully marching up and down outside the door. But they paid no attention to the call of the doctor. Each of them seemed to be impressed with the idea that the protection of the plantation and the lives of all the family depended upon him, and that it would be treason for them to leave their posts.

"Can't you hear me, you black rascals?" demanded the surgeon in a loud tone. "Come here, one of you!"

"Can't leabe de post, Mars'r Doctor," replied one of the men.

Probably there was no enemy within a mile of the fort; but they had been told that they were not to leave their places for anything, and they were disposed literally to obey their orders. But the angry tones of the surgeon had awakened Levi Bedford, who was sleeping at one end of the fort. He sprang to his feet, and discovered the doctor at the couch of his patient.

"Good-morning, Doctor Falkirk," said he. "I did not know you were here."

"I knew I was here, and I ordered those black scoundrels to assist me, and they refused to do so," replied the doctor angrily.

"They only obey their orders, but they rather overdo it. I will assist you, Doctor," added Levi.

"Orders!" exclaimed the professional gentleman contemptuously. "One would think this was a regular garrison."

"That is about what it is," replied the overseer.

"Humbug!" said the surgeon, as he turned to his patient.

Levi called in one of the sentinels, and the bed of the wounded man was drawn out before the door where the light was best, and the doctor proceeded with his work. The morphine pills he had given the patient appeared to have relieved his pain. The operator probed for the ball, and soon found it. Then he dressed the wound with as much care as though the sufferer had been a Kentucky colonel. He had hardly completed his office before Buck dropped asleep under the influence of the powerful medicine he had taken. The bed was moved back without waking him, and Dr. Falkirk passed out of the fort, followed by the overseer.

"Keep the man quiet for a week, and give him anything he wants to eat," said he, as he looked about him at the warlike preparations which had been finished the day before.

"We have three more wounded men in the hospital who need a surgeon," added Levi.

"What are those niggers doing over on the other side of the creek?" asked the surgeon, whose gaze had wandered to the grove at the side of the road. Some of the hands had been directed to bury the man who had fallen behind the tree where he had taken refuge from the shots of the defenders of the plantation.

He had been seen in the act of levelling his gun at the advancing column, and Levi had brought him down before he could discharge his weapon.

"They are burying a man that fell in the skirmish last night," Levi replied to the question of the doctor.

"What skirmish?" inquired Dr. Falkirk, with evident astonishment.

"You don't appear to have heard the news, Doctor," replied the overseer.

"What news? I was called to General Longman's plantation last evening; I spent the night there, and did not get home till half-past eight this morning."

As briefly as possible Levi gave the details of the events of the preceding night, beginning with the meeting at Big Bend, and ending with the final defeat and surrender of the ruffians.

"An Abolition row!" said the doctor contemptuously.

"Not exactly, Dr. Falkirk; it was a Secession row!" added Levi with energy.

"Brought about by the insane wrangling of the traitors to the State of Kentucky!" snapped the surgeon.

"The traitors to the State of Kentucky are loyal to the government of the United States and the Union," protested the overseer.

"There is no longer any United States, and the Union has ceased to exist! The men who are making all this trouble in Kentucky are those who are trying to make war upon the Southern Confederacy, to subdue and enslave a dozen sovereign States!" argued the doctor, almost furiously.

"I reckon it's no use for you and me to argue this question, for we don't live in the same world on that subject," said the overseer, with a smile on his round face. "But Kentucky is for the Union by a large majority, and what you call sovereign States are in rebellion against the lawful authorities of the nation, and the insurrection will be put down just as sure as fate."

"This used to be a free country, though it isn't so now; but every man can have his own opinion as long as he is willing to be responsible for it."

"It isn't exactly a free country as long as the loyal citizens of this county cannot hold a meeting without being attacked by the ruffians of Secession, as was the case at Big Bend last night. Then the same villains came over here in a mob of a hundred to burn Major Lyon's house, and capture his daughters, as they tried to do with Colonel Belthorpe's girls. They did not succeed, and some of them were shot down in the attempt. The right to commit such outrages as these is what you call free; but we at Riverlawn don't understand it in just that way."

"But, according to your own statement, Mr. Bedford, your people had stolen the arms intended for the company of the Home Guards whom Captain Titus Lyon has enlisted," returned the doctor.

"We took possession of the arms and ammunition, including the two guns at those embrasures, to prevent these ruffians from using them against the loyal citizens of the county in carrying out their ideas of freedom," said Levi stoutly. "Do you believe these ruffians, the offscourings of the county, ought to be permitted to burn, ravage, and destroy the homes of some of the most respectable people in this vicinity, Dr. Falkirk?"

"But your people were the aggressors, and I think they were justified in trying to recover the property that had been stolen from them."

"The ruffians issued their threats to burn the mansion of Major Lyon before the arms entered into the question."

The discussion might have continued all day, if Sam, Colonel Belthorpe's house servant, had not ridden up at this moment.

"I come for the doctor, sar," said the man.

"Who is sick at Lyndhall, Sam?" asked Levi with much interest.

"Nobody sick, Mars'r Bedford; but Mars'r Tilford's very bad with his wound, and Mars'r Cunnel send me for the doctor," replied the servant.

"Is this another of your victims, Mr. Bedford?" asked the doctor with a heavy sneer.

"It is Colonel Belthorpe's overseer. He refused to assist in protecting the family from the ruffians, and left the mansion. It seems that he was shot in attempting to join your army, doctor."

"He's a brave fellow! I will go and see him."

"But he deserted your army of ruffians, and crawled back to the house, where the girls nursed him and cared for him. Now the colonel sends for you to patch him up, the ingrate!"

"True to his principles against his employer!"

The doctor was conducted to the hospital, where he did his duty faithfully to those who had been wounded, though Levi reminded him that they belonged to "his army." None of them were in a bad way, and the surgeon said they would be all right in a few days.

All was quiet again at Riverlawn, and the sleepers used most of the day in their beds. On the following morning, after the whole evening had been used in discussing the events of the preceding night, everything went along as usual on the plantation. No more ruffians appeared on the other side of the creek, though Major Lyon and the boys remained on duty at the fort.

"What is to be the end of all these disturbances, Noah?" asked Mrs. Lyon, as the family seated themselves at the breakfast-table the second morning after the battle, as they had come to call the events of that stormy night.

"I think we all understand what is before us. We are to have war, and I don't believe it will end in a hundred days, as the statesman at Washington says," replied Major Lyon; and even some of his family had learned to apply this title to him. "Within a few days we shall begin to form a company of cavalry. I am still of military age, and the boys are old enough to take part in the struggle before us. But Levi will remain on the plantation; and as the hands have proved that they can stand up under fire, he will have the means of protecting you, Ruth."

"Of course we shall be sorry to have you go, but I agree with you, Noah, that your country has a claim upon you which you cannot shirk," replied Mrs. Lyon, struggling to repress a tear.

"Buck Lagger asked me this morning if I

thought he was well enough to be hung," said Levi, perhaps to break off the conversation in that line.

"Do you think of hanging him, Levi?" inquired the planter.

"That is what I promised him; but I leave that matter to you, Major Lyon. He is a murderer at heart, and the bullet from his gun passed within two inches of the top of my head."

"I should not like to have him hung at Riverlawn," added the planter. "I will talk with him, and see what can be done; but there is no law in this part of the country just now."

The family were to dine that day at Lyndhall at one o'clock, so that none of them need be absent after dark. Major Lyon left the house, and was directing his steps towards Fort Bedford for an interview, when he saw Captain Titus Lyon driving over the bridge. He did not care to meet him, but he could hardly avoid doing so, and he stopped in front of the flower-garden. Titus fastened his horse to a post, and approached his brother.

CHAPTER XXXII

THE ARRIVAL OF THE RECRUITING OFFICER

Noah Lyon was not glad to see his brother; but this was a new experience to him, for he had always had a fraternal feeling for him, and had done everything in his power for him when he needed assistance. He was willing to believe that Titus was sincere in his political convictions, though it was impossible for him to understand how he could be a traitor to the Union.

At the North, both of the great parties were united in support of the government, and at his former home Titus would have been almost alone if he had clung to the opinions which now actuated him; for "copperheads" were rare serpents there. Noah's brother would hardly have been one amid the surroundings of his former home. It was evident that Kentucky whiskey and a feeling of revenge, born of his disappointment over the provisions of Duncan's will, had done more to make him a Secessionist than the workings of his own reason.

"I have come to see you once more, Noah," Titus began quite mildly for him, though it was plain to his brother that he was primed with his favorite beverage as usual.

He was not intoxicated in any reasonable sense of the word; and he had plainly resolved to make the interview a peaceable one. Doubtless he had a point to carry, but within a few days he had probably learned more about the character of his brother than he had ever known before. Noah could not say that he was glad to see him, for even a "society lie" was repulsive to him.

"I hope we shall be peaceable and pleasant this time, even if we cannot agree in everything," he replied very gently and with a smile upon his honest face.

"That's just what I want, Noah; and I have always tried to make things peaceable between us," added Titus.

Noah wondered if he believed what he uttered, after coming with a mob to his plantation to burn and ravage his property; but whatever doubts he had, he kept them to himself, for he knew that the thought which was uppermost in his mind, if expressed, would only irritate his brother, and provoke him to wrath.

"I trust you will continue to do so," was his next remark, though he thought that even this was admitting too much.

"There is a question between us, Noah," continued Titus, struggling to retain his quiet demeanor as he approached the point of difference between them. "I won't say a word about the way I have been used up to three days ago, for I want to be on kind of brotherly terms with you, if we don't agree on politics."

"I assuredly desire to be on brotherly terms with you, and it shall not be any fault of mine that we are not brothers in spirit as well as in fact," replied Noah, who became slightly hopeful of Titus, for he had not recently heard him speak so many friendly words.

"There is only one question between us now, and we might just as well come right down to business at once," said Titus, very nervous in his manner, as though his hope of accomplishing anything with the stern patriot his brother had proved to be was only slight. "Of course you know that I mean about the arms."

"I understand you, Brother Titus," replied Noah, exceedingly unwilling to fan the fire that was smouldering in the breast of the leader of the ruffians.

"It seems to me that there ought to be no trouble between two brothers like you and me about settling a question of this kind," continued Titus, still toying with the subject. "Of course you must admit that the arms did not belong to you."

"No more than Fort Sumter and a dozen other places built and maintained by the Union belonged to the insurgents who have taken possession of them," answered Noah very quietly.

"That's another matter," returned the captain, evidently thrown off his base by this home argument.

"It is precisely the same thing to my mind."

"Do you call stealing my property the same thing as a nation taking possession of forts and such things within its own territory, Noah Lyon?"

"Precisely the same thing, though on a smaller scale."

"I used to think you had lots of logic in your head, Noah; but I believe you hain't got none on't left," retorted Titus, relapsing into what he called his "week-day speech." "I was in hopes you had come to sunthin' like reason, and would be ready to give up the property you stole."

"I shall be quite ready to give it up when the insurrectionists give up the property they stole."

"The two things ain't no more like than a' nigger is like a white man," protested Titus, the bad blood, mingled with whiskey, in his veins beginning to boil.

"I think we had better not discuss this question any more, Brother Titus. It only stirs up bad blood, and does not accomplish anything," suggested Noah.

"I s'pose I'm to understand from what you say that you don't mean to give up the arms you stole from me," said Titus, doubling his fist, and holding it near the face of his brother.

"I do not consider that I have any right to deliver the arms to you; for I understand that they were to be used to arm what you call the Home Guards, or, in other words, the ruffians who came over here to burn my house and lay waste my property. I shall not give up the arms to you, or to any other person representing the enemies of the Union. The insurrectionists have set the example of stealing arms, as you call it, and forts, and public buildings by wholesale; and the Secessionists of Kentucky are robbing the Union men of their arms. I hold that the precedent has been well established by those on your side of the question."

"I don't care for your precedents, and I wish my brother would deal with the one question between us."

"I am entirely willing to do so, Brother Titus. You wish me to furnish the brands with which you can burn my house and those of my neighbors."

"What sort of bosh is that?" demanded Titus, who did not see the point.

"If I should return to you the military supplies in my possession, they would be used to arm the horde of ruffians you marched over here to burn my property the other night."

"They would be used to arm my company of the Home Guards; and they are regular under the call of the Governor of Kentucky."

"The Legislature of the State repudiate him, and the people are enlisting the troops he refused to furnish."

"The Legislature is a fraud, and don't rightly

represent the will of the people. I came over here with the Home Guard and other friends of the cause to get the arms. You turned our own weapons against us, and without arms we could do nothing against armed niggers."

"I have put my place in a condition to be defended, and I have called upon the United States government to send a body of troops here to protect the Union people from the outrages of your people."

"They will have a hot time of it when they get here," replied Titus with a sneer.

"In the meantime we shall defend ourselves. We have been attacked"—

"You have not been attacked!" protested the captain. "We came over here to demand the arms. We put up a flag of truce, and wanted to talk with you; but you drove us off, and fired upon us," answered Titus.

"Your people began the attack at the schoolhouse."

"'Tain't so! Some of our men went to the meeting, and you fell upon 'em there."

"They had no business there, for the call was addressed to the Union men of the county. They disturbed the meeting, and we put them out. Then your company gathered in the woods, demanding 'Lyon and his cubs.' My friends stood by me, and the meeting shouldered all the responsibility in regard to the arms. We agreed to get up a company of cavalry for the United States."

"And you mean to arm 'em with the things you stole from me!" almost gasped Captain Titus.

"When a proper officer comes here he will give you a receipt for the property."

"Which would not be worth the paper it is written on to me!"

"Not unless you could show that you were a Union man."

"My men are bent on gettin' them arms, and they will have them!"

"They will have to fight for them," added Noah quietly.

Perhaps the interview would have become still more stormy if Levi Bedford had not approached with a gentleman wearing the uniform of a cavalry officer. Captain Titus did not like the looks of him, and, judging that Noah had proceeded farther than he had suspected in providing for the protection of the loyal people of the county, he beat a hasty retreat; and he drove across the bridge at a rate so furious as to indicate his state of mind.

"Major Lyon, this is Lieutenant Gordon, of the United States Volunteer Service," said Levi, as he approached with the visitor.

"I am very glad to see you, Lieutenant Gordon," added the planter, extending his hand to the officer.

"I am rejoiced to meet you, Major Lyon; and I am glad to find that you are a military man," replied Lieutenant Gordon.

"But I am not a military man, and was never even a private in a military company," replied the major, laughing at the natural mistake of his guest. "I protested against answering to my title till I found it was useless to do so."

"If you are not a major now, perhaps you will be one very soon. I am sent here by Major-General Buell, in reply to your letter to him," added the officer, producing a document which authorized him to enlist, enroll, and muster in a company of cavalry.

"You are the very man I wished most to see," said the planter, after he had glanced at the paper.

"Come to the house, if you please, and we will consider the object of your visit."

"I had some trouble in getting here; for our information is that General Buckner, with a considerable force of the enemy, is moving towards Bowling Green, probably with the intention of occupying it, and I did not deem it wise to go there, as I had been directed to do."

"What you say is news to us," replied the major, as he conducted the officer into the house. "Have you been to breakfast, Lieutenant?"

"I have not, sir. I left the train last night at Dripping Spring, which they told me was the last station before coming to Bowling Green. I found a place to sleep, and a stable for my horse, which I brought down in a baggage car, I started out early this morning to find Riverlawn, and here I am."

The lieutenant was shown to one of the guest chambers of the mansion, and the planter ordered breakfast for him, instructing Aunty Diana to provide the best the house afforded. The officer wanted his saddle-bags, which had gone to the stable with his horse, and they were carried up for him. Before the morning meal was ready he came down, and was presented to Mrs. Lyon and her daughters.

After he had washed and dressed himself, he proved to be what the girls declared was a handsome man. He was not more than twenty-five years old, and had a decidedly military air, and manner. He made himself very agreeable to the ladies; and Dorcas, who was a full-grown woman in stature, wondered if he was to remain long at Riverlawn.

"You are on the very ragged edge of the Rebellion, Major Lyon," said the visitor, as he seated himself at the table. "I should say you were not more than fifteen miles from Bowling Green."

"I suppose you are acquainted with the country about here, Lieutenant?" added the planter.

"Not at all, Major; I was born and always lived in the State of Ohio; and I have never been in this direction farther than Lexington. But I know that Bowling Green is near the junction of two railroads into Tennessee and the South; and the Confederates can't help seeing that it is an important point for them to possess and hold. There will be some fighting in this quarter before long."

"There has been a skirmish or two. The Home

Guards are making some trouble in this vicinity, and I have put my place in a condition to be defended from their assaults," added Major Lyon.

He proceeded to describe the affair at the bridge and on the two roads, in which the officer was much interested. He was particularly delighted with the capture of the arms and ammunition. The planter then conducted him to Fort Bedford.

CHAPTER XXXIII

ONE AGAINST THREE ON THE ROAD

Lieutenant Gordon looked about him with something like amazement as he entered the fort. Levi Bedford and the boys had arranged the arms in racks made by the carpenters. The two Napoleons, as the twelve-pounders are sometimes called, were pointed out at the embrasures, and the aspect of the place was decidedly warlike. Buck Lagger had been removed to the hospital, where he found three of his comrades of the Home Guards, two others having been sent to their homes.

"These are my sons, Lieutenant," said Major Lyon, introducing each of them by name. "They are stout boys, very nearly eighteen years old, and are good riders. They will be the first recruits to put their names on your paper after mine when you enter upon the work of your mission."

"They are the kind of recruits I like to add to our forces, for they are not only stout, but intelligent," replied the officer, as he took from his breast pocket the printed form of document for the enlistment of soldiers. "Where did you get the name of this fort, Major Lyon?"

"From my overseer, the first man you met on my premises. He was formerly connected with an artillery company in Tennessee; but he is a Union man to the core," replied the planter, who proceeded to give Levi the excellent character he deserved.

"Then he will be our fourth recruit?" suggested the lieutenant.

"No, sir; he is about fifty years old, and he is to take charge of my plantation in my absence. But I think there are over a hundred men in this vicinity who are ready to put their names down on your paper. The horses are all ready for them, for they were pledged in the Union meeting of which I told you."

"We shall not need the horses at first," added the lieutenant.

"Not need the horses, sir!" exclaimed Deck, who was listening with all his ears to the conversation. "How are we going to get up a company of cavalry without horses?"

"The company will be first drilled like infantry,

and the exercises with horses come in later," replied the officer with a smile at the eagerness of the boy; and Artie was just as enthusiastic, though he said very little.

"Both of them will make good soldiers, sir, for they have been under fire in a small way," added the father.

"I should say that you have little need of soldiers for the protection of your place, Major Lyon," added the officer, as he looked at the cannon and the breech-loaders arranged around the interior of the fort. "Are these the arms you captured in the cavern?"

"The same, sir; and they have already enabled us to defend ourselves from the mob that came over here to burn my house."

"These muskets must have cost a round sum of money, for they are of the best quality, and have the latest improvements. Unfortunately they are not adapted to the use of cavalry, and we shall need carbines."

"Well, it is something to keep them out of the hands of the enemy," replied Major Lyon. "I suppose we are ready to make a beginning in the business before us, Lieutenant Gordon. What is the first thing to be done?"

"The first thing is to enlist the men," replied the officer, as he took from his pocket a handbill, printed for use in some other locality. "We must post bills like this one all about this vicinity."

"We can't get them printed short of Bowling Green," said Major Lyon, after he had read the placard. "And the Home Guards will pull them down as fast as we can put them up."

"But some of them will be seen, and the news that a recruiting office has been established here will soon circulate. You are between two fires here, and your foes will talk about it even more than your friends. We must have the handbills at any rate."

"Very well. Artie, this will be a mission for you."

"I am ready and willing to do anything I can," replied the quiet boy; and in half an hour he was mounted on a fleet horse on his way to a printing-office.

"I suppose the village of which you speak would be the best place to establish the recruiting office," suggested Lieutenant Gordon, as soon as Artie had gone to the stable for a horse.

"I am afraid not," replied the planter. "I fear

the ruffians who abound in that vicinity would mob you. Why not establish the office here, where we shall be able to protect you?"

"It seems to be too far from any centre of population," said the officer.

"All the better for that; for in the village they would not only mob you, but the ruffians would intimidate those who were willing to enlist. People in this vicinity don't mind going two or three miles when business calls them," continued the planter.

"I shall adopt your suggestion, Major Lyon," returned the recruiting officer, as he proceeded to alter the handbill to suit the locality. "I suppose everybody in this neighborhood will know where to find Riverlawn."

"Everybody in the county," replied the major, as Artie dashed up to the door of the fort, where the officer gave him his instructions, and the planter supplied him with money to pay the bill.

"I think I had better take one of those revolvers in my pocket," suggested Artie. "If I get into any trouble it may be of use to me."

"Do you expect to get into any trouble, my

boy?" asked the major, anxiously gazing into the messenger's face.

"I don't expect any trouble, but something may happen."

"Perhaps I had better send half a dozen of the boys with you," suggested his father.

"The boys?" queried the lieutenant, wondering where they were to come from, as he had seen only two of them.

"I mean the negroes who defended the place the other night," added the planter. "They have learned to handle the breech-loaders, and they would fight for my boys as long as there was anything left of them."

"I dare say they would," replied the officer with a significant smile. "But if you send six negroes armed with breech-loaders to Bowling Green, you may be sure there will be a row."

"Just my sentiments," added Levi Bedford. "I don't think Artie will have any trouble if he goes alone."

"Very well, let him go alone; but I am confident half a dozen of the boys would make it hot for any band that attempted to molest him," said the major; and the messenger departed on his mission.

"Have you an American flag, Major Lyon?" asked the lieutenant when he had gone.

"Two of them, for my brother always celebrated the Fourth of July."

"We always hoist one on a recruiting office."

Under the direction of Levi a flagstaff was erected in front of the fort, and before dinner-time the Star Spangled Banner was spread to the breeze. Major Lyon took off his hat and bowed to it as soon as it was shaken out to the breeze; and cheers were heard from the negroes in the field beyond the stables.

"If you had set that flag over your office in the village, it would have been hauled down and trampled under foot inside of an hour," said the planter.

"Are the people of this vicinity so disloyal as that?" asked Lieutenant Gordon, astonished at the remark. "I supposed the Unionists were in the majority here."

"So they are; but they are not half so demonstrative as the other side."

The bell rang at the door of the mansion for dinner; and while the family were attending to this midday duty, Artie was entering the county town. He had taken his dinner with him, and had eaten it as he approached his destination. There were two printing-offices in the place, and he called at the first one he saw.

"What's this? 'Union Cavalry!'" demanded the printer, as he read the head-line in displayed type.

"What will you charge for printing two hundred copies of that bill, and doing it while I wait?" asked Artie.

"'Riverlawn!'" added the man, as he continued to read the placard. "Who are you, boy?"

"My name is Artemas Lyon, and my father lives at Riverlawn," replied Artie.

"Well, Artemas Lyon, I would not print that bill if your father would give me a hundred dollars a letter for doing it!" stormed the printer, as he tossed the copy back to the messenger with as much indignation in his manner as in his speech.

"All right, sir; if you don't want to do the job you needn't!" replied Artie, as he returned the bill to his pocket and moved to the door.

"Stop a minute, boy! So you are recruiting at

Riverlawn for the Abolition army?" called the printer, who was perhaps a member of the Home Guards. "I want to know something about that business."

"If you want to enlist in the Union army, you can do so at Riverlawn. I am in a hurry, and I can't stop to answer any questions," replied Artie, as he bolted out at the door.

"What are you doing here, Artie Lyon?" called a voice from the other side of the street as he was unhitching his horse.

It was Colonel Cosgrove, though his house was some distance farther up the street. The lawyer came over to him, and he explained the object of his visit to the county town.

"You ought to have come to me at once, Artie," said the colonel, as the messenger showed him the handbill. "That printer runs a Secession paper, and he would lose all his subscribers if it was known that he printed a placard like this. Come with me, and I will get the work done for you."

Artie followed him to the office of a Union paper, and it looked as though it was in a more prosperous condition than the other. The printer readily undertook the work, and promised to have it done by three o'clock in the afternoon. The messenger was invited to the mansion of Colonel Cosgrove, where he dined with the family.

"I signed the letter to General Buell with your father, asking him to send a recruiting officer to this locality," said the colonel, as he conducted his guest to the library. "I am very glad he has come. I should have been in favor of establishing his office in this place if it were not a current report that the town is to be occupied by the Confederates within a short time."

"Father thought Riverlawn would be a better place than Barcreek village for it," added Artie.

"I think he is right."

The messenger was called upon to tell the news of his vicinity, and he mentioned all that had occurred since the fight, including the attempt to murder Levi Bedford, and the capture of Buck Lagger. At three o'clock Artie went to the printing-office, and found the handbills all ready for him. He paid the bill, and went back to the colonel's house for his horse, which had been as well cared for as his rider. He was advised to hurry out of the town, and he galloped his horse

"'STOP, BOY!' SHOUTED THE MAN." Page 413.

for the first mile till he reached the open country. Half a mile ahead of him was a wood.

The young horseman had reduced his speed to a moderate gait before he reached this grove; but he had not gone far before three men stepped out of the bushes and stood in front of him in the road. They had flint-lock guns in their hands, and it looked as though they were there for a purpose.

"Stop, boy!" shouted the man who stood in the middle of the road, with one on each side of him.

"What do you want of me?" demanded Artie, with his right hand on the handle of his revolver.

"I want them handbills you just got printed," replied the spokesman. "We ain't go'n' to have no Abolition troops enlisted round here. And that ain't all nuther; we're gwine to clean out that Major Lyon that sent you over here."

"Hand over the papers and we won't hurt you," added another of the trio.

"I shall not give them up!" replied Artie as decidedly as though he had the new company of cavalry behind him. "Get out of the road, or I will ride over you!"

"You won't give em' up, won't yer?" returned

the man in the middle, as he brought his old gun to his shoulder.

"No!" yelled the messenger, as he fired his revolver at the spokesman.

At the same moment he drove his heels into the flanks of his spirited steed, giving him the rein as he did so. The horse darted ahead like a shot from a gun, and choosing his way between the men, he knocked two of them over, and galloped on his way. The sudden movement of the animal had prevented the men from bringing their guns to bear upon him. The man on his feet fired, and the rider heard a ball whistle near him. In a minute he was out of the range of such weapons, and reached Riverlawn in season for supper.

He delivered the bills to the lieutenant, and told his story. The next morning the early risers saw these placards posted all over Barcreek village, and along the roads for five miles in all directions.

CHAPTER XXXIV

THE FIRE THAT WAS STARTED AT RIVERLAWN

Levi and Deck were the bill-stickers, and the night was chosen as the time to post them, in order that the paste might be well dried and hardened before they were seen. They had taken a wagon, and with the coachman for driver they had gone their round after people generally were asleep. Wherever a flat surface could be found by the light of a lantern, on barns, fences, rocks, and shops, a placard was posted.

It would take the ruffian brigade a long time to pull them all down, after the paste was dry; and the very wrath of these men would assist in advertising the recruiting office at Riverlawn. The fact that the papers were ready for signature could hardly fail to be known all over the vicinity early in the morning, and all over the county in a day or two. The information was already circulating in Bowling Green; for the editor of *The Planter*, at whose office Artie had applied to have the bills printed, had made it known soon enough to enable the three ruffians to make an attempt to suppress the placards.

The Kentuckian was the loyal paper, and would doubtless make at least an item of the fact that the recruiting office had been established. Possibly the other journal would make a "dastardly outrage" of the shot which Artie had fired at the three ruffians who beset him on the road. There was no doubt in the minds of the active men at Riverlawn that the recruiting office would be known to the fullest extent even the day after the bills were posted; for even the women would gossip about it as they went from house to house, and the loafers in the "corner grocery" would have an exciting theme for discussion.

The people had been terrorized by the ruffians, who had banded together as Home Guards in this locality; and they had made noise enough to create the belief among the less demonstrative citizens that the Secessionists were in a majority. But Squire Truman had punctured this bubble by an actual canvass of the inhabitants, and proved, as did the vote of the Legislature, that loyalty was the predominant sentiment.

When Artie Lyon returned from his mission to the county town with the bundle of placards in his possession, there was so much excitement at Fort Bedford that he said nothing about his adventure on the road. Lieutenant Gordon had counselled the sending away of the four wounded ruffians, who had been carefully nursed and fed at the hospital. They were all recovering from their injuries, and all of them walked about the premises during a portion of the day.

"We don't want a lot of spies and enemies in our midst, for they will report everything that is done to their friends who have been permitted to visit them," he reasoned with the planter, and the major agreed with him; and this was the work which was in progress when Artie arrived.

Deck had made a hero of himself at the crosscut, and his brother was not inclined to wear a wreath of laurel for the little exploit on the road. He slept upon it, and the next morning he felt that it was his duty to inform his father of the occurrence, as one of the indications of public sentiment in the county. The ruffians evidently intended that the Union army should not be recruited in the county.

Major Lyon praised him for his spirited conduct, and the lieutenant made him blush with his commendation. But the incident was discussed more as an exponent of the temper of the ruffians than as an exhibition of pluck and courage on the part of the boy.

"You were right in calling these fellows the ruffians, Major Lyon," said the recruiting officer. "I have no doubt there are many respectable Secessionists in this part of the State, but I am confident they do not associate with such fellows as you have had to deal with."

"Such men are simply in favor of neutrality, which I look upon as a fraud and a humbug," replied the planter. "They are gentlemen in the truest sense of the word, and I am only sorry they are on the wrong side of the question."

The American flag was flying on the newly erected staff, and during the forenoon the carpenters were busy preparing the fort for the new use to which it was to be devoted. A skylight was put in the roof to afford better light, a desk was brought from the library, and enclosed in rails for the officer. Dr. Farnwright, who lived at Brownsville, was appointed medical examiner, and the office was all ready for business by noon.

Before that time a dozen men had presented themselves for enlistment, and had signed the roll. A camp for the volunteers was to be established in the vicinity as soon as practicable. The lieutenant had sent off a requisition for uniforms, arms, provisions, and such other supplies as would be needed. At dinner all were in excellent spirits, and the location of the camp was discussed, and was decided after considerable disagreement. When the party returned to the fort they found half a dozen men waiting for the officer. While he was questioning them, a tremendous outcry came from the direction of the mansion.

"Fire! fire!" screamed the two girls, assisted by all the females in the house.

The planter, Levi, and the boys ran with all their might to the point from which the alarm came. Before they reached it a considerable cloud of smoke rose from the rear of the building, indicating the locality of the fire.

"The house is on fire!" screamed Dorcas.

Major Lyon ran into the house; but Levi, as soon as he saw the smoke, rushed around the mansion, followed by the two boys. In the rear of the building was an ell, to which a one-story structure had been added as a storeroom. The flames rose from this part of the house. Against it was heaped up a pile of dry wood and other combustibles, and it was instantly apparent to the overseer that the fire was the work of an incendiary. No time was to be lost, for the flames were rapidly gathering headway, and in a few minutes the whole mansion would be on fire.

The hands began to appear on the spot, and Levi sent the first one to the stable for pitchforks; but he did not wait for them, and began to draw away the combustibles with such sticks as he could obtain. The boys followed his example, and the dry wood, blazing against the side of the storeroom, was soon removed from its dangerous proximity to the building. The work was effectively completed with the pitchforks as soon as they came.

"There are three men running away towards the swamp!" shouted Deck.

"I see them!" added Artie.

"Put the fire out first, and we will attend to them afterwards!" said Levi. "Keep an eye on them while you work, and see where they go."

The burning brands were removed from the

house, but the flames were already communicated to the building. Mrs. Lyon had not gone out at the front door with the girls, but had rushed to the storeroom, where she was soon joined by her husband. All the buckets in the house were brought into use, including half a dozen leather ones that hung in the main hall, and all the women were carrying water to the exposed point. The fire had not yet come through the side of the building, and the buckets were passed out the window to the overseer.

In a few moments the fire was thoroughly drowned out, and everybody breathed more freely. The lieutenant and the recruits had followed the others, and assisted in putting out the fire. Deck and Artie turned their attention to the three men they had seen, and had started in pursuit of them; but Levi called them back. Then he sent to the fort for several revolvers, not doubting that the men who were engaged in this desperate venture were armed.

But he did not wait for them, and told Artie to bring them to him as soon as the messenger returned. Gordon and Deck went with him. The great river was directly in the rear of the mansion, with the road to the county town on its shore. The swamp between the lawn and the road was a quagmire of mud, which was impassable for man or beast. The green from which the estate had been named was high ground, and bordered on the river, with the swamp between them.

"I suppose this fire is the work of the ruffians," said the lieutenant when the party had reached the highest ground in the rear of the house.

"No doubt of that; but it is a mystery to me how any of them got this side of the house without being seen," replied Levi.

"But there is the road I came over yesterday morning," suggested the officer.

"And you can see that low place this side of it, where the ruffians could neither walk nor swim. There is a pond farther along, with a stream from it that flows into Bar Creek," the overseer explained.

While they were on this high land, surveying the surrounding region, Artie brought them the weapons which had been sent for, and informed Levi that his father and the recruits were following the creek, looking for the incendiaries.

"I should say they came across the river above

the bridge," said the lieutenant, pointing in that direction.

"But the rapids run close to the shore, and they would not find very good boating right there," replied the overseer with a smile. "However, we will go over to the river, and beat the edge of the swamp to the pond."

They went to the river; but nothing like a boat could be seen on the shore. Then they followed the swamp till they heard a shot ahead of them.

"That makes it look as though Major Lyon had fallen upon them," said Levi, as he quickened his pace. "There is another and another;" and two shots followed the first one.

The party broke into a run, and soon came in sight of the pond. On its waters was a flatboat, or bateau, in which three men were paddling with all their might towards the shore near the road to Bowling Green. The planter had fired three shots at them; but they were too far off for the range of the revolver.

"Out of the reach of the revolver; and he had better have brought one of the breech-loaders," said the lieutenant. "It looks to me just as though they had a first-rate chance to escape."

"We are not euchred yet," replied Levi, as he ran with all his might in the direction of the pond, but to a point much nearer the road. "I have often thought of this place since the troubles here began. The high ground extends very nearly to the road, over which a bridge goes over a small creek, flowing into the pond. I have crossed this place on a plank to the road."

"Then we are all right."

"We are if I can find the plank. One of the cows got mired here, and it was brought over to use in getting her out. There it is!" exclaimed the overseer, rushing to the spot where it lay.

It was carried to the swamp; and though it was too short to bridge the dangerous place, it assisted, with the help of two long leaps, in carrying them over. It was now seen that the ruffians had a wagon, with which they had probably brought the boat to the pond. The party reached the road just as the incendiaries leaped from the bateau. Levi fired the six shots of his weapon at them, and the others followed his example; but the enemy were too far off, and not one of them appeared to be hit.

The moment they reached the shore they ran

for the road, and struck it at a considerable distance from the pursuers. The ruffians did not wait to recover the team, but bolted with all their might towards Bowling Green. It seemed useless to pursue them; for they had an advantage of a hundred rods, and the overseer was too fat to compete in speed with them.

The wagon was only a haycart, drawn by two mules; and the incendiaries could easily outrun them if they were used for the pursuit. The purpose of the villains had been defeated, and Levi was disposed to be satisfied with this result. The bateau was taken from the water, and loaded upon the wagon. Major Lyon and the recruits started back to the mansion as soon as the ruffians had effected their escape.

The party seated themselves in the boat, and the mules were started for a new home. When they reached the bridge over the upper part of the rapids, they were not a little surprised, not to say startled, to see a crowd of men marching over in the direction of Riverlawn. They were not exactly a mob, for the head of the column was in regular ranks, and the men were armed with muskets.

"What does that mean, Mr. Bedford?" asked the lieutenant.

"The placards we posted last night have waked up the ruffians, and they are coming over here on the same mission as the three we have driven off to Bowling Green," replied Levi, as he whipped up the mules. "They are the ruffians without a doubt, and we are going to have music of some sort before the sun goes down to-night."

The information was carried to Major Lyon, who had reached the fort in advance of them. The ruffians had doubtless made up their minds that a company of cavalry should not be enlisted at Riverlawn, as advertised, and it was evident enough to all that there was to be a fight before this question could be settled.

CHAPTER XXXV

A BATTLE IN PROSPECT ON THE CREEK

So far as the overseer and the boys had been able to observe the crowd on Rapids Bridge, they were in much better condition for an assault than when they came before. The right of the line was formed in ranks, all they could see of the assailants, for they had just begun to cross the river. They were armed with muskets, or something that looked like such weapons.

Levi drove directly to the fort, where Major Lyon was telling those who had not gone with him the result of the visit to the pond. There were only six recruits present, though a dozen had before been enlisted. These were all young men, generally the sons of the farmers of the vicinity, and doubtless adopted the political sentiments of their fathers. They were of a better class than the ruffians morally.

"I did not expect to be besieged so soon, Major Lyon," said Lieutenant Gordon with a pleasant laugh, though he had never been in anything but a skirmish so far.

"We shall hardly be besieged, Lieutenant, for I think it will be a fight as soon as they get near enough to begin it," replied the planter, who was seated on a log, resting himself after the hard tramp he had had after the incendiaries. "But the enemy seem to be better prepared for business than they were when they came before, for you say that all you could see were armed with muskets."

"I could not see at the distance they were from us how well they were armed," added the officer.

"About every family in these parts has one or more persons who do something at hunting in the woods and swamps, and I reckon it would be hard to find a house without a fowling-piece or an old king's arm in it," said Levi.

"They have all got guns of some sort," interposed Simeon Enbank, one of the recruits. "They have been drilling all the time for the last two days in one of Dr. Falkirk's fields."

"I went over to look at them this morning, and the sight of them made me so mad that I came right over here and enlisted," added Robert Yowell.

"Good for you, Yowell!" exclaimed the officer. "Could you see what sort of guns they had?"

"I went in and looked at them; for they were not using them when I was there. They were in line, sort of taking steps, as they do in a dancing-school," answered the recruit.

"But the arms?"

"They were all sorts and kinds, mostly fowling-pieces and old flint-locks that might have been used in the Revolutionary War."

"But we are losing time," said Major Lyon impatiently. "If they had reached the bridge when you saw them, they will be here very soon."

"We don't lose time while we are looking up the condition of the enemy. I believe you are all ready for an attack, and we can do nothing till they reach the other side of the creek. But we can talk while we work," replied the officer. "I suppose these recruits will assist us in the defence of the place?"

The six men all volunteered to perform the service required.

"There are a dozen more men over in the grove," said Ben Decker; "for I had a talk with them as I came along from the old road. They said they expected to stay here all day, and they brought their dinners with them."

This was good news, and Deck was sent over after them. Major Lyon went to the desk, and wrote a brief note to Colonel Belthorpe. He had already ordered all the horses that could be saddled, and Frank was sent to deliver the message the planter had written to Lyndhall. Decker was provided with a steed for his mission, and a wagon was sent for the men a little later.

The negroes who had been slightly drilled in the use of the arms were ordered to report at the fort, and all the hands on the place were summoned from the fields, and held in readiness for anything required of them. The six recruits were drilled for a little while in the use of the breech-loaders. At the same time Levi did what he could to instruct the negroes, though nothing like a military organization could be attempted in the brief space of time available for the purpose.

The twelve-pounders were loaded with canister this time; and Levi, with four of the hands, was placed in charge of the fort. Deck and Artie Lyon were sent down the creek to report the approach of the enemy, and found they had halted

"THE BOYS CLIMBED A BIG TREE TO OBTAIN A BETTER VIEW."
Page 431.

A BATTLE IN PROSPECT ON THE CREEK 431

at the cross roads, evidently to prepare for the attack. The boys climbed a big tree to obtain a better view of the proceedings of the ruffians, as they still called them, though they had reduced themselves to something like an organization.

"There are a lot of wagons on the bridge," said Deck, who was the first to discover them. "What do you suppose that means?"

"There are three mule teams," added Artie, who had taken a higher place in the tree than his brother. "I see now; the wagons are loaded with boats."

"That means that they intend to cross the creek," replied Deck. "They ought to know this at the fort at once; and if you will study up the thing while I am gone, Artie, I will run up and carry the information."

"That is a good scheme; go ahead with it as quick as you can."

Deck descended the tree with a haste which threatened the safety of the bones of his body, and ran with all the speed he could command to Fort Bedford.

Lieutenant Gordon was drilling the eighteen recruits, the number from the grove on the other side of the creek having arrived, and Levi was training the negroes in the rear of the fort. All the men had been supplied with muskets and rounds of ammunition. No attention was given to facing, wheeling, or marching; for the use of the weapon was more important than any other detail in the brief space of time available.

Deck reported to his father, who was observing the drill of the Africans, and in the hearing of Levi. It was not a mere accident that Squire Truman was seen approaching the fort from the bridge; for he had observed the movement among the ruffians in the village, and had seen that the column was moving by a roundabout road in the direction of the Rapids Bridge. He had no horse, but he had started at once on foot for Riverlawn, to apprise the planter of the danger that menaced him.

"It is time to do something," said the major, after he had welcomed the young lawyer. "The ruffians have a wagon-train loaded with boats in their rear, as my son has just informed me. We will adjourn to the fort and call in the lieutenant."

The information was imparted to the officer, and he joined the others in the fort.

"They intend to make it easy work for us to repel them," said the lieutenant with a smile.

"You are the only military man among us just now, Lieutenant, and I place you in command of all the forces," added Major Lyon. "Levi had some experience in the artillery many years ago."

"I don't aspire to any command," added the overseer. "I will obey orders as a private; and that is all I ever was in the artillery."

"But I shall do something better for you," replied Captain Gordon, as they began to call him from this time. "You are a good soldier, Mr. Bedford, and I shall make an officer of you at once. You will limber up your two guns, and haul them down to the boathouse. Have you any gunners?"

"Plenty of them, Captain; for I have trained enough of the hands to handle a full battery," answered Levi.

The planter had ordered both horses and wagons to be assembled in the rear of Fort Bedford, in readiness for any emergency. A pair of horses were promptly harnessed to each gun by the enthusiastic negroes whom the overseer had trained for battery service, and the artillery was soon on its way to the anticipated field of action. A supply of ammunition was sent down by a wagon.

The major and the squire mounted a couple of steeds, and rode to the front of the fort, a horse having been sent for the use of the new commander. The recruits were standing in line, leaning on their weapons; but they seemed to be engaged in a lively conversation. As the lieutenant approached, Jim Keene, one of the recruits, stepped forward with an awkward attempt to be polite, and addressed the officer: —

"Captain Gordon, we are not going into the army with niggers," said he in a very decided tone. "We ain't going to drop down to the level of niggers, and we want to take our names off that paper."

"Not a single negro has been enlisted, and will not be," replied Captain Gordon.

"But there is a squad of niggers marching down to the creek with muskets in their hands," added Keene, pointing to the detachment that followed the guns, with Levi at their head, mounted on his favorite colt.

"If we had a sufficient force of white men here, we should not call in the negroes as fighting men," interposed Major Lyon. "That Home Guard that has just crossed the bridge over the river consists of over a hundred men, and this time they are armed with guns. We can muster only twenty-four white men at present to beat them off. The other night we called upon the hands to help defend the place because no others were to be had; and to some extent the same is true to-day. My house has been set on fire, and that mob are coming to burn my buildings and capture my wife and daughters. If the white man won't fight for me, the negro will!"

"That alters the case," replied Keene. "We didn't understand it before, and we will fight for you, one and all;" and all the other recruits shouted their acquiescence with one voice.

"No negroes will be enlisted for the army, for there are no orders to that effect," added Captain Gordon.

"That's enough!" exclaimed Enbank. "We will stand by Major Lyon as long as there is a Secesher in sight."

"And you will find the negroes as stiff under fire as any white man ought to be," said Major Lyon, as he galloped down to the boathouse, followed by Squire Truman.

Artie, up in the tree, had kept his eyes wide open, but there was nothing more to be seen. Deck returned to him, and took his place near him. The enemy was still halted at the cross roads. The wagon-train had come up with the main body, and stopped in the road at the side of the creek. Whoever directed the movements of the column had evidently blundered, for the assailants did not appear to know what to do next.

"There is only one boat on each wagon, which is drawn by two mules," said Artie in the tree.

"They must have expected to get the boats into the water before they were discovered," added Deck. "Perhaps they would have done so if we had not happened to see them crossing the bridge when we were coming up after the hunt for the firebugs."

"There comes our artillery," continued Artie, as Levi's section of a battery galloped down the descent from the fort.

At this moment a bullet from the enemy struck a branch of the tree just above Artie's head. The boys had been discovered; and some one, with a better weapon than most of those with which the guards were armed, had fired upon them.

"Get behind the trunk, Artie!" shouted Deck, a position he had secured before. "Now use your musket, my boy!"

They were near enough at their lofty position to make out individuals at the cross roads, which were distant hardly more than double the width of the creek. Deck had seen one man, who wore a semi-uniform, that took a very active part in the movement. Having assured himself that this person was not his uncle, the enterprising young soldier took careful aim at him, and fired. Artie discharged his piece a moment later.

"I hit the man in uniform!" exclaimed Deck, with no little exultation. "A man is tying up one of his arms."

Major Lyon heard the shot, and shouted to the boys to come to the boathouse; and they obeyed the order, keeping the trunks of the trees between themselves and the enemy as far as possible. They were no longer needed in the tree, for the ruffian band could be plainly seen from the boathouse, which was at a safe distance from the enemy.

CHAPTER XXXVI

THE SECOND BATTLE OF RIVERLAWN

The enemy did nothing, and seemed to be still in a state of confusion and uncertainty as to what they should do. The new commander of their forces was certainly even more stupid than Captain Titus had been. As Deck had suggested, he had expected to surprise the defenders at Riverlawn, so far, at least, as to get their boats into the water before they discovered that they were attacked.

"If they had any plan of attack it is a failure," said Captain Gordon, as he and the planter were seated on their horses watching the enemy from the front of the boathouse. "One of the recruits informs me that they have a leader in the person of a captain from the Confederate army in Tennessee, who was either sent for by Captain Titus, or was despatched by General Buckner to organize recruits for the Southern army."

"I should say that his first business would be

to prevent recruiting for the Union forces," replied Major Lyon.

"Whatever he is, he has made a mess of it," added Captain Gordon.

"But what did he expect to do?" asked the planter.

"Of course he expected to put his pontoons into the water, and send over a force of from thirty to fifty men before they were discovered. If he had done that, they could have acted as sharpshooters from behind the trees on this side. They are just out of range of our muskets now, though the twelve-pounders would catch them with a single shot of canister."

"But I don't wish to have any more of them killed and wounded than is absolutely necessary," said the planter.

"You desire to carry on the war on peace principles," answered the captain with a smile. "You don't seem to understand that the war has actually begun, and the more damage we can do the enemy, the better it will be for us."

"You are in command, and I shall not interfere with your operations," said Major Lyon, as he rode off to the point where Levi was training his gunners.

The recruits in front of the boathouse were impatient for something to be done. They were from the country around the village of Barcreek. The frequent outrages against Union men and families had kindled a feeling of hatred in them, and they were anxious to retaliate. The influence of certain men like Colonel Cosgrove and Colonel Belthorpe had created more Union sentiment than prevailed in many of the Southern counties of the State, and the loyal men had been terrorized from the first indications of trouble.

"Why don't we fire at them, Captain?" demanded Enbank.

"Why don't you fire at the moon? Because you are too far off, and nothing is to be gained by it," replied the commander. "I am waiting for the enemy to make a movement of some kind; and as soon as they do so, you shall have enough of it, I will warrant you."

"They are doing something now!" exclaimed Sam Drye.

"The mule-teams are in motion!" exclaimed Major Lyon, returning to the front of the building.

"I see they are," replied Captain Gordon;

"and there is a movement up the new road, as you call it."

"What does that mean?"

"Probably it is intended to cover the launching of the boats. I think the reprobates are in earnest this time," added the commander.

About fifty men started up the new road, and immediately broke into a run. The territory between the new and the old road was covered with trees of large growth, though rather too sparsely to be a wood, but was rather a grove. For about twenty rods above the cross roads the trees had been cut off, and it was a stump field. As soon as the detachment reached the grove they scattered and took refuge behind the trunks of the big trees.

"That is the idea, is it?" said Captain Gordon. "They intend to pick us off from their covert. We must do the same thing. Scatter, my men; and fire at will as you see a head."

The recruits obeyed the order, and were sheltered behind the big trees by the time the enemy reached the positions they had chosen. A desultory firing was begun on both sides of the creek. The commander and the major were on horseback, and they could not protect themselves as the recruits did, and they rode to the rear of the boat-house. They found that Levi had organized a shovel brigade there. The Magnolia had been taken out of the water to prevent it from being captured by the marauders, and had been placed behind the boathouse.

Levi had moved the craft about twenty feet from the building, and had propped it up, with the keel nearest to the creek. This was as far as he had proceeded when the officer presented himself on the ground. Twenty negroes, armed with shovels, which had before been brought down in the wagon, were standing ready for orders.

"What in the world are you doing now, Levi?" asked the planter, when he saw what had been done.

"I am throwing up a breastwork, so that my men can work the guns without being shot down by the enemy on the other side of the creek," replied the overseer.

"A capital idea!" exclaimed Captain Gordon.

"But you are putting it behind the boathouse, man!" shouted the major, who thought he had detected Levi in an egregious blunder.

"These negroes are worth from five hundred to a thousand dollars apiece if you want to sell them, and not many of them would be left if I should set them to digging in the open," replied Levi, laughing at his own argument. "Those ruffians could pick them off at their leisure, and we might as well not have any artillery if the cannoneers are to be shot down as fast as they show themselves. I will warrant that fellow in command on the other side has picked out his best riflemen for duty in the grove."

"The negroes are not for sale," replied the planter. "I should as soon think of selling one of my sons as one of them. But the boathouse is between you and the enemy, Levi."

"How long do you think it will take me with the force at hand to move the boathouse out of the way, Major Lyon?" demanded the overseer with a very broad smile.

"I indorse Mr. Bedford's work," added Captain Gordon, who had turned to observe the operation of the enemy at the cross roads. "They are not making a good job of their work."

As soon as the recruits had been ordered to the trees, and before the detachment sent to the grove had obtained their positions, Deck and Artie had obeyed the commander's order in hot haste. They had chosen a couple of trees on the very verge of the quagmire which lay between the lawn and the road to the south; and when the ruffians attempted to move the mules, both of them opened fire upon the animals.

Both of the boys were good shots, and they hit the mark every time. The mule, though one of the most useful beasts in the world, is very uncertain at times. The testimony of soldiers is to the effect that mules object to being under fire. The two boys were near enough to each other to talk together, and they had agreed to fire into different teams, and they had wounded one in each of them. The two that had been hit not only made a disturbance, braying furiously, but they communicated the scare to the others. The mule drivers could do nothing with them, and in a minute or two the whole of them were all snarled up, and the men were obliged to unhitch them from the wagons and lead them away.

The animals were so terrified that they bolted up the new road in spite of the drivers, and turned in at the bridge, which seemed to promise them a place of security, just as Colonel Belthorpe and his party galloped up to it. The mules were permitted to take the lead. Major Gadbury and Tom were with the planter of Lyndhall. Major Lyon saw them, and, by a roundabout course, joined them in season to prevent them from coming within range of the sharpshooters in the grove.

It did not take the planter of Riverlawn long to explain the situation; and he was informed that twenty Lyndhall negroes, under the lead of Uncle David, in wagons, were on their way to the seat of danger. The horses were left in charge of the servants, and the party made their way to the fort, where they armed themselves with breechloaders, and took places behind the trees with the recruits.

At the cross roads the enemy were attempting to get the boats to the creek by hauling the wagons by man-power. It was a long pull for them, but they succeeded at the end of a couple of hours. The party in the grove and the one on the lawn were careful about showing themselves, and the firing was continued on both sides without producing any decided result. But by this time Levi had completed his breastwork. Rather to make a smoke than for any other purpose, both of the twelve-pounders were discharged, aimed into the grove.

While the smoke hung about the boathouse, for one of the pieces had been fired on each side of it, all hands seized hold of the building, lifted it from its foundations, and bore it some distance towards the mansion. The cannon were then drawn into the hastily constructed fort, loaded with round shot this time, and were ready for use. The cracking of the rifles in the grove had been quite lively during this operation, and two of the negroes were wounded.

By this time the first of the boats had been filled with men, who were paddling it with all their might to a clump of bushes near the trees where Deck and Artie were sheltered. Both of them fired into the crowd in the boat. But it was hardly under way before Levi had brought one of his guns to bear upon it. He was very careful in pointing the piece, and the solid shot struck the craft squarely on its bow, knocking the thing all to pieces. The black gunners cheered, and were almost mad with enthusiasm.

Another of the boats which had just been

launched had to be used to pick up the men from the first. They were taken to the shore. Then some sort of a contention seemed to be stirred up among the party, the nature of which could be easily understood, for it was almost sure death to embark in the boats. In the mean time the shots from the recruits and others behind the trees were picking them off, and the dispute ended in the whole of them taking to their heels and fleeing towards the bridge.

The fire from the grove seemed to be suspended at the same time; for the sharpshooters could not help seeing that the plan of attack, whatever it was, had failed. Colonel Belthorpe and Major Lyon came out from behind their trees. Captain Gordon, who was a cavalry officer, thought it was time for his arm of the service to come into action to harass the retreat of the enemy, if nothing more, and he called in all the recruits from their covert, and ordered as many men as could be mounted to rally at the bridge.

Twenty-four mounted men, including those from Lyndhall, were mustered, each with a breech-loader, in the absence of sabres and carbines. Captain Gordon led them down the new road to the grove. The force occupying it had fled to the old road, and were hurrying to the Rapids Bridge. Among the trees they found two men killed and three badly wounded. Each of them had a rifle on the ground near him, and they were weapons of excellent quality.

The cavalry party followed the fugitives to the bridge, and at the intercession of Major Lyon they were permitted to escape; for he was confident they would not make another attack upon Riverlawn, at least not till they had an organized regiment for the purpose.

While they were upon the ground, Tom Belthorpe and Major Gadbury signed the enlistment papers, as Deck and Artie had done before, and the Lyndhall party went home. The recruits were dismissed for a week, and ordered to report at Riverlawn at the end of that time.

The second battle had been fought and won, and there was no present danger of another attack, though patrols were kept along the creek till the camp was formed the following week. The two attacks upon Riverlawn was the current topic of conversation all over the county for the next week; and so far from damaging the Union cause, it stimulated the recruiting, and at the end of the week Lieutenant Gordon had the names of a full company on his roll. He had reported his success, and had received orders to enlist another company.

The government supplied everything that was required, including sabres, carbines, uniforms, ammunition, and lumber for barracks. Steamboats from Evansville came up the river loaded with supplies; and as the water was high from unusual rains, they landed their cargoes at the boathouse pier, enlarged for the purpose. Each boat was provided with a guard, for they were occasionally fired upon from the shore. Another officer and several non-commissioned officers were sent to the camp.

Barracks and stables were built, and the drill was kept up very diligently. Riverlawn was no longer between two fires, for they were now all on one side. Before, the fight had been a sort of neighborhood quarrel; but now it had become a national affair. The outrages upon Union men ceased in that locality, though they still occurred in other parts of the State. At the end of a month two companies of cavalry had been enlisted, forming a squadron, if another could be raised.

About this time the Home Guard, under command of Captain Titus Lyon, marched to Bowling Green for the purpose of joining the Confederate army that was expected there. They went with such arms as they had used in the second battle of Riverlawn, and without uniforms. They had a hard time of it; for they had no supplies, and suffered from hunger and cold in the cool nights. Titus's two sons, Sandy and Orly, were enrolled in the company; but both of them deserted, though they had not been mustered in, and went back to their mother, where they could at least get enough to eat. The captain could not go home, for it required his presence and all his skill and energy to keep his recruits from abandoning the company.

Noah Lyon saw nothing more of his brother after his visit to Riverlawn when the lieutenant arrived. After he had gone to the South, his wife and daughters called at the mansion, and declared that they were left without money or means of support, except so far as they could obtain it from the little farm.

Deck and Artie Lyon, whose career as soldiers is to appear in these volumes, now appeared wearing the uniform of cavalrymen, with sabres clinking at their sides. They have been under fire, though not in a pitched battle. They are frequent visitors on Sundays at Lyndhall, and Kate Belthorpe has what her father called "a violent admiration for Captain Deck," as he still insists upon styling him, assured that, if he is not of that rank now, he will be in due time. The next volume will present the two boys and others engaged in actual warfare; and what they did will be found in "IN THE SADDLE."

OLIVER OPTIC'S BOOKS

All-Over-the-World Library. By OLIVER OPTIC. First Series. Illustrated. Price per volume, $1.25.

1. **A Missing Million;** OR, THE ADVENTURES OF LOUIS BELGRADE.
2. **A Millionaire at Sixteen;** OR, THE CRUISE OF THE "GUARDIAN MOTHER."
3. **A Young Knight Errant;** OR, CRUISING IN THE WEST INDIES.
4. **Strange Sights Abroad;** OR, ADVENTURES IN EUROPEAN WATERS.

No author has come before the public during the present generation who has achieved a larger and more deserving popularity among young people than "Oliver Optic." His stories have been very numerous, but they have been uniformly excellent in moral tone and literary quality. As indicated in the general title, it is the author's intention to conduct the readers of this entertaining series "around the world." As a means to this end, the hero of the story purchases a steamer which he names the "Guardian Mother," and with a number of guests she proceeds on her voyage. — *Christian Work, N. Y.*

All-Over-the-World Library. By OLIVER OPTIC. Second Series. Illustrated. Price per volume, $1.25.

1. **American Boys Afloat;** OR, CRUISING IN THE ORIENT.
2. **The Young Navigators;** OR, THE FOREIGN CRUISE OF THE "MAUD."
3. **Up and Down the Nile;** OR, YOUNG ADVENTURERS IN AFRICA.
4. **Asiatic Breezes;** OR, STUDENTS ON THE WING.

The interest in these stories is continuous, and there is a great variety of exciting incident woven into the solid information which the book imparts so generously and without the slightest suspicion of dryness. Manly boys will welcome this volume as cordially as they did its predecessors. — *Boston Gazette.*

All-Over-the-World Library. By OLIVER OPTIC. Third Series. Illustrated. Price per volume, $1.25.

1. **Across India;** OR, LIVE BOYS IN THE FAR EAST.
2. **Half Round the World;** OR, AMONG THE UNCIVILIZED.
3. **Four Young Explorers;** OR, SIGHT-SEEING IN THE TROPICS.
4. **Pacific Shores;** OR, ADVENTURES IN EASTERN SEAS.

Amid such new and varied surroundings it would be surprising indeed if the author, with his faculty of making even the commonplace attractive, did not tell an intensely interesting story of adventure, as well as give much information in regard to the distant countries through which our friends pass, and the strange peoples with whom they are brought in contact. This book, and indeed the whole series, is admirably adapted to reading aloud in the family circle, each volume containing matter which will interest all the members of the family. — *Boston Budget.*

LEE AND SHEPARD, BOSTON, SEND THEIR COMPLETE CATALOGUE FREE.

OLIVER OPTIC'S BOOKS

The Blue and the Gray—Afloat. By OLIVER OPTIC. Six volumes. Illustrated. Beautiful binding in blue and gray with emblematic dies. Cloth. Any volume sold separately Price per volume, $1.50.

1. Taken by the Enemy.
2. Within the Enemy's Lines.
3. On the Blockade.
4. Stand by the Union.
5. Fighting for the Right.
6. A Victorious Union.

The Blue and the Gray—on Land.

1. Brother against Brother.
2. In the Saddle.
3. A Lieutenant at Eighteen.
4. On the Staff.
5. At the Front.
6. An Undivided Union.

"There never has been a more interesting writer in the field of juvenile literature than Mr. W. T. ADAMS, who, under his well-known pseudonym, is known and admired by every boy and girl in the country, and by thousands who have long since passed the boundaries of youth, yet who remember with pleasure the genial, interesting pen that did so much to interest, instruct, and entertain their younger years. 'The Blue and the Gray' is a title that is sufficiently indicative of the nature and spirit of the latest series, while the name of OLIVER OPTIC is sufficient warrant of the absorbing style of narrative. This series is as bright and entertaining as any work that Mr. ADAMS has yet put forth, and will be as eagerly perused as any that has borne his name. It would not be fair to the prospective reader to deprive him of the zest which comes from the unexpected by entering into a synopsis of the story. A word, however, should be said in regard to the beauty and appropriateness of the binding, which makes it a most attractive volume." — *Boston Budget.*

Woodville Stories. By OLIVER OPTIC. Six volumes. Illustrated. Any volume sold separately. Price per volume, $1.25.

1. Rich and Humble; OR, THE MISSION OF BERTHA GRANT.
2. In School and Out; OR, THE CONQUEST OF RICHARD GRANT.
3. Watch and Wait; OR, THE YOUNG FUGITIVES.
4. Work and Win; OR, NODDY NEWMAN ON A CRUISE.
5. Hope and Have; OR, FANNY GRANT AMONG THE INDIANS
6. Haste and Waste; OR, THE YOUNG PILOT OF LAKE CHAMPLAIN.

"Though we are not so young as we once were, we relished these stories almost as much as the boys and girls for whom they were written. They were really refreshing, even to us. There is much in them which is calculated to inspire a generous, healthy ambition, and to make distasteful all reading tending to stimulate base desires." — *Fitchburg Reveille.*

The Starry Flag Series. By OLIVER OPTIC. In six volumes. Illustrated. Any volume sold separately. Price per volume, $1.25.

1. The Starry Flag; OR, THE YOUNG FISHERMAN OF CAPE ANN.
2. Breaking Away; OR, THE FORTUNES OF A STUDENT.
3. Seek and Find; OR, THE ADVENTURES OF A SMART BOY.
4. Freaks of Fortune; OR, HALF ROUND THE WORLD.
5. Make or Break; OR, THE RICH MAN'S DAUGHTER.
6. Down the River; OR, BUCK BRADFORD AND THE TYRANTS.

"Mr. ADAMS, the celebrated and popular writer, familiarly known as OLIVER OPTIC, seems to have inexhaustible funds for weaving together the virtues of life; and, notwithstanding he has written scores of books, the same freshness and novelty run through them all. Some people think the sensational element predominates. Perhaps it does. But a book for young people needs this, and so long as good sentiments are inculcated such books ought to be read."

LEE AND SHEPARD, BOSTON, SEND THEIR COMPLETE CATALOGUE FREE.

OLIVER OPTIC'S BOOKS

Army and Navy Stories. By OLIVER OPTIC. Six volumes. Illustrated. Any volume sold separately. Price per volume, $1.25.

1. The Soldier Boy; OR, TOM SOMERS IN THE ARMY.
2. The Sailor Boy; OR, JACK SOMERS IN THE NAVY.
3. The Young Lieutenant; OR, ADVENTURES OF AN ARMY OFFICER.
4. The Yankee Middy; OR, ADVENTURES OF A NAVY OFFICER.
5. Fighting Joe; OR, THE FORTUNES OF A STAFF OFFICER.
6. Brave Old Salt; OR, LIFE ON THE QUARTER DECK.

"This series of six volumes recounts the adventures of two brothers, Tom and Jack Somers, one in the army, the other in the navy, in the great Civil War. The romantic narratives of the fortunes and exploits of the brothers are thrilling in the extreme. Historical accuracy in the recital of the great events of that period is strictly followed, and the result is, not only a library of entertaining volumes, but also the best history of the Civil War for young people ever written."

Boat Builders Series. By OLIVER OPTIC. In six volumes. Illustrated. Any volume sold separately. Price per volume, $1.25.

1. All Adrift; OR, THE GOLDWING CLUB.
2. Snug Harbor; OR, THE CHAMPLAIN MECHANICS.
3. Square and Compasses; OR, BUILDING THE HOUSE.
4. Stem to Stern; OR, BUILDING THE BOAT.
5. All Taut; OR, RIGGING THE BOAT.
6. Ready About; OR, SAILING THE BOAT.

"The series includes in six successive volumes the whole art of boat building, boat rigging, boat managing, and practical hints to make the ownership of a boat pay. A great deal of useful information is given in this Boat Builders Series, and in each book a very interesting story is interwoven with the information. Every reader will be interested at once in Dory, the hero of 'All Adrift,' and one of the characters retained in the subsequent volumes of the series. His friends will not want to lose sight of him, and every boy who makes his acquaintance in 'All Adrift' will become his friend."

Riverdale Story Books. By OLIVER OPTIC. Twelve volumes. Illustrated. Illuminated covers. Price: cloth, per set, $3.60; per volume, 30 cents; paper, per set, $2.00.

1. Little Merchant.
2. Young Voyagers.
3. Christmas Gift.
4. Dolly and I.
5. Uncle Ben.
6. Birthday Party.
7. Proud and Lazy.
8. Careless Kate.
9. Robinson Crusoe, Jr.
10. The Picnic Party.
11. The Gold Thimble.
12. The Do-Somethings.

Riverdale Story Books. By OLIVER OPTIC. Six volumes. Illustrated. Fancy cloth and colors. Price per volume, 30 cents.

1. Little Merchant.
2. Proud and Lazy.
3. Young Voyagers.
4. Careless Kate.
5. Dolly and I.
6. Robinson Crusoe, Jr.

Flora Lee Library. By OLIVER OPTIC. Six volumes. Illustrated. Fancy cloth and colors. Price per volume, 30 cents.

1. The Picnic Party.
2. The Gold Thimble.
3. The Do-Somethings.
4. Christmas Gift.
5. Uncle Ben.
6. Birthday Party.

These are bright short stories for younger children who are unable to comprehend the Starry Flag Series or the Army and Navy Series. But they all display the author's talent for pleasing and interesting the little folks. They are all fresh and original, preaching no sermons, but inculcating good lessons.

LEE AND SHEPARD, BOSTON, SEND THEIR COMPLETE CATALOGUE FREE

OLIVER OPTIC'S BOOKS

The Great Western Series. By OLIVER OPTIC. In six volumes. Illustrated. Any volume sold separately. Price per volume, $1.25.
1. Going West; OR, THE PERILS OF A POOR BOY.
2. Out West; OR, ROUGHING IT ON THE GREAT LAKES.
3. Lake Breezes; OR, THE CRUISE OF THE SYLVANIA.
4. Going South; OR, YACHTING ON THE ATLANTIC COAST.
5. Down South; OR, YACHT ADVENTURES IN FLORIDA.
6. Up the River; OR, YACHTING ON THE MISSISSIPPI.

"This is the latest series of books issued by this popular writer, and dealt with life on the Great Lakes, for which a careful study was made by the author in a summer tour of the immense water sources of America. The story, which carries the same hero through the six books of the series, is always entertaining, novel scenes and varied incidents giving a constantly changing yet always attractive aspect to the narrative. OLIVER OPTIC has written nothing better."

The Yacht Club Series. By OLIVER OPTIC. In six volumes. Illustrated. Any volume sold separately. Price per volume, $1.25.
1. Little Bobtail; OR, THE WRECK OF THE PENOBSCOT.
2. The Yacht Club; OR, THE YOUNG BOAT BUILDERS.
3. Money-Maker; OR, THE VICTORY OF THE BASILISK.
4. The Coming Wave; OR, THE TREASURE OF HIGH ROCK.
5. The Dorcas Club; OR, OUR GIRLS AFLOAT.
6. Ocean Born; OR, THE CRUISE OF THE CLUBS.

"The series has this peculiarity, that all of its constituent volumes are independent of one another, and therefore each story is complete in itself. OLIVER OPTIC is, perhaps, the favorite author of the boys and girls of this country, and he seems destined to enjoy an endless popularity. He deserves his success, for he makes very interesting stories, and inculcates none but the best sentiments, and the 'Yacht Club' is no exception to this rule." — *New Haven Journal and Courier.*

Onward and Upward Series. By OLIVER OPTIC. In six volumes. Illustrated. Any volume sold separately. Price per volume, $1.25.
1. Field and Forest; OR, THE FORTUNES OF A FARMER.
2. Plane and Plank; OR, THE MISHAPS OF A MECHANIC.
3. Desk and Debit; OR, THE CATASTROPHES OF A CLERK.
4. Cringle and Crosstree; OR, THE SEA SWASHES OF A SAILOR.
5. Bivouac and Battle; OR, THE STRUGGLES OF A SOLDIER.
6. Sea and Shore; OR, THE TRAMPS OF A TRAVELLER.

"Paul Farringford, the hero of these tales, is, like most of this author's heroes, a young man of high spirit, and of high aims and correct principles, appearing in the different volumes as a farmer, a captain, a bookkeeper, a soldier, a sailor, and a traveller. In all of them the hero meets with very exciting adventures, told in the graphic style for which the author is famous."

The Lake Shore Series. By OLIVER OPTIC. In six volumes. Illustrated. Any volume sold separately. Price per volume, $1.25.
1. Through by Daylight; OR, THE YOUNG ENGINEER OF THE LAKE SHORE RAILROAD.
2. Lightning Express; OR, THE RIVAL ACADEMIES.
3. On Time; OR, THE YOUNG CAPTAIN OF THE UCAYGA STEAMER.
4. Switch Off; OR, THE WAR OF THE STUDENTS.
5. Brake Up; OR, THE YOUNG PEACEMAKERS.
6. Bear and Forbear; OR, THE YOUNG SKIPPER OF LAKE UCAYGA.

"OLIVER OPTIC is one of the most fascinating writers for youth, and withal one of the best to be found in this or any past age. Troops of young people hang over his vivid pages; and not one of them ever learned to be mean, ignoble, cowardly, selfish, or to yield to any vice from anything they ever read from his pen." — *Providence Press.*

LEE AND SHEPARD, BOSTON, SEND THEIR COMPLETE CATALOGUE FREE.

www.ingramcontent.com/pod-product-compliance
Lightning Source LLC
Chambersburg PA
CBHW022109300426
44117CB00007B/651